Computer Applications

IN

Reading

Third Edition

Jay S. Blanchard
Texas Tech University

George E. Mason
University of Georgia

Dan Daniel
Houston, Texas, Independent School District

Published by the

International Reading Association

Newark, Delaware 19714

To Ira E. Aaron, President of the International Reading
Association 1983-1984, and Alumni Foundation Distinguished
Professor Emeritus of Reading, University of Georgia.

Copyright 1987 by the
International Reading Association, Inc.

Library of Congress Cataloging-in-Publication Data

Blanchard, Jay S.
  Computer applications in reading.

  Rev. ed. of Computer applications in reading/George E.
Mason, Jay S. Blanchard, Danny B. Daniel. 2nd ed. 1983.
  Includes bibliographies and index.
  1. Reading – United States – Data processing.   2. Read-
ing – United States – Data processing – Bibliography.   3.
Computer assisted instruction – United States. I. Mason,
George E. II. Daniel, Dan. III. Computer applications in
reading. IV. Title.
LB1050.37.M37   1987   428.4'0285   87-3503
ISBN 0-87207-785-3

Contents

INTERNATIONAL READING ASSOCIATION

The International Reading Association attempts, through its publications, to provide a forum for a wide spectrum of opinions on reading. This policy permits divergent viewpoints without assuming the endorsement of the Association.

Foreword

C *omputer Applications in Reading* enters its third edition as a chronicle of research, programs, and uses of computers in reading. An index of the rapid changes that have taken place in the use of computers in reading is that this edition has a new and different set of references from that in the earlier editions. These form a body of recent literature that supersedes and augments the more than 900 citations included in the second edition. Many of the speculations and predictions included in the earlier editions have come to pass, often sooner than predicted. This edition includes topics that were barely more than fantasy in 1979 when the first edition was published.

The impediments to widespread educational adoption of computers have changed since 1979. The potential of computers in education has been linked to the costs of both hardware and software. Hardware capabilities of computers have also limited their educational utility. Slow processing speed, restricted memory capacity, lack of voice recognition and synthesis, and poor quality graphics have all played (in the past) a role in keeping the computer from becoming a dominant force in education. And much of the software was of dubious quality.

However, costs for microcomputer hardware have continued to spiral down while capabilities have greatly improved. Microcomputer systems can now perform tasks that required mainframe computers only a few years ago. Although hardware development usually outpaces software development, computer materials for use in reading are significantly improved. This is due in part to improved capacities of computers and in part to the efforts of major reading materials publishers who have finally become convinced of the reality of the computer in schools. Consequently, the use of microcomputers is continually expanding in education generally and in reading specifically.

Just as hardware costs are approaching affordability for most schools, a persistent problem has begun to loom larger than ever before. We have begun to realize that our broad based systematic knowledge of how to teach reading is inadequate to create software that will take advantage of the new, different, and expanded capabilities of computers. While computer technology has provided a dizzying array of new potentials, our knowledge of how to teach reading remains geared to older and more stable technologies. Teachers and students often find themselves more comfortable with convenient texts and tasks that are "friendly" if not entirely effective or satisfactory.

Nevertheless, the computer "revolution" in reading will probably not be deflected from success. We have had convincing recent demonstrations of the effectiveness and the cost effectiveness of computers as instructional intervention devices, despite the claims of inadequate software and expensive hardware. Computers have become too pervasive, their promise too enticing, and their cost too irresistible to ignore. As educators, students, and parents are exposed to computers, more applications will be generated.

What we must strive to achieve is an integration of innovative uses of computers with our traditional knowledge of reading and reading instruction. We must also become aware of what we need to know (about both computers and reading) to increase effective uses of computers in reading and instruction. When such a synthesis can be produced, we will have reached the final phase of the computer "revolution" in reading.

Until then, this work is the most thorough compilation of the recent research on and applications of computers in reading, reflecting our current state of knowledge and practice. It provides us with an encouraging summary of what has been and can be done with computers.

Michael L. Kamil
University of Illinois at Chicago

Introduction

I t is important to note that in this edition of *Computer Applications in Reading* most annotations and comments from the earlier editions have been deleted. However, a few historically important references have been retained for those who might not have access to earlier editions. The format of the third edition is somewhat different from earlier editions for reasons of economy. All references, both annotated and nonannotated, are arranged in alphabetical order by year of publication.

The third edition of *Computer Applications in Reading* contains twelve chapters. Chapter 1 provides a broad view of computer applications in education. Chapter 2 describes computer applications in reading with special sections on LOGO, cloze procedure, language experience approach, special education, spelling, Native American and bilingual reading instruction, and English as a second language and foreign language education. Chapter 3 introduces the reader to software evaluation guidelines (including IRA's Criteria for the Selection and Utilization of Nonprint Media for the Reading Curriculum) and includes references about the development of computer based reading programs and projects. Chapter 4 reviews computer based research on teaching reading, reading assessment, and psychological and physiological aspects of the reading process. Chapter 5 presents references about word processing, writing, and reading. Chapter 6 offers some explanations for the puzzling questions surrounding computer based readability and text analysis. Chapter 7 presents references to computer based activities in reading readiness and beginning reading. Chapter 8 discusses computer managed reading instruction. Chapter 9 details advances in computer based speech technology and reading instruction. Chapter 10 focuses on text legibility and computers. Chapter 11, The Optical Era and Reading, provides references about recent developments with CD ROMS and CDIS. Chapter 12 speculates on the importance of other emerging applications in computer based reading; namely, simulations, artificial intelligence, programing and authoring systems, telecommunications and satellite communications, and robots. Appendix A is a comprehensive listing of companies that produce or distribute reading and language arts software.

Appendix B describes integrated learning systems that contain reading and language arts software.

Special thanks go to MaryAnn Jones of the Ralls, Texas, Public Schools, Susan Awbrey of Computer Curriculum Corporation, and to the Colleges of Education at the University of Georgia and Texas Tech University. In addition, the authors wish to acknowledge the efforts of the reviewers: Richard L. Carner, Michael P. French, and James R. Layton. Preparation of this text was supported in part by a grant from Texas Tech University.

JSB
GEM
DBD

1

Computer applications in education

I t is possible that the computer will become an educational friend to *all* students within the next decade. Indeed, the computer probably will become an important part of all classroom instruction. However, the computer is still in its horse and buggy days, and its impact on education is just beginning.

It was not until the early 1960s that American colleges and universities began to develop the first computer based educational programs. Development projects were launched by partnerships among universities, the government, and computer manufacturers (e.g., IBM System 1500 and Stanford University). The programs developed were mainly for elementary and secondary education. They ran on mainframe, time sharing computers. Unfortunately, this approach to computer based education did not spark enough widespread public interest for continued support. As federal funding decreased, so did the involvement of American colleges and universities, and prior to the introduction of the microcomputer only a few computer based education projects were in operation. But the introduction of the microcomputer aroused great public interest. Soon there were hundreds and then thousands of microcomputers, not only in American schools but also in the schools of many countries (notably in Europe and the Far East).

An overview of selected applications in education

Diverse computer applications in education and reading continue to grow. Several years ago computers were used principally for drill and practice activities with few innovations. Today, drill and practice activities are just one use for computers in education. Some of these uses are introduced in this chapter; they will be discussed in greater detail in later chapters.

Testing

Computers can administer virtually all types of assessment instruments (with or without teacher support): achievement and aptitude tests and interest and reading inventories, whether norm referenced or criterion referenced. These instruments can be administered in group or individual settings. For example, Kendall-Hunt offers a computer based reading assessment instrument, in both English and Spanish, that can evaluate reading performance with or without teacher support. (See Appendix A for addresses of software publishers.)

Information and instruction management

Computers can ease most educational record keeping tasks by managing data derived from any number of sources. Computers can schedule classes, plan cafeteria menus, arrange bus routes, keep immunization records, dial the telephone numbers of absentees, and manage or prescribe most types of instructional activities. When these activities are coordinated with test administration and materials management, the computer can play a major role in the total instructional program in any subject, including reading.

Drill and practice

Computers can be used to present information in drill and practice formats for instruction and review purposes. In the past few years, much progress has been made in the refinement of drill and practice programs, especially by companies such as the Computer Curriculum Corporation and the Control Data Corporation-PLATO. (See Appendix B.) Although much maligned, drill and practice activities can provide valuable instructional support for the classroom teacher.

Tutorial/dialogue

Many computer based instructional programs are available that feature computer and student dialogue. These programs are called tutorials or dialogue programs because their algorithms make decisions about student performance; they alter (branch) the program content, level, or rate. These decisions and the accompanying adjustments in the program increase the likelihood of student success in mastering the program content.

Simulations

Computers can convey information through programed experiences that imitate reality. These computer generated models of the real world allow teachers and students to role play decisions without the consequences often associated with the real world (danger, expense, time). Today, many fine simulations are available for school use.

Telecommunications/information retrieval

Computer telecommunications can provide easy and inexpensive access to information as well as the ability to correspond using electronic mail. Telecomputing in its commonest form requires a computer, a telephone, a modem, a subscription to a telecommunications service such as CompuServe (5000 Arlington Boulevard, Columbus, Ohio 43220), and the appropriate telecommunications software. Teachers and students in any location that has phone service can get information on virtually any topic by searching on-line databases.

Word processing

Teachers and students using word processing can focus on all aspects of language skills, including prewriting, grammar, punctuation, composing, editing, and proofreading. Word processors that focus on many aspects of the writing process include The Writing Workshop (Milliken) and Electric Writing (Creative Publications). Similar programs that feature only prewriting activities are Proteus and Proteus, Jr. (Research Design Associates). These programs are designed to help students collect their thoughts during the initial stages of composing.

In the past few years, word processors have been integrated (in one program) with databases and spreadsheets. Integrated word processing programs present unique opportunities for teachers and students in all curricular areas. Appleworks (Apple Computer) is an example of an integrated program; it contains a word processor, database, and spreadsheet. Those interested in the application of integrated word processing programs throughout the school curriculum may wish to read Trends in Educational Computing: Decreasing Interest and the Changing Focus of Instruction in the May 1986 issue of *Educational Researcher,* or contact The Scholastic Teacher Network: Integrating Computers into the Curriculum (Scholastic). In addition, several word processing programs now contain activities that permit applications across the curriculum. For example, Scholastic PFS:

Curriculum Data Bases and Appleworks: Data Bases (Scholastic) contain activities in U.S. history, U.S. government, world geography, physical science, language arts (poetry, mythology, literature, composition), climate, and U.S. Constitution. Students and teachers can use these previously developed databases or create their own to help organize informtion.

Utilities

There are many computer based programs (not designed to be educational) that support educational activities. These teacher utilities are programs that enable teachers to create word search puzzles, signs, greeting cards, worksheets, word lists for games, and other material useful for instruction. An example is Print Shop (Broderbund), a program that allows teachers and students to create almost any kind of printed display (greeting cards, letterheads, stationery, posters).

Interactive fiction

Computers can help teachers and students *create* and *complete* stories. Much like simulations, interactive fiction programs allow students to build their own stories from computer generated story fragments. The number of possible story outcomes is broad enough so students will not readily write all the stories. One good example is Winnie the Pooh in the Hundred Acre Woods (Disney).

Also available are writing programs that help students create fiction. Examples of such programs include Story Tree (Scholastic) and The Playwriter Series—Tales of Me, Adventures in Space, Mystery, Castles and Creatures (Woodbury Software). Recently, Grolier Educational Software introduced a new twist to interactive fiction programs. In the programs entitled Treasure Hunter, The Secrets of Science Island, Hospital, and Farewell Alaska (Knowledge Explorer Series), students are expected to use a reference source (*New Book of Knowledge Encyclopedia*) in order to complete the interactive fiction. A similar program is entitled Where in the World Is Carmen Sandiego? (Broderbund). This interactive fiction thriller requires the use of *The World Almanac* for successful completion.

Videodisks and compact disks

Computers can support and control high speed, text/image storage devices. Computer controlled videodisks and compact disks give educators the advantages of both television imagery and computerized print display and branching. Computers using videodisks and compact disks undoubtedly will display much of the text material in classrooms of the future.

Speech

Producing speech. Computers can be made to speak—at least after a fashion. Currently, there are two forms of computer generated speech: digitized and synthesized. Digitized speech refers to the storage and recall of prerecorded human speech. Synthesized speech is usually constructed by an additive process using discrete phonemes programed to be combined into sound units listeners will interpret as words. Nothing is prerecorded; the computer constructs "speech" as its program dictates. Each type of speech is available in reading and language arts programs.

Optical character readers (OCRs) can speak and read. The Kurzweil Reading Machine (Kurzweil Computer Products, Waltham, Massachusetts, a subsidiary of the Xerox Corporation, 1341 W. Mockingbird, Dallas, Texas 75247) can read a document and translate print to speech. Classroom applications of OCRs are limited because of the cost ($20,000-$40,000).

Listening to speech. Computers also can respond to speech. Voice entry terminals (VETs) allow users to control the computer with voice commands. As problems with variations in individual speech patterns, limited vocabulary recognition, background noise, dialect, and price are solved, computers will respond to spoken commands.

Programing and problem solving

Computers can be used to teach problem solving, both through curricula specially designed to teach a particular problem solving skill and through the teaching of programing techniques. Among the programs created to foster problem solving are Gertrude's Secrets, Moptown Hotel, and Rocky's Boots (The Learning Company).

It is generally assumed that teaching programing techniques can help students develop many types of problem solving skills. Teaching students to program is a difficult task that can be simplified by using an authoring language. With an authoring language such as SuperPILOT (Apple Computer), virtually any student can develop original programs combining print displays with graphics.

Summary

The computer has become an effective instructional tool for teachers. The potential advantages of this tool seem to outweigh the potential disadvantages, but there are some problems. Nevertheless, the many applications to testing, information and instruction management, drill and practice activities, tutorial/dialogue activities, simulations, telecommunications/information retrieval, word processing, utilities, interactive fiction, videodisks/compact disks, speech, and problem solving are constantly increasing the usefulness of the tool.

The references in Chapter 1 can help clarify past and present roles of our new tool and help us better predict the future of its use in education.

References

1965

Dick, W. The development and current status of computer based instruction. *American Education Research Association,* 1965, *2* (1), 41-54.

1966

Bitzer, D., Lyman, E., and Easley, J. The uses of PLATO: A computer controlled teaching system. *Audiovisual Instruction,* 1966, *11* (1), 16-21.
　　Reviews the uses of the PLATO system in various kinds of instruction. Includes a description of hardware components.

1968

Atkinson, R., and Wilson, H. Computer assisted instruction. *Science,* 1968, *162,* 73-77.

Bundy, R. Computer assisted instruction—where are we? *Phi Delta Kappan,* 1968, *49* (9), 424-429.
　　Provides an overview of the status of computer assisted instruction as of 1968, with a brief summary of results from research. Makes several recommendations about areas in which further research is needed, reviews the research limitations of past projects, and comments on the future of computer assisted instruction.

Trippon, M. PLATO at work. *Phi Delta Kappan,* 1968, *49* (9), 439-441.

1969

Adair, J. Computer assisted instruction in adult basic education. In J. Mangano (Ed.), *Strategies of adult basic education.* Newark, DE: International Reading Association, 1969.
　　Discusses selling points of CAI: Instructional programs may be prepared to meet the differing needs of individuals; computer programs can sequence materials; CAI can provide immediate feedback; CAI makes continuous diagnosis easier; and with CAI, a teacher can deal with more students.

Butler, C. CAI in New York City: Report on the first year's operation. *Educational Technology,* 1969, *9* (10), 84-87.

Jerman, M. Promising developments in computer assisted instruction. *Educational Technology,* 1969, *9* (8), 10-18.

Wilson, H., and Atkinson, R. *Computer assisted instruction — a book of readings.* New York: Academic Press, 1969.

1970

Alpert, D., and Bitzer, D. Advances in computer based education. *Science,* 1970, *167,* 1582-1590.

Dick, W., Latsa, R., and Rivers, L. Sources of information in computer assisted instruction. *Educational Technology,* 1970, *10* (3), 165-169.

Reports results of a 1969 survey of public schools, universities, and research/development centers to determine the extent of computer assisted instruction. Discusses several programs.

Elementary school sets up own minicomputer data bank. *Educational Technology,* 1970, *10* (4), 89.

Describes a minicomputer used at Juliette Elementary School in Elk Grove Village, Illinois, believed to be the first elementary school computer installation in the United States. The computer had 8K of memory.

Feldhusen, J., and Szabo, M. A review of developments in computer assisted instruction. *Educational Technology,* 1970, *10* (3), 90-97.

Alerts the reader to potential sources of information on computer assisted education.

Suppes, P., Jamison, D., and Butler, C. Estimated costs of computer assisted instruction for compensatory education in urban areas. *Educational Technology,* 1970, *10* (4), 49-57.

1971

Baker, F. Computer-based instructional management systems: A first look. *Review of Educational Research,* 1971, *41* (1), 41-70.

Describes computer based instructional management systems existing in 1971. Provides a complete review of early CMI programs; mentions some CAI programs. Author hypothesizes that computer based instructional management has greater possibilities than computer assisted instruction because of the cost.

Hall, K. Computer assisted instruction: Problems and performance. *Phi Delta Kappan,* 1971, *52* (10), 628-631.

Points out problems and successes in CAI implementation.

1972

Barnes, D., and Schrieber, D. *Computer assisted instruction: A selected bibliography.* 1972. (ED 063 769)

Provides the most extensive and complete bibliography of computer uses in education up to 1971, with 835 entries.

Levien, R., Barro, S., Blackwell, R., Comstock, G., Hawkins, M., Hoffmayer, K., Holland, W., and Mossman, C. *The emerging technology: Instructional uses of the computer in higher education.* New York: McGraw-Hill, 1972.

Provides a detailed report of technology elements included in the Carnegie Commission Report on Higher Education.

Vinsonhaler, J., and Bass, R. A summary of ten major studies on CAI drill and practice. *Educational Technology,* 1972, *12* (7), 29-32.

Summarizes the results of ten CAI programs, three reading related: Stanford University, INDICOM — Pontiac, Michigan, and Harcourt Brace Jovanovich.

1973

Cartwright, G., and Cartwright, C. A computer assisted instruction course in the early identification of handicappped children. *Journal of Teacher Education*, 1973, *24* (2), 128-134.

Clark, R. *The best of ERIC: Recent trends in computer assisted instruction.* 1973. (ED 076 025)

> Provides an annotated bibliography of computer assisted instruction up to 1973 at elementary, secondary, junior college, community college, and university levels.

Hall, K., and Mitzel, H. CARE: Computer assisted renewal education—an opportunity in Pennsylvania. *Audio Visual Instruction*, 1973, *18* (1), 35-38.

> Describes CARE, a computer project to bring fundamentals of remediation to teachers of handicapped children.

Merrill, M., and Boutwell, R. Instructional development: Methodology and research. In F. Kerlinger (Ed.), *Review of research in education.* Itasco, IL: F. Peacock, 1973.

1974

Dirr, P. *Computers in education: A bibliography for the instructional technology course for teachers.* 1974. (ED 105 677)

> Lists 78 references from 1968 to 1974 on the uses of computers in education, many of which deal with reading.

Hall, K., Cartwright, P., and Mitzel, H. A triumph for CAI. *Phi Delta Kappan*, 1974, *55*, 70-72.

Swanson, A. The computer as a tool of instruction. An annotated bibliography of selected 1972-1973 books and reports. *AEDS Journal*, 1974, *7* (1), 92-96.

1975

Baker, F. *The computer in the school.* Bloomington, IN: Phi Delta Kappa, 1975.

> Gives an overview of computer assisted and computer managed instruction, including information on PLATO, TICCIT, LOGO, and PLAN. Also includes the author's opinions on present and future capabilities of computers in education.

Eastwood, L., and Ballard, R. The PLATO IV CAI system: Where is it now? Where can it go? *Journal of Educational Technology Systems*, 1975, *3* (4), 267-284.

Fletcher, J. *Computer applications in education training: Status and trends.* 1975. (ED 108 681)

> Provides a review of computer based applications to military training. Some reading programs are mentioned: PLATO IV, Chicago Public Schools, TICCIT, Stanford University, Florida State University, Penn State University, and the University of California.

1976

Beard, M. *Computer assisted instruction: The best of ERIC, May 1973-May 1976.* 1976. (ED 125 608)

> Contains an annotated bibliography of articles about the entire spectrum of computer assisted and managed instruction up to May 1976, including such topics as PLATO, TICCIT, research, teacher training, authoring languages, and costs.

Bukoski, W., and Korotkin, A. Computer activities in secondary education. *Educational Technology,* 1976, *16* (1), 9-22.

Surveys the use of computers in secondary schools up to 1976.

Bunderson, C., and Faust, G. Programmed and computer assisted instruction. In N. Gage (Ed.), *National social studies education yearbook,* Part 1. Chicago: University of Chicago, 1976.

Computer tutor. *American Education,* 1976, *12* (5), 4.

Describes Tel-Catch, a pilot program serving homebound school children in New York State. One hundred children were able to dial a computer and receive both audio and video instruction.

Smith, S., and Sherwood, B. Educational uses of the PLATO computer system. *Science,* 1976, *192,* 344-352.

1977

CAI gets credit for dramatic achievement gains for minorities. *Phi Delta Kappan,* 1977, *59* (4), 290-291.

Seidel, R., and Rubin, M. (Eds.). *Computers and communication: Implications for education.* New York: Academic Press, 1977.

1978

Atkinson, R., Attala, E., Bitzer, D., Bunderson, C., Charp, S., and Hirshbuhl, J. Futures: Where will computer assisted instruction (CAI) be in 1990? *Educational Technology,* 1978, *17* (4), 60-63.

Baker, F. *Computer managed instruction: Theory and practice.* Englewood Cliffs, NJ: Educational Technology Publications, 1978.

Committee on Science and Technology, Subcommittee on Domestic and International Scientific Planning, Analysis and Cooperation, Congress of the United States. *Computers and the learning society.* 1978. (ED 162 643)

Gives the views of noted authorities on the impact of computers in education as of 1978. Excellent reading for those interested in the history of computer applications in education.

Molnar, A. *The next great circle in American education.* 1978. (ED 191 733)

Predicts the future of computer applications in education. Contains a 1972-1977 bibliography.

1979

Piel, D. *Microcomputers GOTO school.* 1979. (ED 172 776)

Discusses using the computer to teach logical thinking skills to sixth grade students at Bose Elementary School, Kenosha, Wisconsin.

Smith, L. Microcomputers in education. *AEDS Monitor,* 1979, *18,* 18-20.

Discusses the history of computers in education, including early leaders in the field.

Van Dusseldorf, R., and Spunk, D. Microcomputers: The selection and application in education. *AEDS Monitor,* 1979, *13* (1).

Consists of an entire issue devoted to microcomputers in education, with eleven articles discussing the issues.

1980

Chambers, J., and Bork, A. *Computer assisted learning in U.S. secondary/elementary schools.* 1980. (ED 202 461)

Discusses the evolution of computer assisted instruction in the public schools. An interesting sidelight describes how PLATO showed positive gains in math achievement on an Educational Testing Service test, but reading did not.

Fitting, M. *Computer use in Santa Clara County schools.* 1980. (ED 212 253)

Gull, R. A successful transition from mini to microcomputer assisted instruction: The Norfolk (Public Schools) experience. *Educational Technology,* 1980, *20* (2), 41-42.

Hinton, J. *Individualized learning using microcomputer CAI.* 1980. (ED 196 409)
Gives a review and extensive bibliography on microcomputers in individualized learning.

Joiner, L., Silverstein, B., and Ross, J. Insights from a microcomputer center in a rural school district. *Educational Technology,* 1980, *20* (5), 36-40.

Papert, S. *Mindstorms: Children, computers, and powerful ideas.* New York: Teachers College Press, 1980.

Taylor, R. *The computer in the school: Tutor, tool, tutee.* New York: Teachers College Press, 1980.

1981

Computers in the schools. *Educational Technology,* 1981, *21* (10).
Consists of an entire issue devoted to the topic of computers in the schools. State of the art review for 1981.

Dickerson, L., and Pritchard, W. Microcomputers and education: Planning for the coming revolution in the classroom. *Educational Technology,* 1981, *21* (1), 7-12.
Warns of the need for teachers and society in general to be computer literate.

Frierl, S., and Roberts, N. Computer literacy bibliography. In J. Thomas (Ed.), *Microcomputers in the schools.* New York: Oryx Press, 1981.

Gleason, G. Microcomputers in education: The state of the art. *Educational Technology,* 1981, *21* (3), 7-12.
Reviews CAI in education up to 1981 and provides some historical background about computers.

Hall, K. Computer based education. The best of ERIC, June 1976-August 1980. 1981. (ED 195 288)

Luehrmann, A. Planning for computer education—problems and opportunities for administrators. *NASSP Bulletin,* 1981, *64* (444), 62-69.
Discusses starting laboratory courses in computing.

Seidel, R. (Ed.). *Computer literacy.* New York: Academic Press, 1981.

Terzian, P. *Microcomputers in public schools: Albany, Schenectady, and Saratoga Counties of New York State.* 1981. (ED 212 291)

Thomas, J. (Ed.). *Microcomputers in the schools.* Phoenix, AZ: Oryx Press, 1981.

1982

Barrett, B., and Hannafin, M. Computers in educational management: Merging accountability with technology. *Educational Technology,* 1982, *22* (3), 9-12.
Discusses eight factors relating to the success of a CMI program, all of which apply to CMI in reading programs.

Bejar, I. Videodisks in education. *BYTE,* 1982, *7* (6), 78-104.

> Discusses state of the art development as of 1982. Includes choice of computers and videodisk players and integrating both, software, courseware, and suppliers of hardware and software.

Bork, A. Learning — not hardware — is the issue. *Electronic Education,* 1982, *1* (2), 12-14, 25.

Braum, L. Computer-aided learning and the microcomputer revolution. *Programmed Learning and Educational Technology,* 1982, *18* (4), 223-229.

> Provides an overview of computer based educational activities since 1975.

Burke, R. *CAI sourcebook.* Englewood Cliffs, NJ: Educational Technology Publications, 1982.

Caldwell, R. The case for and against computer-based education. *Performance and Instruction,* 1982, *21* (8), 34-35.

Caldwell, R. The case for and against computer-based education. *Performance and Instruction,* 1982, *21* (9), 36-37.

Clay, K. *Microcomputers in education: A handbook of resources.* 1982. (ED 235 790)

Computer age in education. *Phi Delta Kappan,* 1982, *63* (5), 303-322.

> Contains articles with diverse points of view about computers in education. Titles include The Silicon Age and Education, Bringing the Microcomputer into the Junior High: A Success Story from Florida, and Instructional Computing in 2001.

Davies, G., and Higgins, J. *CILT information guide 22: Computers, language, and language learning.* London: Centre for Information of Language Teaching and Research, 1982.

Dorsey, O., and Burleson, J. *Automated learning, individual instruction and computers in the small schools classroom.* 1982. (ED 228 003)

> Explores some of the problems and possible solutions inherent in implementing CAI and CMI in small school classrooms.

Evans, C. An invitation to the (near) future. *Today's Education,* 1982, *71* (2), 14-17.

Fisher, G. Computer use in self-contained classrooms. In J. Rodenstein and R. Lambert (Eds.), *Microcomputers in vocational education.* Madison, WI: University of Wisconsin, Vocational Studies Center, 1982, 319-320.

Gold, J. New technology partners: Video and computers. *Personal Computing,* 1982, *6* (4), 64-70.

> Discusses the future of video and computers with specific applications to education.

Hawkins, J. *The flexible use of computers in classrooms.* 1982. (ED 252 188)

Hawkins, J. Sheingold, K., Gearhart, M., and Berger, C. Microcomputers in schools: Impact on the social life of elementary classrooms. *Journal of Applied Developmental Psychology,* 1982, *3,* 361-373.

Joiner, L., Vensel, G., Ross, J., and Silverstein, B. *Microcomputers in education: A nontechnical guide to instructional and school management applications.* Holmes Beach, FL: Learning Publications, 1982.

Leiblum, M. Computer-managed instruction: An explanation and overview. *AEDS Journal,* 1982, *15* (3), 126-142.

Library services to gifted youth. *Top of the News,* 1982, *38* (4), 301-344.
> Discusses in nine articles the diverse services offered to gifted youth by libraries. Includes a treatment of CAI and CMI and provides references.

Miller, B. Bringing the microcomputer into the junior high: A success story from Florida. *Phi Delta Kappan,* 1982, *63* (5), 230.
> Describes the start of the Miami Lakes Junior High School computer based education activities.

Office of Technology Assessment, Congress of the United States. *Informational technology and its impact on American education.* Washington, DC: U.S. Government Printing Office, 1982. (GPO Stock No. 052-003-00888-2)
> Suggests both hope and concern for information technology and education: hope because it appears that technology can improve education not only in the schools but also the home; concern because technology will "profoundly" affect education in unpredictable ways.

Samojeden, E. *The use of computers in the classroom.* 1982. (ED 225 117)
> Describes educational computer use, including modeling and simulation, CAI, CMI, information storage and retrieval, statistical analysis, and educational games. Explains the integration of CASSIS (Computer Assisted Study Skills Instruction) into the course of study at St. Cloud State University in Minnesota. Provides additional information on selection of computer systems and appropriate software. Appendix lists software sources and computing magazines.

Schwartz, H. Monsters and mentors: Computer applications for humanistic education. *College English,* 1982, *44,* 141-152.

Smith, C. *Microcomputers in education.* Chichester, England: Ellis Norwood Limited, 1982.

Uhlig, G. *Microcomputer literacy and teacher education in the southeastern U.S.* 1982. (ED 226 721)
> Tells results of a survey of 134 colleges of education in eight southeastern states, suggesting that "teacher training institutions in the eight southeastern states largely have not responded to the challenge of microcomputer technology." Florida, with a state adopted policy of educational computing, was noted as having a leadership position in the integration of computer technology into teacher training programs.

1983

Adams, A., and Jones, E. *Teaching humanities in the microelectronic age.* Milton Keyes, England: Open University Press, 1983.
> Contains chapters of interest to reading professionals. Chapter 6, The Language Arts Curriculum, discusses adventure/story generators and word processing/writing.

Armstrong, J. The microcomputer in elementary education: Learning can be enjoyable. *Educational Computer Magazine,* 1983, *3* (5), 18.

Becker, H. *Microcomputers in the classroom—dreams and realities.* 1983. (ED 217 872)
> Warns educators not to "uncritially accept every computer-based anything that comes to the market." Explores the computer's role in the instructional delivery system via drill and practice activities, reteaching and remedial in-

struction, CMI, simulations, information retrieval/word processing, and computer programing.

Boruta, M. Computers in schools: Stratifier or equalizer? *The Quarterly Newsletter of the Laboratory of Comparative Human Cognition*, 1983, *5*, 51-55.

Center for Social Organization of Schools. *School uses of microcomputers: Reports from a national survey.* No. 1 (April 1983), No. 2 (June 1983), No. 3 (October 1983), No. 4 (February 1984). Baltimore: Johns Hopkins University, 1983-1984.

Surveys the impact of computers in education.

Char, C. *Research and design issues concerning the development of educational software for children.* Technical Report No. 14. New York: Bank Street College of Education, Center for Children and Technology, 1983.

Committee on Education and Labor, House of Representatives, Ninety-Eighth Congress, First Session. *Hearing on the national center for personal computers in education.* Washington, DC: U.S. Government Printing Office, 1983.

Computers: A kaleidoscopic view. *Phi Delta Kappan*, 1983, *65* (2), 103-131.

Contains eleven articles on computer applications in education, all of which might be of interest to reading educators. Titles include Reflections on the Educational Potential and Limitations of Microcomputers, The Information Society: Byting the Hand that Feeds You, and Terminal Time in the Classroom.

Department of Education, Office of Educational Research and Improvement. *Computers in education: Realizing the potential.* Washington, DC: U.S. Government Printing Office, 1983.

Contains proceedings and papers from a conference sponsored by the Department of Education, November 1982, Pittsburgh, Pennsylvania. Titles include Technologies for Learning, Paradigms for Computer-Based Education, and Research on Reading Education.

Floeger, F. *The effectiveness of microcomputers.* 1983. (ED 246 876)

Grady, T., and Gawronski, J. *Computers in curriculum and instruction.* Alexandria, VA: Association for Supervision and Curriculum Development, 1983.

Lathrop, A., and Goodson, B. *Courseware in the classroom: Selecting, organizing, and using educational software.* Menlo Park, CA: Addison-Wesley, 1983.

Lesgold, A. *Computers in education: Realizing the potential.* 1983. (ED 235 784)

Reports on a 1982 research conference examining the potential of computers in education. Concludes "striking improvement in the quality and productivity of instructional computer systems is attainable with a coherent and sustained research investment." Summarizes basic cognitive research, prototype research, and related research issues. Includes thirteen invited papers dealing with computers in education and classroom application.

Lesgold, A. When can computers make a difference? *Theory into Practice*, 1983, *22*, 247-252.

Loftus, G., and Loftus, E. *The psychology of video games.* New York: Basic Books, 1983.

Discusses the impact of videogames on children and how the psychology surrounding the success of videogames can be used to improve educational activities.

Marling, W. What do you do with your computer when you get it? *Focus: Teaching Language Arts*, Spring 1983, 48-53.

Marvin, C., and Winther, M. Computer-ease: A twentieth-century literacy emergent. *Journal of Communication,* 1983, *33,* 92-108.
>Discusses some relationships between computer literacy and literacy in general.

O'Donnell, H. Beyond computer literacy. *Journal of Reading,* 1983, *27* (1), 78-80.
>Discusses the impact of computer literacy on society with seven ERIC/RCS resources serving as focal points.

Ogletree, E., and Haskins, T. *Microcomputers in schools: A research review.* 1983. (ED 252 187)
>Reviews studies on computer applications in education.

Oliver, M. *Computer literacy for teachers.* 1983. (ED 234 742)
>Gives a very general treatment of the basics in computer literacy. Suggests "computers are only tools that can help teachers do their job." Emphasis is on teacher use for classroom management and instruction.

Patterson, J. Theoretical secrets for intelligent software. *Theory into Practice,* 1983, *22,* 267-271.

Patterson, J., and Patterson, J. *Putting computer power in schools: A step-by-step approach.* Englewood Cliffs, NJ: Prentice-Hall, 1983.

Pogrow, S. *Education in the computer age: Issues of policy, practice, and reform.* Beverly Hills, CA: Sage, 1983.

Prince, A. *The ghost of computers past, present, and future: Computer use for preservice/inservice reading programs.* 1983. (ED 239 242)
>Suggests the possibility of improved efficiency and effectiveness of teacher learning in colleges of education by using computer assisted instruction and simulations. Concludes that the availability of preplanned, meaningful educational training can give professors more time for classroom supervision and individual and group interaction.

Rheingold, H. Video games go to school: Classroom computers could bring about a profound transformation in the way children learn. *Psychology Today,* 1983, *17* (9), 37-43.

Schorr, B. Many schools buying computers find problems using them. *Wall Street Journal,* April 7, 1983, *27,* 45.

Shavelson, R., Winkler, J., Stasz, C., and Robyn, A. *Teachers' instructional uses of microcomputers.* Santa Monica, CA: Rand Corporation, 1983.

Tucker, M. Computers in schools: A plan in time saves nine. *Theory into Practice,* 1983, *22,* 313-320.

White, M. (Ed.). *The future of electronic learning.* Hillsdale, NJ: Erlbaum, 1983.
>Contains seven papers presented at a conference held at Teachers College, Columbia University, April 1982. Titles include Public Policy and Electronic Learning, Learning by Doing Revisited for Electronic Learning Environments, How Children Learn from Electronic Sources, and Toward a Psychology of Electronic Learning.

Winkler, J., and Shavelson, R. *Successful uses of microcomputers in classroom instruction.* Santa Monica, CA: Rand Corporation, 1983.

1984

Anchorage Borough School District. *Scope and sequence for computer education.* 1984. (ED 252 188)
>Tells one school district's ideas on how to organize computer education curricula.

Ascher, C. *Microcomputers: Equity and quality in education for urban disadvantaged students.* 1984. (ED 242 801)

Examines the possibility of computers in education causing a disparity among students. One survey's data indicate 66 percent of affluent school districts have computers, compared to 41 percent of less wealthy school districts. Schools serving disadvantaged students are urged to give equitable exposure to computers and to structure CAI to fit the needs of those students.

Auten, A. A guide to purchasing a microcomputer. *Journal of Reading,* 1984, *26* (3), 268-271.

Reviews nine resources available on how to choose a computer for classroom or computer lab use.

Becker, H. Computers in schools today: Some basic considerations. *American Journal of Education,* 1984, *93* (1), 22-39.

Explores the computer's role in education with a lengthy section on computers and writing instruction. Becker believes that "by far the most significant advantage of a computer-based writing system is the minimal effort required to make changes in one's text." He cautions that word processors are irrelevant if students are not motivated to improve their text.

Bitter, G., and Camuse, R. *Using a microcomputer in the classroom.* Reston, VA: Reston, 1984.

Bork, A. Education and computers: The situation today and some possible futures. *T.H.E. Journal,* 1984, *12* (3), 92-97.

Caster, T. What they won't teach you in your programming course. *The Reading Teacher,* 1984, *38* (1), 123-124.

Suggests some of the problems teachers will face as they try to use computers in their classrooms — outlets, breakdowns, traffic patterns, and group size.

Committeee on Education and Labor, House of Representatives, Ninety-Eighth Congress, Second Sesson. *Hearing on computer education.* Washington, DC: U.S. Government Printing Office, 1984.

Committee on Science and Technology, House of Representatives, Ninety-Eighth Congress, Second Session. *H.R. 3750, The computer literacy act, and H.R. 4628, The national educational software act.* Washington, DC: U.S. Government Printing Office, 1984.

Computers and education. *Creative Computing,* 1984, *10* (11), 163-188.

Contains articles devoted to the history of microcomputers in education, including Computers, Children, and Learning: One Complete Iteration; Reflections on Educational Computing; and Personal Computers Invade the Classroom.

Crovello, T. Evolution of educational software. *The American Biology Teacher,* 1984, *46* (3), 140-145.

Traces the development of both computer hardware and educational software. Computer integrated curriculum, artificial intelligence, and videodisk technology are described as realistic expectations in education's future.

Dreyfus, H., and Dreyfus, S. Putting computers in their proper place: Analysis versus intuition in the classroom. *Teachers College Record,* 1984, *85* (4), 578-601.

Grabe, M. Evaluating the educational value of microcomputers. *Computers in the Schools,* 1984, *1* (4), 35-44.

Presents some ideas on how to evaluate microcomputer applications in the schools.

Herrmann, A., and Gallagher, B. (speakers). *Using the computer in the classroom: Approaches and issues.* Cassette Recording No. 74329-012. Urbana, IL: National Council of Teachers of English, 1984.

International Reading Association Computer Technology and Reading Committee. Guidelines for educators on using computers in the schools. *The Reading Teacher,* 1984, *38* (1), 80-81.

International Reading Association Computer Technology and Reading Committee. Guidelines for educators on using computers in the schools. *Journal of Reading,* 1984, *28* (1), 63-65.

Kleinman, G. *Brave new schools: How computers can change education.* Reston, VA: Reston, 1984.

Liebling, C. Creating the classroom's communicative context: How teachers and microcomputers can help. *Theory into Practice,* 1984, *23* (3), 323-238.

Menosky, J. Computer literacy and the press. *Teachers College Record,* 1984, *85* (4), 615-621.

Meyers, J. *Computer awareness activities and computer curriculum, K-5.* 1984. (ED 254 197)
> Presents over one hundred computer awareness activities for students in elementary schools.

Microcomputers: A revolution in learning. *Theory into Practice,* 1984, *22* (4).
> Contains eleven articles of possible interest to reading professionals, including When Can Computers Make a Difference?, Classrooms and Computers as Instructional Settings, and Theoretical Secrets for Intellectual Software.

Noble, D. Computer literacy and ideology. *Teachers College Record,* 1984, *85* (4), 602-614.
> Criticizes the public's need for computer literacy.

Organization for Economic Cooperation and Development. *The impact of the new information technologies on learning processes in formal education.* 1984. (ED 258 546)
> Provides a European perspective on computers in education.

Pantiel, M., and Petersen, B. *Kids, teachers, and computers: A guide to computers in the elementary school.* Englewood Cliffs, NJ: Prentice-Hall, 1984.

Peterson, D. (Ed.). *Intelligent schoolhouse: Reading on computers and learning.* Reston, VA: Reston, 1984.

Simpson, B. Heading for the ha-ha. *Teachers College Record,* 1984, *85* (4), 622-630.
> Talks about a "ha-ha," an unseen, unpenetrable barrier. Computers, despite their appeal, will not unlock any of the secrets of good education. Computers appear to be nothing more than educational aids.

Suchor, C., and Jester, V. Computer caveats. *English Education,* 1984, *16* (3), 181-185.
> Reviews ten sources about computers, children, and education.

Teacher Education Conference Board. *Teaching learning with computers: Position paper.* 1984. (ED 248 885)

Tolman, M., and Allred, R. *The computer and education: What the research says to the teacher.* 1984. (ED 252 173)

Toward the advancement of microcomputer technology in special education. *Peabody Journal of Education,* 1984, *62* (1).

Contains twelve articles on computers and special education, some of which might be of interest to reading professionals.

Visions of the future in educational computing. *Phi Delta Kappan,* 1984, *66* (4), 239-258.

Contains six articles on computer applications in education. Titles include Computers in Education Today—and Some Possible Futures, Educational Computing: The Burden of Insuring Quality, and Forget It! Forget It!

Winkler, J., Shavelson, R., Stasz, C., Robyn, A., and Feibel, W. *How effective teachers use microcomputers for instruction.* Santa Monica, CA: Rand Corporation, 1984.

1985

Alessi, S., and Trollip, S. *Computer-based instruction: Methods and development.* Englewood Cliffs, NJ: Prentice-Hall, 1985.

Provides information for reading professionals who want to author their own computer based instruction activities.

Barrett, S. When you wish upon a CPU: Truly integrating the personal computer into the classroom. *Educational Technology,* 1985, *25* (9), 21-23.

Bork, A. *Personal computers for education.* New York: Harper & Row, 1985.

Bramble, W., and Mason, E. *Computers in schools.* New York: McGraw-Hill, 1985.

Brown, J. Process versus product: A perspective on tools for communal and informal electronic learning. *Journal of Educational Computing Research,* 1985, *1* (2), 179-201.

Suggests that new computer based learning environments should feature a process approach to learning rather than a product approach.

Calfee, R. Computer literacy and book literacy: Parallels and contrasts. *Educational Researcher,* 1985, 14 (5), 8-13.

Suggests that different instructional approaches to literacy training can be related to the ways schools teach computer literacy.

Callison, W. *Using computers in the classroom.* Englewood Cliffs, NJ: Prentice-Hall, 1985.

Clark, G. Using computers to enhance thinking. *Electronic Education,* 1985, *4* (4), 20, 27.

Describes how the interaction between computers and children can lead to better thinking skills.

Cline, H. *The electronic schoolhouse: The IBM secondary computer education program.* Hillsdale, NJ: Erlbaum, 1985.

Describes IBM's computer education program from the perspective of Educational Testing Service researchers who evaluated the programs in more than one hundred schools.

Coburn, P., Kelman, P., Roberts, N., Synder, T., Watt, D., and Weiner, C. *Practical guide to computers in education,* second edition. Reading, MA: Addison-Wesley, 1985.

Computers in education: Where do we go from here? *Educational Technology,* 1985, *25* (1).

Consists of an entire issue containing articles about the impact of computers in education.

Costanzo, W. Language, thinking, and the culture of computers. *Language Arts,* 1985, *62* (5), 516-523.

Discusses the impact of videogames, adventure games, and programing on students. Suggests some reasons for the impact.

Cuban, L. *Teachers and machines: The classroom use of technology since 1920.* New York: Teachers College Press, 1985.

Dronka, P. Computer integration into instruction is stuck; experts blame unclear optimal uses and three implementation problems. *ASCD Update,* 1985, *27* (5), 1, 6-8.

Criticizes computers in education. Author reports that many experts feel computers do not have and, in the foreseeable future, will not have a positive impact on education. Limited access to machines, limited software, and inexperienced teachers of the computer contribute to the criticism. Also discusses the findings of the Johns Hopkins University survey, How Schools Use Microcomputers.

Huber, L. Computer learning through Piaget's eyes. *Classroom Computer Learning,* 1985, *6* (2), 39-42.

Discusses the demands of using computers with students in three stages of Piaget's development process: preoperational, concrete, and formal.

Instructional uses of new technology. *NASSP Bulletin,* 1985, *69.*

Contains eleven articles on computers and learning, including Instructional Uses of New Technology; Language Laboratories: What Have We Learned?; Computer-Assisted Instruction: Possibilities and Problems; and The Forgotten Medium – Are We Too Visually Dependent?

Is this the good life on a chip? *IRT Communication Quarterly,* Spring 1985, 3.

Tells the views of Jere Brophy and Patrick Hannon (staff members at the Institute for Research on Teaching, Michigan State University) on the development of computer software for classroom use. The authors suggest that "software designers have not taken into account an important feature of classroom life: Classroom instruction is group-based." Also, computer based activities are "not worth the trouble" and have been "oversold." However, computers do have the potential to help teachers and students in simulation exercises, computer graphics, and word processing.

Lepper, M. Microcomputers in education. *American Psychologist,* 1985, *40* (1), 1-18.

Mojkowski, C. 10 essential truths to help you plan for technology use. *Tech Trends,* 1985, *30* (7), 18-22.

Lists ten essential truths: Computers are tools, new technology is a catalyst for curriculum revitalization, teachers and administrators need more and better training, microcomputers have their limitations, our definitions of computer literacy need clarity, computer education programs must be evaluated, most software is inadequate, technology is a catalyst for increased planning for school systems, technology will alter the organization of schools, and computers are inherently subversive.

Newman, D. Functional environments for microcomputers in education. *Quarterly Newsletter of the Laboratory of Comparative Human Cognition,* 1985, *7* (2), 51-56.

Discusses how the computer operates in a "functional learning environment." In particular, how can LOGO, simulations, and networking help students realize that these activities have a purpose for future learning?

Norris, W. Improving education through technological innovation. *T.H.E. Journal,* 1985, *12* (10), 65-68.
Offers the views of the chief executive officer of Control Data Corporaton on the many ways technology can help education.

Nowlin, W., and Friedstein, H. A guide to information utilities for educators. *Educational Technology,* 1985, *25* (9), 29-32.

O'Donnell, H. Teaching teachers to use computers. *English Education,* 1985, 17 (1), 54-61.
Reviews available ERIC/RCS documents and provides an adapted evaluation scheme for determining teacher computer competency at three levels of awareness: basic, curriculum, and technological.

Phi Delta Kappa. *Planning for microcomputers in curriculum.* Bloomington, IN: Phi Delta Kappa Center on Evaluation, Development, and Research, 1985.

Reidesal, C., and Clements, D. *Coping with computers in the elementary and middle schools.* Englewood Cliffs, NJ: Prentice-Hall, 1985.
Contains a chapter on reading and language arts that discusses sample reading programs and word processing.

Rowntree, D. *Educational technology in curriculum development.* New York: Teachers College Press, 1985.

Salmon, P. Technological challenges to the education profession. *Electronic Learning,* 1985, *5* (3), 17-20.

Sawada, D. New metaphoric images for computers in education. *Educational Technology,* 1985, *25* (12), 15-20.

Schwandt, L., and Wiederanders, D. Microcomputers and the ultimate goal of education. *Educational Technology,* 1985, *25* (8), 32-33.

Sloan, D. (Ed.). *The computer in education: A critical perspective.* New York: Teachers College Press, 1985.

Smith, R. School of the future—from the assembly line to the job shop model. *AEDS Monitor,* 1985, *24* (3, 4), 6, 27.

Sturdivant, P. Technology in the classroom—students preparing for the world of tomorrow. *AEDS Monitor,* 1985, *24* (3, 4), 8-10.
Describes the Houston Independent School District's Department of Technology Computer Concepts program. The program features a problem solving curriculum using word processing.

Summer, E. Microcomputers as a new technology innovation in education: Growth of the related journal literature. *Educational Technology,* 1985, *25* (8), 5-14.
Shows how the growth of computer applications in education can be traced by the number and types of journals printing articles about the topic.

Whiting, J. New directions in educational computing: Coming changes in software and teaching strategies to optimize learning. *Educational Technology,* 1985, *25* (9), 18-20.

Wright, E., and Forcier, R. *The computer: A tool for the teacher.* Belmont, CA: Wadsworth, 1985.
Suggests how and when to use computers in the classroom. Of particular interest is Chapter 8, which contains a section on classroom applications of language arts programs.

1986

Becker, H. Our national report card: Preliminary results from the new Johns Hopkins survey. *Classroom Computer Learning,* 1986, *6* (4), 30-33.

Reports survey results: More teachers are using computers than in the past; close to 10 percent of secondary teachers in English and social studies use computers for instruction; most elementary teachers are using computers for CAI and secondary teachers are using CAI for computer programing and computer literacy; more male than female students are using computers in the schools; computer theft is not a problem in the schools; and many schools have insufficient computer resources.

Carnoy, M., and Loop, L. (Eds.). *Computers and education: Which role for international research?* A report on the Stanford/Unesco symposium, March 10-14, 1986, Stanford University School of Education. Paris, France: Unesco, 1986.

Presents proceedings of a symposium on worldwide understanding of the role of educational technology in educational systems and the identification of needs for further research at the international level.

McClintock, R. Into the starting gate: On computing and the curriculum. *Teachers College Record,* 1986, *88* (2), 191-215.

Raises many questions (and provides a few answers) about the future of computers as "education machines." Required reading for anyone pondering the future of educational computing in whatever forms it might take.

National Task Force on Educational Technology. Transforming American education: Reducing the risk to the nation. *T.H.E. Journal,* 1986, *14* (1), 58-67.

Presents a comprehensive report by the task force to the Secretary of Education. The report discusses transforming education, the status of technology in education, the potential for technology in education, educational applications of technology, effects on education, beginning the transformation, recommendations, and concluding comments. Educators interested in computer based educational applications should read this report.

Piorot, J. Computer literacy: What is it? *Electronic Learning,* 1986, *5* (4), 33-36.

Provides an up to date treatment of problems surrounding the term *computer literacy.*

Salomon, G., and Gardner, H. The computer as educator: Lessons from television research. *Educational Researcher,* 1986, *15* (1), 13-19.

Cautions that useful lessons learned from research about televised instruction should not be forgotten. Describes what should have been learned from televised instruction and what computer based research can do to overcome the same errors.

Scheffler, I. Computers at school? *Teachers College Record,* 1986, *87* (4), 513-528.

Casts doubt on most of the educational and social precepts that currently drive computer based education. Suggests in a general sense that most of what we should value in education is "beyond the reach of algorithms" and hence today's computer based education efforts.

Shillingburg, P. *The teacher's computer book.* New York: Teachers College Press, 1986.

Presents forty student projects that use computers in the classroom. The activities are designed for elementary and middle school students.

Snyder, T., and Palmer, J. *In search of the most amazing thing: Children, education, and computers.* Reading, MA: Addison-Wesley, 1986.

Suggests that the instructional practices contained in most of our computer based educational programs are ineffective and that more exploration and discovery programs are needed.

Sununu, J. Will technologies make learning and teaching easier? *Phi Delta Kappan,* 1986, *68* (4), 220-222.

Presents the National Governors' Association recommendations on technology and the schools plus a seventeen item action agenda. The recommendations include state supported demonstrations of cost effective, efficient school sites; state supported research and development; state supported marketing mechanisms; and state supported development plans for using technologies and training teachers.

1987

Shane, H. *Teaching and learning in a microelectronic age.* Bloomington, IN: Phi Delta Kappa Educational Foundation, 1987.

Discusses the impact of the computer on our daily lives and on elementary and secondary education.

2
Computer applications for reading instruction

T he first computer applications in reading education were offered on mainframe, time sharing computers. Schools had relatively little interest in computers because the cost of using mainframe computers was high and the rigid drill and practice programs were not enticing. The microcomputer solved the problem of high computer costs, but early microcomputer based reading software was low quality. Fortunately, the reading software of the 1980s is much improved, and the quality continues to improve even though developing quality reading software is a Herculean task.

There are compelling reasons why the quality of reading and language arts software should continue to improve. First, publishers of traditional reading instruction materials are converting their materials for computer based delivery whenever feasible. This represents an enormous financial commitment by the publishers.

Second, inexpensive, powerful, fast, and reliable microcomputers are now readily available. Although Apple Computer dominates the educational computer marketplace, most of the other microcomputer manufacturers are interested in reaping the millions of dollars schools spend annually on computers and software.

Third, the growth of the educational software market has provided financial incentive for research and development efforts. Computer manufacturers are beginning to commit large amounts of resources toward the development and marketing of reading and language arts software. For example, IBM's Writing to Read System (developed by John Henry Martin) is becoming increasingly popular in kindergarten and first grade classrooms. IBM has helped to develop many other programs for reading and language arts instruction; for example, the Reading for Meaning Series, the Reading for Information Series, and the Language Series. Another recent IBM program, PALS (Principle of the Alphabet Literacy System, developed by John

Henry Martin), is an interactive videodisk, personal computer, adult literacy program similar in concept to the Writing to Read Program. (For a complete listing of computer based education software and hardware companies, see Appendix A).

Fourth, schools and school districts are switching the focus of their computer purchases from hardware to software. This increase in demand for educational software should reinforce publishers' increased financial commitment to quality programs.

Fifth, the newer reading software allows the teacher or student some control of content. While the algorithms of programs cannot be readily changed by teachers or students, they do allow change to the content. For instance, a teacher who wants children to practice their basal reader vocabulary words with a computer can do so by using an authoring scheme (if one is available as a part of the microcomputer program).

In summary, the microcomputer reading software of the late eighties promises to fulfill many of the unmet promises made about earlier computer based instruction programs. Reading software is improving and will continue to improve, but we have a long way to go.

The references in this chapter describe computer based reading and language arts programs for both children and adults in classroom and clinic settings.

References

1966
Atkinson, R., and Hansen, D. Computer assisted instruction in initial reading: The Stanford project. *Reading Research Quarterly,* 1966, *2,* 5-25.
> Describes the purposes of the CAI reading project, its organization, its potential for research, equipment used, and commands necessary to create one complete lesson. Also explains the six strand reading curriculum.

1967
Spache, G. A reaction to computer assisted instruction in initial reading: The Stanford project. *Reading Research Quarterly,* 1967, *3* (1), 101-110.
> Evaluates the Stanford reading project, listing six misconceptions inherent in the work of the project and discussing questionable research.

1968
Atkinson, R. The role of the computer in teaching initial reading. *Childhood Education,* 1968, *44,* 464-470.

1969
Charp, S., and Wye, R. Computer assisted instruction in a large school system. *Journal of Educational Data Processing,* 1969, *6* (1), 28-39.
> Describes the first large school system (Philadelphia) implementation of CAI, which included more than 200 hours of reading activities. Activities

included recognition of sentences, recognition and use of key words, labeling and categorizing concepts, seeing the relationship between sentences and sentence order, ordering and sequencing ideas and sentences, distinguishing general from specific topics, finding and understanding details, selecting topic sentences, drawing sound conclusions, and following directions. Also points out that 254 hours were required to create 1 hour of CAI.

1970

Hannan, T. Computer assisted instruction—state of the art summary. *Audiovisual Instruction,* 1970, *15* (6), 93-94.

Reviews the INDICOM project, an elementary reading and mathematics project in Pontiac, Michigan.

Wilson, H., and Fitzgibbons, N. Practice and perfection: A preliminary analysis of achievement data from the CAI Elementary English Program. *Elementary English,* 1970, *47* (4), 576-579.

1972

Atkinson, R., and Fletcher, J. Teaching children to read with a computer. *The Reading Teacher,* 1972, *25* (4), 319-327.

Describes the "strand" structure of a drill and practice program designed to supplement reading instruction in grades one to three. Also provides a flow chart and sample exercises with cost estimates.

Fletcher, J., and Atkinson, R. Evaluation of the Stanford CAI program in initial reading. *Journal of Educational Psychology,* 1972, *63,* 597-602.

Provides a detailed analysis of scores for forty-four matched pairs of subjects. Results indicated that five and one-half months of CAI yielded significant gains in reading among first grade students; boys were helped more by CAI than were girls; and significant results were obtained in sentence and paragraph comprehension, areas hardly touched by the CAI program.

Fletcher, J., and Suppes, P. Computer assisted instruction in reading: Grades 4-6. *Educational Technology,* 1972, *12* (8), 45-49.

Describes implementation of Computer Curriculum Corporation's reading curriculum using a minicomputer with 33 student TTY terminals.

Strang, H. An automated approach to remedial reading. *Psychology in the Schools,* 1972, *9,* 433-439.

Describes a program of automated remedial reading instruction available to grade six students as soon as they failed any classroom reading tasks. Children making use of this program outperformed controls in word accuracy and task completion.

1973

Atkinson, R., Fletcher, J., Lindsey, E., Campbell, J., and Barr, A. Computer assisted instruction in initial reading: Individualized instruction based on optimization procedures. *Educational Technology,* 1973, *13* (8), 27-37.

Describes an eight strand drill and practice curriculum. Also describes how monitoring student performance can allow the computer to prescribe more practice for either slow students or difficult items. Suggests a method for computing the amount of study time needed to reach a given score on a reading achievement test.

Elliot, P., and Videbeck, R. Reading comprehension materials for high school equivalency students on the PLATO IV computer based education system. *Educational Technology*, 1973, *13* (9), 20-22.

> Discusses the development of a program to train adults to pass the GED (high school equivalency) test using the PLATO IV terminal.

Litman, G. *CAI in Chicago*. 1973. (ED 087 423)

> Tells how CAI in reading proved effective in raising reading scores in a 1973 project using Computer Curriculum Corporation software and computers.

Majer, K. Computer assisted instruction and reading: How, what, when, and where? *Educational Technology*, 1973, *13* (9), 23-26.

1974

Atkinson, R. Teaching children to read with a computer. *American Psychologist*, 1974, *29*, 169-178.

> Discusses three levels of optimization of instruction: decision making within an instructional strand (which items to present, how to present them, and when to schedule review), decision making about allocation of instructional time to the various strands or skills with reading, and decision making about distribution of terminal use time among students.

Golub, L. A computer assisted literacy development program. *Journal of Reading*, 1974, *17* (4), 279-284.

> Discusses LITE, a literacy program developed at Pennsylvania State University.

Obertino, P. The PLATO reading project: An overview. *Educational Technology*, 1974, *14* (2), 8-13.

> Presents the aims of the PLATO Elementary Reading Curriculum (PERC) and details the program development.

1976

Venezky, R., Chicone, S., and Perry, J. *On-line diagnosis of reading difficulties*. 1976. (ED 141 791)

1977

Venezky, R., Perry, J., Chicone, S., and Pittleman, S. *Summary of studies for an on-line reading diagnosis system*. 1977. (ED 138 967)

Yeager, R. *The reading machine*. 1977. (ED 142 990)

> Describes the PLATO Elementary Reading Curriculum.

1978

Johnson, D., Pittleman, S., Schwenker, J., and Perry, J. *On-line diagnosis of reading difficulties*. 1978. (ED 162 277)

> Describes three studies conducted to evaluate various paradigms for assessing vocabulary knowledge on-line: synonym in context, synonym out of context, cloze, oral recognition, and self-screening. Authors conclude that no single format is superior for the assessment of vocabulary knowledge.

1979

Buckley, E., and Rauch, D. *Pilot project in computer assisted instruction in adult basic education*. 1979. (ED 197 202)

> Reports a three year study that found CAI in reading "to be an effective supplementary learning medium for ABE students." Students used the ABE pro-

gram from Computer Curriculum Corporation, which contains word attack skills, vocabulary skills, literal and inferential skills, and work related study skills.

1980

Blanchard, J. Computer assisted instruction in today's reading classrooms. *Journal of Reading,* 1980, *23,* 430-433.

Explains briefly the terms computer assisted instruction (CAI) and computer managed instruction (CMI). Presents a history of computer based reading programs and of bilingual and handicapped reading programs.

Brebner, A., Hallworth, H., McIntosh, E., and Wonter, C. *Teaching elementary reading by CMI and CAI.* 1980. (ED 198 793)

Describes a K-8 CMI reading program with some prescriptive CAI components initiated by Belvedere-Parkway Elementary School. The CMI program consisted of 329 education objectives and tests marketed through the Educational Development Corporation. The CAI component featured drill and practice and tutorial programs involving structural analysis skills. Teachers reported increased reading performance and positive attitudes toward the program and reading.

Computer based instruction: A new decade. *Proceedings of the annual conference of the Association for the Development of Computer Based Instructional Systems.* 1980. (ED 194 047)

Contains two papers of interest to reading educators—The University of Akron's Computer Based Education Network: A Report on Activities and Results of a Five Year Study and Microprocessor Applications in Reading Instruction, Diagnostic Testing, and Evaluation.

Heuer, R. Reading comprehension for the SOL-20. *Creative Computing,* 1980, *6* (4), 38-39.

Describes an early computer based comprehension activity using one of the first microcomputers to appear in the schools.

Mason, G. Computerized reading instruction: A review. *Educational Technology,* 1980, *20* (10), 18-22.

Discusses three early attempts to teach reading: Stanford, PLATO, and TIC-CIT. Describes several computer based reading programs, including DOVACK and the Talking Typewriter. Discusses computer based college reading programs and computer reading programs for elementary and secondary schools.

Thompson, B. Computers in reading: A review of applications and implications. *Educational Technology,* 1980, *20* (8), 38-41.

Provides a history of computer applications in reading up to 1980.

1981

Brandt, R. On reading, writing, and computers: A conversation with John Henry Martin. *Educational Leadership,* 1981, *39* (1), 60-64.

Describes a system developed by John Henry Martin by which children can learn to read and write with a simplified alphabet and interactive computer programing. Martin discusses the aspects of his program being field tested.

Mason, G., and Blanchard, J. Computerized reading in the eighties. In E. Dishner, T. Bean, and J. Readence (Eds.), *Reading in the content areas: Improving classroom instruction.* Dubuque, IA: Kendall/Hunt, 1981.

Rauch, M., and Samojeden, E. *Computer assisted instruction: One aid for teachers of reading.* 1981. (ED 204 702)

> Discusses a college CAI reading program at St. Cloud State University.

1982

Frederiksen, J., Warren, B., Gillotte, H., and Weaver, P. The name of the game is literacy. *Classroom Computer News,* 1982, *2* (5), 23-27.

> Discusses a rationale for using computer arcade games to teach reading and describes experimental games being field tested. The games include Speed, the rapid recognition of letter clusters in words; Racer, pronouncing displayed words; and Ski Jump, context plus slower and slower tachistoscopic word presentation.

Henny, M. *Development and use of microcomputer reading programs.* 1982. (ED 215 302)

Judd, D. Microcomputer use in teaching adult reading. In D. Gueulette (Ed.), *Microcomputers for adult learning: Potentials and perils.* Chicago, IL: Follett, 1982.

Kepner, H. The computer in language arts and reading. In H. Kepner (Ed.), *Computers in the classroom.* Washington, DC: National Educational Association, 1982.

Langer, J. *Computer technology and reading instruction: Perspectives and directions.* 1982. (ED 214 131)

Lesgold, A. Computer games for teaching of reading. *Behavior Research and Instrumentation,* 1982, *14* (2) 224-226.

> Offers suggestions for selecting topics for computer based reading instruction, indicating that words, word meanings, and speed of processing are places to start.

Mason, G. *Advantages and disadvantages of the computer as a teacher of reading.* 1982. (ED 214 131)

Mason, G., and Blanchard, J. Reading teachers put the computer to work. *Classroom Computer News,* 1982, *2* (5), 44-45.

Mewcomb, S. PLATO's "finest and most expensive." *Electronic Education,* 1982, *1* (2), 12-14.

Milner, J. (Ed.). *Micro to mainframe in English education.* Urbana, IL: National Council of Teachers of English, 1982.

> Contains eight essays on computer based applications in English/language arts education.

Neufeld, H. *Reading, writing, and algorithms: Computer literacy in the schools.* 1982. (ED 211 959)

O'Donnell, H. Computer literacy, Part I: An overview. *The Reading Teacher,* 1982, *35* (4), 490-493.

> Uses Resources in Education (RIE) and Current Index to Journals in Education (CIJE) to form the nucleus for a review of computer applications in reading.

O'Donnell, H. Computer literacy, Part II: Classroom applications. *The Reading Teacher,* 1982, *35* (5), 614-617.

> Provides a general treatment of the distinctions between computer assisted instruction and computer managed instruction and their applications in reading.

Paisley, W., and Chen, M. *Children and electronic text: Challenges and opportunities of the new literacy.* 1982. (ED 225 530)

Zucker, A. The computer in the school: A case study. *Phi Delta Kappan*, 1982, *63* (5), 317-319.

> Describes the introduction of a minicomputer in the 1975-1976 school year at Milton Academy in Massachusetts. Reading teachers used maze type activities with the computer.

1983

Anderson, B. A primer for classroom uses of microcomputers in reading. *Reading Psychology*, 1983, *4* (2), 157-161.

> Describes instructional uses, especially for diagnosis and prescription of reading problems, as part of what teachers need to know about microcomputers. Also covers evaluation guidelines and sources of software reviews for teachers.

Beyers, C. Telephone gives drill new twist. *Electronic Education*, 1983, *3* (2), 52-53.

> Describes a service of Computer Curriculum Corporation (CCC), Dial-a-Drill. Through the use of a home telephone, students can access an instructional computer. The computer provides six to ten minutes of drill and practice activities on arithmetic, spelling, and reading. The students interact with the computer through the numbers and symbols on the dials of their telephones. Describes a summer pilot project involving Dial-a-Drill.

Blanchard, J.S., and Daniel, D.B. The second coming of computers in reading: Hope or hysteria? *Reading Psychology*, 1983, *4* (2), iii-vii.

> Notes that computers have been involved in reading instruction since the early 1960s, but few are aware of earlier efforts. The authors discuss the realities of today's microcomputers in reading instruction and suggest future advances.

Daniel, D., and Blanchard, J. Trends in educational microcomputing: Implications for the language arts. *Computers, Reading and Language Arts*, 1983, *1* (2), 18-22.

> Identifies current trends in microcomputing, including the word processing boom, cost effectiveness of computer hardware, greater quantity of educational software, and curriculum integration of CAI. Analyzes the effect of technical trends (new computer languages, expanded memory, and specialized microprocessors). Provides suggestions to aid educators in responding to these approaches.

Davis, J., and Davis, H. (Eds.). *Computers in teaching English*. Urbana, IL: National Council of Teachers of English, 1983.

> Contains twenty-five articles on computers and English/language arts education.

Davis, K. (Ed.). *The computerized English class*. Urbana, IL: National Council of Teachers of English, 1983.

> Contains seven articles on computers and English/language arts education.

Fech, B. Computer assisted instruction—beyond drill and practice. *Computers, Reading and Language Arts*, 1983, *1* (1), 44-46.

> Comments on the state of CAI from an international perspective in 1983.

Gabriel, D. *The mainframe computer in a basic reading and writing class*. 1983. (ED 239 710)

Describes some instructional problems and advantages associated with mainframe computer use in the basic reading and writing classes at Cuyoga Community College.

Geoffrion, L., and Geoffrion, O. *Computers and reading instruction*. Reading, MA: Addison-Wesley, 1983.

Consists of an entire text that should be of interest to reading professionals. Sample chapter titles include The Computer-Based Reading Classroom, Reading Readiness, and Word Identification.

Kearn, S. Make room for computers in language arts. *AEDS Monitor*, 1983, *21* (7, 8), 28-30.

Advocates having English teachers become involved in using computers for instructional purposes and suggests why and how they should go about it.

Kling, M. *Reading and computers*. Paper presented at the Sixteenth Annual Reading Conference of the Reading Center of Rutgers University, 1983.

Kuchinskas, G. 22 ways to use a microcomputer in reading and language arts classes. *Computers, Reading and Language Arts*, 1983, *1* (1), 11-16.

Discusses drill and practice, tutoring, assessment, record keeping, prescriptions, interactive language programs, readability, language analysis, cloze passage generation, vocabulary list generation, test item generation, objectives production, inventories, word processing, videodisks, data banks, simulations, computer programing, staff development, research, and computer literacy.

Lesgold, A. A rationale for computer-based reading instruction. In A. Wilkinson (Ed.), *Classroom computers in schools*. New York: Academic Press, 1983.

Begins with some implications from reading research that apply to computer based instruction. The author believes that two important uses of computers in reading are to provide practice in word recognition skills and to provide better diagnostic information on student progress. The article discusses why these are important uses for the computer.

Mason, G. The computer in the reading clinic. *The Reading Teacher*, 1983, *36* (6), 504-507.

Focuses on the computer as a valuable tool for reading clinicians and remedial teachers and suggests ways computers can assist with instruction. Includes descriptions of the computer as diagnostic test administrator, accuracy trainer, game partner, and provider of review and repetition. Describes a variety of software.

Mason, G. Which computer teaches reading best? *The Reading Teacher*, 1983, *37* (1), 104-106.

Discusses the costs of computers, color quality, print displays, user friendliness, and software.

Mason, G., Blanchard, J., and Daniel, D. Computer applications in reading – part 1 of an excerpt. *Computers, Reading and Language Arts*, 1983, *1* (3), 19-23.

Mason, G., Blanchard, J., and Daniel, D. Computer applications in reading – part 2 of an excerpt. *Computers, Reading and Language Arts*, 1983, *1* (4), 30-34.

Perfetti, C. Reading, vocabulary, and writing: Implications for computer-based instruction. In A. Wilkinson (Ed.), *Classroom computers and cognitive science*. New York: Academic Press, 1983.

States that computer based reading programs should involve the interplay of word coding, conceptual knowledge, and comprehension strategies. Discusses how these three activities can be used in computer based reading programs that provide both instruction and practice.

Rauch, M. *Using computer assisted instruction in a reading and study skills course.* 1983. (ED 240 522)

Discusses a test wiseness and study skills program (CASSI) used with students at St. Cloud State University. The study skills program covers an introduction to study skills, motivation and achievement, time management, reading textbooks, notetaking, concentration, improving memory, procrastination, exams, and test anxiety.

Richardson, J. What a difference an hour makes: A computer literacy workshop for reading students. *Virginia College Reading Educator's Journal,* 1983, *4* (1), 39-46.

Rupley, W., and Chevrette, P. Computer assisted reading instruction: A promising tool for enhancing teacher effectiveness. *Reading World,* 1983, *22* (3), 236-240.

Gives a brief history of CAI since the mid 60s. Suggests advantages of CAI in reading programs: individualized instruction, immediate feedback, increased motivation, and active involvement in the learning experience.

Russ-Eft, D., and McLaughlin, D. Ideas for courseware in reading, writing, and communication skills. *Computers, Reading and Language Arts,* 1983, *1* (3), 27-33.

Explores the issue of limited availability of high quality reading, writing, and communication courseware. Recommends clearer design guidelines in reading and writing software and increased incentives for the courseware developer and teachers using the newly developed materials.

Schuelke, D., and King, T. New technology in the classroom: Computers and communication and the future. *T.H.E. Journal,* 1983, *10* (6), 95-100.

Summarizes and discusses computer based research (circa 1983) on reading comprehension, composition, and organization communication and information use. In addition to the discussions on computer based research, the authors make a strong case for the development of a model for computer/ classroom/education. This model would provide guidance in the development of educational programs that could feature instruction on computer based interpersonal, organizational, and bibliographic communication resources. Provides twenty-six references and a lengthy list of on-line databases.

Standiford, S., Jaycox, K., and Auten, A. *Computers in the English classroom.* 1983. (ED 228 654)

Includes four areas in a "primer" for teachers: a nontechnical explanation of how a computer works, computerized instructional strategies, computer applications in language arts instruction, and resources for software evaluation. Concludes with a detailed list of references.

Wedman, J. Reading skills. *Media and Methods,* 1983, *19* (6), 25, 27.

Willis, J., Johnson, D., and Dixon, P. *Computers, teaching and learning: A guide to using computers in schools.* Beaverton, OR: Dilithium Press, 1983.

Zaharias, J. Microcomputers in the language arts classroom: Promises and pitfalls. *Language Arts,* 1983, *60* (8), 990-995

Suggests that present (circa 1983) applications of microcomputers to education fall into three categories: computer assisted instruction, information processing, and computer managed instruction. Describes the potential impact of each category as well as nine negative attributes of language arts software. Provides fifteen references.

1984

Alexander, C. *Microcomputers and teaching reading in college.* Research Monograph Series Report No. 8. New York: Instructional Resource Center, City University of New York, 1984.

Burnett, J., and Miller, L. Computer assisted learning and reading: Development of the product or fostering the product? *Computers and Education,* 1984, *8,* 145-150.

Chew, C. (Ed.). *Computers in the English program: Promises and pitfalls.* Urbana, IL: National Council of Teachers of English, 1984.

Includes fourteen articles on computers in English/language arts education.

Douglass, M. *Reading in the age of the computer.* Forty-Eighth Yearbook of the Claremont Reading Conference. 1984. (ED 251 823)

Collects twenty-six articles dealing with Reading in the Age of the Computer. Topics include the electronic environment, creative thinking via the computer, LOGO language, software evaluation, and CAI in writing and reading programs.

Fagan, E. Evaluation of selected approaches to computing in reading and language arts. *Computers, Reading and Language Arts,* 1984, *1* (4), 38-40.

Discusses the computer based education philosophies of Suppes, Luehrmann, Bork, and Papert as they relate to reading and language arts.

Fredericks, A. Parents, computers, and the reading program. *The Reading Teacher,* 1984, *37* (9), 918-919.

Suggests ways schools and teachers can help support their computer programs: computer open house, lending, minicourses, TV programs, and so on.

Gerhard, C. *Reading and technology: Tangibles and intangibles.* 1984. (ED 252 826)

Discusses the relationships between technology and reading.

Jobe, R. *Explore the future: Will books have a place in the computer classroom?* 1984. (ED 243 102)

Urges teachers to make a commitment to reading, to encourage sharing good books, and to make classroom reading periods an important part of the day's instruction. Analyzes a representative sample of children's books published in 1983 according to age, type, price, number of pages, and audience appeal.

Kamil, M. Computers, literacy and teaching reading. In J. Baumann and D. Johnson (Eds.), *Reading instruction and the beginning teacher: A practical guide.* Minneapolis, MN: Burgess, 1984.

Liebling, C. Creating the classroom's communicative context: How teachers and microcomputers can help. *Theory into Practice,* 1984, *23* (3), 232-238.

Linville, W., and Waterman, D. Now that you have a computer. In V. Gibbs (Comp.), *Reading, the core of learning.* Proceedings of the Annual Reading Conference. 1984. (ED 241 903)

Gives evidence of the proliferation of computer hardware and software in education: Indiana State University's MICRONET, an educational network for schools and corporations; books, catalogs, and magazine articles on a variety of computer related topics; professional associations that supply computer information, college and university computer courses; and classroom teacher involvement in both CAI and CMI. Provides addresses of companies offering computer catalogs.

Lynn-Mullen, J. Using literature to prepare students for the world of computers and technology. *Computers, Reading and Language Arts,* 1984, *2* (1), 33-34.

Explores how contemporary literature can familiarize students with technology and computers. Mentions a diversity of titles.

Mason, G. Programs for supplementing your basal. *The Reading Teacher,* 1984, *37* (7), 680-681.

Describes how basals now have supplemental computer activities (testing, instruction, information management) that accompany the readers. Cites several examples.

Mason, G. The computer and reading—cautions and comments. *The Reading Teacher,* 1984, *38* (2), 249-250.

Addresses some concerns about computer use with children.

Miller, K., and Stolarski, R. Computer matching of reading lab materials to students' needs. *Computers, Reading and Language Arts,* 1984, *2* (1), 13-15.

Describes a system that produced individualized computer assisted reading instruction for college students. Program goals included improvement of vocabulary and reading comprehension as well as acquisition of study skills.

Ohanian, S. IBM's "Writing to Read" program: Hot new item or same old stew? *Classroom Computer Learning,* 1984, *4* (8), 30-33.

Provides a critical evaluation of the IBM writing program for kindergarten and first grade students.

O'Neal, F. An alternative model for computer-assisted instruction in an educational environment. *T.H.E. Journal,* 1984, *11* (8), 113-117.

Describes the third year of operation for the Waterford School and speculates on the possible accomplishments of the fourth year (1984-1985). Fourth year research and development activities include the testing of a K-12 reading and writing curriculum.

Scanlan, N. Reading related skills and strategies for the computer age. *Computers, Reading and Language Arts,* 1984, *2* (1), 16-18.

Offers approaches for teaching skills that can enable students to successfully use computers in "the computer age." Considers computer related concepts, levels of comprehension, problem solving techniques, study strategies, and employability skill training.

Solomon, G. Computers are for English too! *Computers, Reading and Language Arts,* 1984, *2* (1), 31-32.

Introduces the varieties of CAI available through PROJECT ETC—English through Computers at Taft High, South Bronx.

Suchor, C. *1984 report on trends and issues in English.* 1984. (ED 239 290)

Summarizes reports on educational trends and issues by the National Council of Teachers of English commissions on composition, curriculum, language, literature, media, and reading. Raises various issues related to computer assisted instruction.

Vacc, N. Computers in language arts: Potential benefits and problems. *Journal of Educational Technology Systems,* 1984, *13* (1), 15-22.

Explores the computer's potential in listening, reading, speaking, writing, and literature instruction. Observations include some benefits of CAI as well as potential problems.

1985

Balajthy, E., and Reinking, D. Micros and the first R. *Electronic Learning,* 1985, *5* (1), 45-50.

Discusses computer based reading activities as they relate to reading readiness, word recognition, vocabulary, and comprehension. Also includes a software directory.

Ewing, J. (Ed.). *Reading and the new technologies.* London: Heinemann Educational Books, 1985.

Contains nineteen articles including Reading and the new technologies; The book in 2000; and Reading, writing and learning with microcomputers.

Fredericks, A. Reading opportunities using classroom microcomputers. *The Reading Teacher,* 1985, *38* (4), 488-489.

Suggests seven ways teachers can use microcomputers for reading and language arts activities in their classrooms: make crossword puzzles (Crossword Magic), have students rewrite documentation for others to use, have students review software and publish the reviews, prepare computer bulletin boards, start a computer club, prepare computer book jackets for school books, and have students prepare questions about software for other students to answer.

Greer, S. KoalaPad: Pictures have a place in your classroom. *The Computing Teacher,* 1985, *13* (2), 14-29.

Suggests how a KoalaPad can be used to support language arts and reading activities.

Jarchow, E. Meeting the computing needs of language arts teachers. *Computers, Reading and Language Arts,* 1985, *2* (2), 27-29.

Discusses what language arts teachers might need or want to know about computer applications. Also mentions potential computer based extracurricular activities.

Karbal, H. (Ed.). All about reading and technology. *Michigan Reading Association Journal,* 1985, *18* (2).

Features articles on computer applications in reading. Titles include The use of computers in the reading program; Reading and computers: A partnership; and Rom, ram, and reason.

Mason, G. Communications received—an international view. *The Reading Teacher,* 1985, *38* (7), 713-715.

Provides information about international efforts in computer applications for reading instruction and related areas.

Mason, G. Computer bulletin boards: Constantly renewed material. *The Reading Teacher,* 1985, *39* (1), 123-124.

Newman, J. Online: Vision and wisdom. *Language Arts,* 1985, *62* (3), 295-300.

Discusses from a philosophical standpoint the potential impact of computers on education as seen through the vision of two authors: Papert and Chandler. Papert is best known for LOGO and his hopes for LOGO as embodied in *Mindstorms: Children, computers, and powerful ideas.* Chandler has produced a book "written for all who share a concern for young children's learning and the social impact of technology." Newman discusses both books and the views of the authors. Other portions of the article include an introduction to Microzine (Scholastic), a computer based bimonthly magazine that contains educational software activities, and to QUILL, a writing tool for children.

Rotenberg, L. Booting up for reading: Two nationwide programs that use computers to teach reading. *Educational Microcomputer Annual*, 1985, *1* (1), 132-135.

Discusses the IBM Writing to Read program as well as the WICAT individualized reading instruction system (IRIS).

Starshine, D. Free and inexpensive software for teaching the language arts. *The Computing Teacher*, 1985, *13* (3), 19-21.

Surgey, P., and Scrimshaw, P. *Who controls CAL? The case of TRAY.* Report No. 49. Milton Keynes, England: The Open University, 1985.

Discusses who controls the learning environment in a CAL program: programer, teacher, student. (TRAY is a program designed to develop various language skills in which the learners try to reconstruct an initially invisible text chosen by the teacher.)

Thompson, M. Beyond the computer: Reading as a process of intellectual development. *Computers, Reading and Language Arts*, 1985, *2* (2), 13-15, 43.

Investigates the role of computers in education, emphasizing that technology should never replace teacher-student interaction.

Valuk, R. Tutors on computers. *Phi Delta Kappan*, 1985, *67* (3), 233.

Tells how fifth and sixth graders serve as before school tutors for second and third graders using drill and practice programs.

Wilson, L. TICCIT: A computer-based success story. *T.H.E. Journal*, 1985, *12* (7), 94-95.

Describes TICCIT (timeshared interactive computer controlled information television), which has been involved in computer based instruction for several decades. Today TICCIT is involved in on the job basic skills reading programs with the Army (with the Hazeltine Corporation) and English as a second language programs at Brigham Young University.

Wood, B. Computers and reading at the secondary school, college, and adult levels. *Journal of Reading*, 1985, *28* (8), 750-752.

Discusses several innovative computer based applications that may have an impact on reading and writing instruction for adults. They include the word processing approach to language experience, finding the best language arts software, advancing comprehension strategy research, and learning to read and write with personal computers.

1986

Balajthy, E. A preservice training module in microcomputer applications. *Journal of Reading*, 1986, *30* (3), 196-200.

Suggests a training module on computers and reading for teachers.

Kinzer, C. A five part categorization for use of microcomputers in reading classrooms. *Journal of Reading*, 1986, *30* (3), 226-232.

Describes a categorization scheme involving learning about microcomputers, learning from microcomputers, learning with microcomputers, learning about thinking with microcomputers, and managing learning with microcomputers. Discusses each category.

Layton, K. Interactive text adventures. *The Reading Teacher,* 1986, *40* (3), 378-380.

Mason, G. Recent reading computer books of interest. *The Reading Teacher,* 1986, *39* (5), 490-492.
> Discusses computer books of interest to teachers of reading and language arts.

Mason, G. Doing it cheaply: Renting or using programs in the public domain. *The Reading Teacher,* 1986, *40* (1), 122-124.
> Provides sources of free reading and language arts software.

Merrell, J. Capitalizing on the computer to capture children's interest in reading. *The Reading Teacher,* 1986, *40* (2), 250-252.
> Explains that using computers can help motivate remedial and reluctant readers to want to read.

Scrimshaw, P. *What can be learned from TRAY: Practioners' perceptions.* Report No. 55. Milton Keynes, England: The Open University, 1986.
> Discusses survey research that revealed an absence of any "shared priorities" by teachers reviewing TRAY for possible classroom applications. Evidently, teachers select reading and language arts software for some reasons different from others and the developers.

Scrimshaw, P. *Teaching TRAY to teachers.* Report No. 56. Milton Keynes, England: The Open University, 1986.
> Examines the reasons why teachers adopt reading and language arts software. The researchers found that teachers have many reasons for adopting software: some good, some bad, and some unpredictable.

1987

Balajthy, E. Computers and reading/language arts: Will we try to cure the problem with turpentine? *Computers in the Schools,* 1987, *4* (1), 48-56.
> Helps answer questions about where the computer will fit into the reading/language curriculum.

Feeley, J., Strickland, D., and Wepner, S. Computer as tool: Classroom applications for language arts. *Computers in the Schools,* 1987, *4* (1), 1-10.
> Presents an integrated approach to the use of computers for language arts activities.

Mason, G. Computer instruction all over the world. *The Reading Teacher,* 1987, *40* (4), 491-492.
> Reports on worldwide computer efforts to teach reading as presented by a few of the participants at the Eleventh World Congress of the International Reading Association in July 1986.

Mason, G. The relationship between computer technology and the reading process: Match or misfit. *Computers in the Schools,* 1987, *4* (1), 11-17.
> Discusses several models of the reading process and relates them to computer technology.

Sinatra, R. Holistic applications in computer-based reading and language arts programs. *Computers in the Schools,* 1987, *4* (1), 68-77.
> Discusses features of a holistic program with examples of several types of holistic computer programs in reading and language arts education.

Wepner, S., and Kramer, S. Organizing computers for reading instruction. *Computers in the Schools,* 1987, *4* (1), 38-47.
> Tells how school districts can develop successful computer based reading and language arts programs.

LOGO references

1981

Eyster, R. Seymour Papert and the LOGO universe. *Creative Computing*, 1981, *7* (12), 70-74.

> Describes the author's impressions of a two week workshop conducted by Seymour Papert on the use of the LOGO computer language.

Papert, S. Computers and computer cultures. *Creative Computing*, 1981, *7* (3), 84-92.

> States that since computers will be increasingly privately owned, there will be less conforming and more control of education by the learner who will buy programs in the open market. Better for the child to be a programer than to be programed.

1982

Hereford, N. Let's forget about drill and practice. . .computers are objects to think with: An *Instructor* interview with Seymour Papert. *Instructor*, 1982, *91* (7), 86-89.

> Reiterates Papert's belief that children should not be drilled by computers; children should learn to program and control the computer.

Steffin, S. A challenge to Seymour Papert. *Educational Computer*, 1982, *2* (4), 34-36.

> Challenges several of Papert's assertions: medium can be a mode of instruction, electronics can reverse developmental processes, and the medium can design and implement instructional strategies.

1983

Weintraub, H. Putting LOGO to work. *The Computing Teacher*, 1983, *11* (2), 52-55.

> Describes how to use the list processing capacity of LOGO and provides a sample program to help explain various features.

1984

Dale, E. *LOGO's problem-solving potential.* 1984. (ED 254 199)

Kramer, S. Word processing in a LOGO environment. *Electronic Learning*, 1984, *3* (6), 70.

> Proposes that word processors can be effective in the schools because they offer opportunities for creating safe learning environments, provide structure, treat errors as new ideas, and provide opportunities for students to share their work.

Odom, M. The effects of learning the computer programming language LOGO on fifth and sixth grade students' skills of analysis, synthesis and evaluation. *Dissertation Abstracts International*, 1984, *45* (8), 2390A.

> Describes a research project in which fifth and sixth grade students learned MIT LOGO. Through pre and posttest data, it was concluded both analysis skills and evaluation skills increased significantly. Indicates a need for further investigation of programing activities that might benefit synthesis skills.

1985

Duncan, M. Computer programs and learning styles. *Computers, Reading and Language Arts*, 1985, *2* (2), 8-12, 24.

> Notes the impact of CAI (LOGO and speech synthesis) on learning styles (auditory, visual, and audiovisual). Results suggest improved achievement, regardless of the learner's style or computer's modality.

Genishi, C., McCollum, P., and Strand, E. The interactional richness of children's computer use. *Language Arts,* 1985, *62* (5), 526-532.

> Focuses on kindergartners' oral language patterns while using LOGO. The researchers maintained that students' oral language interactions with a partner while using the computer were just as important as their interactions with the computer. Also, using the computer can be a very socializing activity between students.

Hoffer, B., and Semmes, P. Haiku and Nim: LOGO in the language arts. *AEDS Monitor,* 1985, *23* (7, 8), 19-22.

> Explains how LOGO was used in college composition classes to help freshmen develop writing abilities in Haiku.

Horner, C., and Maddux, C. The effect of LOGO on attributions toward success. *Computers in the Schools,* 1985, *2,* 45-54.

> Finds that LOGO has a positive effect on personal responsibility and attitude toward success in learning disabled junior high school students.

Perkins, D. The fingertip effect: How information-processing technology shapes thinking. *Educational Researcher,* 1985, *14* (7), 11-17.

> Raises a cautionary flag about the benefits now and in the future of many educational activities that surround LOGO and word processing. Assesses both the positive and negative aspects of using LOGO and word processing.

Wresch, W. Using LOGO to teach writing and literacy skills. *The Computing Teacher,* 1985, *13* (1), 24-26.

> Describes how to use LOGO to create and manipulate lists and to put words into context. The LOGO list making capabilities can be used in various reading activities.

1986

Siann, G., and Macleod, H. Computers and children of primary school age: Issues and questions. *British Journal of Educational Technology,* 1986, *17,* 133-144.

> Describes a study in which six year old children, some of whom used LOGO and some of whom did not, were compared on interviews, picture completion, map reading, and a test of laterality. There were no differences between the two groups.

1987

Papert, S. Computer criticism versus technocentric thinking. *Educational Researcher,* 1987, *16* (1), 22-30.

> Criticizes recent developments in the teaching of LOGO as well as research pitting LOGO groups against non-LOGO groups as a test of the efficacy of LOGO. Papert refers to the recent developments in LOGO instruction and research as examples of technocentric thinking.

Cloze procedure references

1978

Hines, T., and Warren, J. A computerized technique for producing cloze text material. *Educational Technology,* 1978, *18,* 56-58.

> Provides a cloze text generating program with options on length of blank and deletion pattern.

1983

Hedges, W., and Turner, E. The cloze test becomes practical for use by the classroom teacher. *Computers, Reading and Language Arts,* 1983, *1* (2), 11-12.

> Describes a computer assisted cloze test used to determine text readability. After every fifth word has been removed from the prose selection, students complete the passage by supplying the missing words. Through computer presentation and scoring, cloze results can identify the students' independent, instructional, or frustration reading level.

Niesser, D. Computerized cloze test. *The Computing Teacher,* 1983, *10* (6), 62-63.

1984

Montgomery, J. Cloze procedure: A computer application. *The Computing Teacher,* 1984, *11* (9), 16-20.

> Suggests ways word processors can be used to create instructional cloze activities.

Literacy references

1984

Blanchard, J. U.S. Armed Services computer assisted literacy efforts. *Journal of Reading,* 1984, *28* (3), 262-265.

> Describes current attempts to combat illiteracy among U.S. Armed Services members. Might have applications in nonmilitary settings.

1985

Technology for Literacy Project. *Conference on adult literacy and computers.* St. Paul, MN: Technology for Literacy Center, 1985.

> Reports conference proceedings on six issues: quality software, software for levels 0-4, technology, instruction effectiveness, management, and access.

Language experience approach references

1970

Serwer, B., and Stolurow, L. Computer assisted learning in the language arts. *Elementary English,* 1970, *47,* 641-650.

> Describes plans for ORACLE, a computer aided language experience reading program.

1982

Barber, B. Creating BYTES of language. *Language Arts,* 1982, *59* (5), 472-475.

> Describes first grade students using the microcomputer to generate language experience stories. Students can type in their own stories or the teacher can do it for them. Students receive a copy of their story.

1983

Morrison, V. Language experience with microcomputers. *The Reading Teacher,* 1983, *36* (4), 448-449.

> Explains that language experience stories can be used with young children in a computer based word processing environment. Brief suggestions are provided on how to use word processing with language experience stories.

1984

Smith, N. *The word processing approach to language experience.* 1984. (ED 249 465)

> Identifies and summarizes key points of ten articles that give both theoretical background and practical suggestions for using word processing in the language experience classroom.

1985

Grabe, M., and Grabe, C. The microcomputer and the language experience approach. *The Reading Teacher,* 1985, *38* (6), 508-511.

> States that microcomputers and language experience stories can be used in tandem by students at all grade levels. Authors describe how the computer can help students with language experience stories.

Moxley, R., and Barry, P. Spelling with LEA on the microcomputer. *The Reading Teacher,* 1985, *39* (3), 267-273.

> Presents using Terrapin LOGO 2.0 in LEAS as one way to help four year olds develop spelling skills.

Smith, N. The word processing approach to language experience. *The Reading Teacher,* 1985, *38* (6), 556-559.

> Suggests that the interaction between teachers and students that are brought about by using word processing and language experience activities help to minimize many disadvantages of LEAS. The article also mentions what teachers should know about implementing computer based LEAS in their classrooms.

Special education references

1971

Sklar, B. *A computer classification of normal and dyslexic children using spectral estimates of their electroencephalograms.* Unpublished doctoral dissertation, University of California, Los Angeles, 1971.

> Describes a study in which, using the computer, twelve dyslexic children were differentiated from normal age and sex matched children based on spectral estimates of their EEG readings. The greatest differences were in the parietooccipital region during rest with the eyes closed.

Troxel, D. Automated reading of the printed page. *Visible Language,* 1971, *5,* 125-144.

> Explains automated reading in print leading to character codes that can be processed to produce Braille, spelled speech, or synthesized speech.

1978

Howe, J. Using technology to educate pupils with communication difficulties. *T.H.E. Journal,* 1978, *5* (5), 36-39.

1980

Spring, C., and Perry, L. *Computer assisted instruction in word decoding for educationally handicapped children.* 1980. (ED 201 075)

1981

Berenbon, H. The word board. *Creative Computing,* 1981, *6* (4), 64-68.

> Lists and describes two uses of a technique in which keys are covered with word tags. Suggests that speech impaired people may use the technique.

Geoffrion, L., and Goldenberg, E. Computer based exploratory learning systems for communication handicapped children. *Journal of Special Education*, 1981, *15,* 325-332.

Mason, G. The computer as a teacher of the disabled reader. *Journal of Research and Development in Education*, 1981, *14* (4), 97-101.

> Describes how reading clinicians are using computers in diagnosing and teaching students.

1982

Earle, W. Eyetracker. *Technology Illustrated*, 1982, 9.

> Describes how children who can control only their eyes can have a voice and writing capabilities with a device developed by researchers at Carnegie-Mellon University.

Geoffrion, L. Reading and the nonvocal child. *The Reading Teacher*, 1982, *35* (6), 662-668.

> Includes a section on CBELS (Computer Based Exploratory Learning Systems) and the author's own work on CARIS, with LOGO, and with computer mail (deaf children).

LeCavalier, D., Vaughan, S., and Wimp, M. Putting microcomputer technology to work for our hearing impaired students. *American Annals of the Deaf*, 1982, *14* (2), 224-226.

> Describes the impact of CAI on the Hearing Handicapped Program at Jefferson County Public Schools, Colorado. A detailed evaluation form for hearing impaired software is included.

Loughlin, A. *Furrowfield School Programmes for the Texas Instruments*. 1982. (ED 256 136)

> Presents some ways Speak and Spell and Spelling ABC were used with learning and behavioral disordered students.

1983

Boettcher, J.V. Computer-based education: Classroom application and benefits for the learning-disabled student. *Annals of Dyslexia*, 1983, *33,* 203-219.

> Describes a computer based reading comprehension program designed for learning disabled students. Examines the role of the instructor in productive CAI and emphasizes the necessity of choosing materials appropriate for students' needs.

Brawley, R.J., and Peterson, B.A. Interactive videodisc: An innovative instructional system. *American Annals of the Deaf*, 1983, *128* (5), 685-700.

> Describes a three year project that developed an interactive computer videodisk system for language and reading skill instruction for hearing impaired students.

Fulton, R., Larson, A., and Worthy, R. The use of microcomputer technology in assessing and training communication skills of young hearing impaired students. *American Annals of the Deaf*, 1983, *128* (5), 570-576.

> Explains some uses of "a prototype interactive computer controlled audiovisual system" with hearing impaired preschoolers. Examines CAI in simple reading tasks and the assessment of bimodal interactions/interferences.

Grossman, R. On line. *Journal of Learning Disabilities*, 1983, *16* (7), 429-431.

> Details practical applications of the computer in the school setting, including the reading clinic.

McDermott, P., and Watkins, M. Computerized vs. conventional remedial instruction for learning-disabled pupils. *Journal of Special Education,* 1983, *17* (1), 81-88.

Reports findings of a study measuring effectiveness of CAI with learning disabled children. A comparison of the posttest data for experimental and control groups revealed no significant differences in achievement after one year of instruction. Suggests certain achievement assessments may be insensitive to achievement gains made by LD students.

Zorn, R. Micromiracles for the learning disabled. *Instructional Innovator,* 1983, *28* (4), 26-28.

Describes how junior high LD students receive reading, mathematics, and language arts CAI. Improved learning opportunities are combined with improved self image, independent thinking skills, appreciation of learning, and equitable instruction.

1984

Abegglen, S. The efficacy of computer-assisted instruction with educationally handicapped high school students. *Dissertation Abstracts International,* 1984, *45* (10), 3109A.

Tells about educationally handicapped students who received computer assisted reading and mathematics instruction. A comparison of pre and posttest achievement scores suggests CAI is beneficial in raising those students' achievement levels.

Howe, J. Putting cognitive psychology to work teaching handicapped children to read. *School Psychology International,* 1984, *5* (2), 85-90.

Tells how word decoding skills were taught to mildly physically and mentally handicapped students via the computer with a touch sensitive screen. Significant gains were noted by students receiving CAI over an 18 month period.

Kerchner, L., and Kistinger, B. Language processing/word processing: Written expression, computers and learning disabled students. *Learning Disability Quarterly,* 1984, *7* (4), 329-335.

Describes the process approach that allows students to learn grammar rules, spelling, and punctuation as they develop writing skills. Hypothesizes that learning disabled students can gain writing proficiency through intergration of the word processor into the process approach. Positive achievement in reading and written language was made by LD students using the combined instruction.

Kirkland, E. *Writing to read: A computer-based language experience, writing and reading system, as used with handicapped children.* 1984. (ED 248 480)

Explains the Writing to Read program: "What I can say, I can write and what I write, I can read!" This computer based teaching system enables students to write words, sentences, and stories using the alphabet and 42 phonemic English sounds. Learning is continually reinforced as the child sees the word, hears the word, says the word, and writes the word. An observation checklist for identifying possible language and learning disorders is included.

Main, J. *Computer assisted teaching comparisons with handicapped: Final report.* 1984. (ED 256 865)

Explains that CAI programs in word recognition were used with low level, nonreading adults with some success.

Murphy, J. *The development and use of a language arts computer software program appropriate for special needs children.* 1984. (ED 254 348)

Reports a research report that indicates mixed results for drill and practice language arts (vocabulary, spelling, mechanics and expression) programs with handicapped students (second–sixth grades). Vocabulary and spelling skills improved; the other skills did not.

Prinz, P., and Nelson, K. *A child-computer-teacher interactive method for teaching reading to young deaf children.* 1984. (ED 247 720)

Describes research focused on CAI designed for the learning styles of deaf children at the Pennsylvania School for the Deaf. Graphic representations of pictures to illustrate word meanings, printed words, readily changeable keys, and access to new words and graphics give teachers opportunity to individualize courseware for student needs.

Prinz, P., and Nelson, K. Reading is fun – with a keyboard, a hat, and an alligator. *Perspectives for Teachers of the Hearing Impaired,* 1984, *3* (1), 2-4.

Describes using computers to assist students at the Pennsylvania School for the Deaf with communication skills and instructional involvement. Suggests enhanced reading skills and language usage can result from CAI with the hearing impaired.

Spring, C., and Perry, L. *Computer-assisted instruction in word-decoding for educationally handicapped children.* 1984. (ED 201 075)

Torgesen, J. Instructional uses of microcomputers with elementary age mildly handicapped children. *Special Services in the Schools,* 1984, *1* (1), 37-48.

Evaluates the current uses of computers to teach handicapped children.

1985

Capalbo, W. *A microcomputer software guide for special educators.* 1985. (ED 252 197)

Jones, M. Success and the word processor. *Media & Methods,* 1985, *21* (7), 42, 28.

Presents a word processor's success story in a writing class for learning disabled high school students.

Rosegrant, T. Using the microcomputer as a tool for learning to read and write. *Journal of Learning Disabilities,* 1985, *18* (2), 113-115.

Reports that several elementary students with reading and writing difficulties improved their skills with CAI.

Weisgerber, R., and Rubin, D. Designing and using software for the learning disabled. *Journal of Reading, Writing and Learning Disabilities International,* 1985, *1* (2), 133-138.

Presents a software program that will help students learn letter configuration.

1986

Harper, J., and Ewing, N. A comparison of the effectiveness of microcomputer and workbook instruction on reading performance of high incidence handicapped children. *Educational Technology,* 1986, *26* (5), 40-45.

Finds that microcomputer delivery of reading instruction (reading a passage and answering questions) was more effective than workbook delivery of reading instruction. Analysis of attention to task behavior revealed that the microcomputer delivery was as effective as a workbook delivery of reading instruction.

Spelling references

1972

Holland, J., and Doran, J. Teaching classification by computer. *Educational Technology,* 1972, *13* (12), 58-60.

Describes a spelling classification program that uses a touch sensitive screen.

1976

Thompson, M. *The effects of spelling pattern training on spelling behavior of primary elementary students: An evaluative study.* Unpublished doctoral dissertation, University of Pittsburgh, 1976.

Details research in which experimental second grade subjects were given CAI sound-letter correspondence training for twenty-four to thirty-five minutes, three times weekly, for a school year. The on-line CAI work was supplemented with workbook pages. Experimental subjects outperformed control subjects on all posttests, one of which was a test of ability to read whole words.

1980

Nolen, P. Sound reasoning in spelling. *The Reading Teacher,* 1980, *33* (5), 538-542.

Discusses the advent of affordable computer assisted means for spelling practice and instruction. Also describes potential dangers and new demands of computer based spelling activities.

Nolen, P. Electronic aids in spelling. *Language Arts,* 1980, *57* (2), 178-179.

1983

Edmonton Public Schools. *Using the computer to teach spelling.* 1983. (ED 252 861)

Presents the results of a study using CAI in spelling with third graders. Students using the CAI spelling program learned to spell better than those who used conventional methods.

Hasselbring, T., and Owens, S. Microcomputer-based analysis of spelling errors. *Computers, Reading and Language Arts,* 1983, *1* (1), 26-31.

Presents research on the Computerized Test of Spelling Errors (CTSE). Suggests that the CTSE can be a reliable way to diagnose spelling problems.

1984

Hasselbring, T. Using a microcomputer for imitating student errors to improve spelling performance. *Computers, Reading and Language Arts,* 1984, *1* (4), 12-14.

Discusses a program entitled "Computerized Spelling Remediation" and presents research evidence as to its effectiveness. The program uses an imitation plus modeling teaching strategy.

Teague, G.V., Wilson, R.M., and Teague, M.G. Use of computer assisted instruction to improve spelling proficiency of low achieving first graders. *AEDS Journal,* 1984, *17* (4), 30-35.

Describes commercial software spelling packages that permit teachers to change the content of the lessons and that can make a difference in the spelling achievement of first grade students experiencing difficulty learning to spell. Using Apple computers, first graders used spelling programs for twenty-five minutes a day for twenty days. Instruction featured placing words in alphabetical order, word puzzles, unscrambling letter order of words, and writing words in sentences.

1986

Balajthy, E. Using microcomputers to teach spelling. *The Reading Teacher,* 1986, *39* (5), 438-443.

Offers suggestions on what to look for in spelling software: colorful and interesting programs, voice synthesis to present words, a way to add new words, feedback, review of misspelled words, and recordkeeping.

Native American and bilingual education references

1977

Students use talking computer in Dallas bilingual program. *Phi Delta Kappan,* 1977, *59* (4), 234.

Describes an ESEA Title VII and Title IV-C program which uses a computerized voice synthesizer to reinforce reading and language arts programs.

1980

Bell, S., and Wells, B. A new approach to teaching reading using cloze and computer assisted instruction. *Educational Technology,* 1980, *20* (3), 49-51.

Describes the CAI project directed by the All Indian Pueblo Council. The project helped elementary Pueblo students to develop better reading skills through culturally relevant reading materials and the cloze procedure. A HP2000F computer was used to provide lesson materials employing a modified cloze procedure. The article describes how the program worked and gives a sample lesson.

1981

Maller, P. Indians told language by computer. *Green Bay Press Gazette,* July 19, 1981.

Describes funded program designed to teach speaking and reading of Ojibwe to Wisconsin Chippewas using PLATO.

1982

Saracho, O. The effects of a computer assisted instruction program on basic skills achievement and attitudes toward instruction of Spanish speaking migrant children. *American Educational Research Journal,* 1982, *19* (2), 201-219.

Tells how 128 children received supplementary CAI in reading and mathematics using programs from Computer Curriculum Corporation. At the conclusion, the CAI group had high achievement test scores.

1984

Edeburn, C., and Jacobi, C. *Computer assisted instruction for Native American students.* 1984. (ED 252 336)

Provides an evaluation of the first year phase of the federally funded program Computer Assisted Instruction for Bilingual/Bicultural Students in Rapid City, South Dakota, area school districts. Summary data are provided.

Fletcher, J., and Sawyer, T. *Computer-aided instruction in education basics for Indian students.* 1984. (ED 247 053)

Explains, through proceedings of the 1983 Indian Education Conference, the project design and planning for CAI in word recognition, reading comprehension, and mathematics for Native American, Native Alaskan, and American Indian students. Recommendations for project implementation are made by six resource persons in Indian education.

Ramos, N. The utilization of computer technology in a bilingual classroom. *Dissertation Abstracts International*, 1984, *45* (9), 2748A.

Urges the use of computer assisted instruction in bilingual education programs. Research data indicate significant improvement by limited English proficiency students who had received seven weeks of computer assisted English instruction.

1985

Jacobi, C. Project DISC: Developing Indian software curriculum. *The Computing Teacher*, 1985, *12* (7), 12-16.

Discusses a CAI in reading project with Native Americans in Rapid City, South Dakota.

1986

Sweet, S. Cross cultural computing. *Electronic Learning*, 1986, *5* (4), 48-51, 73.

Discusses six bilingual education demonstration projects using a computer. All the projects appear to involve reading as a component. Projects include both Spanish and Native American language instruction.

English as a second language and foreign language education references

1984

Aoki, P. Limitations of current microcomputers for foreign language training. *Foreign Language Annals*, 1984, *17* (4), 409-412.

Explains that the Department of Defense foreign language requirement stipulates students must show level three language proficiency, demonstrating near perfect reading and listening comprehension in the native language. Suggests CAI is a viable component of level three instruction, but adds the computer should be capable of sufficient text display, higher level interaction, storage of lesson files, and manipulation of lengthy passages.

Aoki, P., Eddy, P., Holmes, G., Pusack, J., and Wyatt, D. Working group report: A proposal for a prototype computer-based reading course. *Foreign Language Annals*, 1984, *17* (4), 421-422.

Recommends CAI in teaching foreign language reading skills. Using the language's alphabet, syntax, morphology, vocabulary, and sound-symbol correspondence, the curriculum's design would take the nonreader to intermediate proficiency. Layered assistance (highlighting key words or phrases); student performance tracking; graphic/video support; and a motivating, appealing format should be consolidated into the program.

Curtin, C., and Shinall, S. Computer-assisted reading lessons. *CALICO Journal*, 1984, *1* (5), 12-16.

Describes a college level computer assisted foreign language project and cognitive and affective changes.

Holmes, G. The computer and limitations. *Foreign Language Annals*, 1984, *17* (4), 413-414.

Asks whether the benefits of computer assisted language learning are cost effective in terms of time, energy, and money. Suggests that other media may better provide instructional foreign language activities.

Hope, G. *Using computers in teaching foreign languages.* 1984. (ED 246 695)
Provides suggestions for computer applications in developing foreign language skill. Aspects of building vocabulary files, classifying words, practicing words, grammar, writing, reading, speaking, and listening and culture are discussed. CMI (including testing, placement, and grading) in the foreign language classroom is described. Detailed guidelines are included for evaluating software. An annotated bibliography on foreign language CAI is also available.

Jameison, J., and Chapelle, C. *Prospects in computer assisted language instruction.* 1984. (ED 253 062)
Discusses CAI in foreign language reading instruction as well as in other areas of foreign language curricula.

King, M. The impact of computer assisted instruction on the acquisition of English as a second language. *Dissertation Abstracts International,* 1985, *46* (6), 1604A.
States that ESL students (K–eighth grade) can profit from CAI programs in English.

Mydlarski, D., and Paramskas, D. PROMPT: A template system for second-language reading comprehension. *CALICO Journal,* 1984, *1* (5), 3-7.
Discusses a computer assisted college level authoring system for foreign language instruction.

Wyatt, D. *Computers and ESL.* 1984. (ED 246 694)
Presents a thorough treatment of CALL (computer assisted language learning) as related to ESL (English as a second language) instruction. Provides techniques for integrating CALL into existing programs and specific subject areas. In addition, a number of sources for CALL software and information are listed.

Wyatt, D. Computer-assisted teaching and testing of reading and listening. *Foreign Language Annals,* 1984, *17* (4), 393-405.
Describes the computer's role in foreign language reading and listening skill development. Aspects of instruction (highly structured, traditional strategies), collaboration (interaction in student initiated activities) and facilitation (word processing) are considered.

1985

Hughett, H. *Introduction to computer aided instruction in the language laboratory.* 1985. (ED 225 170)

Kyle, P. *The communicative computer compares: A CALL design project for elementary French.* 1985. (ED 258 456)
Describes a PLATO computer lesson on the Olympic games that simulates a written conversation between a French student and the computer. The format includes the student reading a text and typing a response.

1987

Dalgish, G. Some uses of computers in teaching English as a second language: The issue of control. *Computers in the School,* 1987, *4* (1), 57-65.
Explains how CAI can be used correctly and incorrectly with ESL instruction.

3
Evaluating and developing reading software

Despite an enormous increase in the number of programs in the marketplace, the majority of reading and language arts programs still emphasize drill and practice, largely because drill and practice programs are easier and less costly to create than are more complex programs. Simpler, less costly programs are also less likely to be pirated than are more costly programs. The cost of complex programs has led to extensive piracy in the schools, where personnel justify it as a necessary money saving activity. Because of piracy problems, some publishers are unwilling to risk costly research and development efforts. Copy protection schemes provide one answer to the problem, but software developers and publishers are looking beyond these costly schemes. Site licensing and software rentals are two potential solutions. Also, some newer software programs allow the buyer to make as many copies as desired, but copies can be made only from the purchased disk; programing features of the purchased disk – the "master disk" – do not permit copies to be made from other copies.

The future, however, might reveal that software companies have removed copy protection devices from their programs because the schemes are troublesome as well as costly, and they do not stop piracy. Consequently, the future for research and development of complex reading and language arts programs is uncertain.

Evaluating reading software

Each week some publisher announces a "new" program for reading or language arts instruction. The plethora of programs may be helpful for reading instruction, but teachers need help in learning about what software is available and in selecting the software most appropriate for their students. The publications in the following list provide information on reading and language arts software. Following that list are the IRA criteria for the selection and utilization of nonprint media in the reading curriculum and questions teachers should ask the salesperson about computer based reading and language arts programs, which also can be useful to teachers who are selecting software.

Review sources

California Library Media Consortium, TECC Clearinghouse, San Mateo County Office of Education, 333 Main Street, Redwood City, California 94063

Chime Newsletter, Clearinghouse of Information on Microcomputers in Education, Oklahoma State University, 108 Gunderson, Stillwater, Oklahoma 74078

Classroom Computer Learning (formerly Classroom Computer News), 19 Davis Drive, Belmont, California 94002

Closing the Gap, P.O. Box 68, Henderson, Minnesota 56044

Computing Teacher, The International Council for Computers in Education (ICCE), University of Oregon, 1787 Agate Street, Eugene, Oregon 97403

Curriculum Review, 517 South Jefferson, Chicago, Illinois 60607

Educational Computer, 3199 De La Cruz, Santa Clara, California 95050

Educational Technology, 140 Sylan Avenue, Englewood Cliffs, New Jersey 07632

Educational Software Reviews, Scholastic, P.O. Box 2038, Mahopac, New York 10541

Electronic Learning, Scholastic, P.O. Box 2038, Mahopac, New York 10541

EPIE Micro-Courseware PRO/FILES, Educational Products Information Exchange Institute, P.O. Box 839, Water Mill, New York 11976

InfoWorld, 1060 March Road, Suite C-200, Menlo Park, California 94025

Journal of Learning Disabilities, 11 East Adams Street, Chicago, Illinois 60603

Journal of Special Education Technology, Association of Special Education, Utah State University, Logan, Utah 84322

The Mathematics Teacher, 1906 Association Drive, Reston, Virginia 22091

Media & Methods, 1511 Walnut Street, Philadelphia, Pennsylvania 19102

Media Review, P.O. Box 425, Ridgefield, Connecticut 06877

MicroSIFT Courseware Evaluation, Northwest Regional Educational Laboratory, 300 SW Sixth Avenue, Portland, Oregon 97204

Popular Computing, 70 Main Street, Peterborough, New Hampshire
  03458
The Reading Teacher (Computer Software Reviews) International Reading
  Association, 800 Barksdale Road, P.O. Box 8139, Newark, Delaware
  19714
School Library Journal, 205 East 42 Street, New York, New York 10017
Science Teacher, National Science Teachers Association, 1742 Connecti-
  cut Avenue, NW, Washington, DC 20009
SECTOR, Exceptional Children Center, Utah State University, Logan, Utah
  84321
Simulations & Games, 275 South Beverly Drive, Beverly Hills, California
  90212
Software Encyclopedia, R.R. Bowker, 205 East 42 Street, New York, New
  York 10017
Software Reports, Trade Service Publications, 10996 Torreyana Road, San
  Diego, California 92121
Software Review, 520 Riverside Avenue, Westport, Connecticut 06880
Teaching and Computers, Scholastic, P.O. Box 2038, Mahopac, New York
  10541

IRA Criteria for the selection of nonprint media for the reading curriculum*

Print media include printed material in book, pamphlet, magazine, or
newspaper form. Nonprint media include any other means of conveying
information including television, radio, computer, music, games,
audiotape, film, videodisk, videotape, and cable TV.

1. Materials shall support and be consistent with the general educational
   goals of the school district.
2. Materials shall contribute to the objectives of the instructional program.
3. Materials shall be appropriate for the age, social, and emotional development and interest of the students for whom the materials are selected.
4. Materials shall present a reasonable balance of opposing sides of con-
   troversial issues so that students may develop the practice of critical
   reading and thinking. When no opposing side of an issue is currently

*Criteria recommended by the 1983-1984 IRA Nonprint Media and Reading Committee and
approved by the IRA Board of Directors, May 1984.

available, the nature of the bias will be explicitly discussed and explained to the students.

5. Materials shall provide a background of information which will enable pupils to make intelligent judgments in their daily lives.
6. Materials shall provide a stimulus for creative reading, writing, listening, and thinking.
7. Material shall reflect the pluralistic character and culture of society. Materials shall foster respect for minority groups, women, and ethnic groups.
8. Materials shall be of acceptable technical quality, such as clear narration, synchronized pictures and sound.
9. Materials should be selected on the basis of their aesthetic quality, providing students with an increasing appreciation of the world around them.
10. Materials should encourage affective responses and further humanistic concerns.

IRA Criteria for the utilization of nonprint media in the reading curriculum*

1. Teachers should be fully trained in the use of audiovisual equipment before operating it in the classroom setting.
2. Nonprint media should be ready to operate prior to its scheduled use to avoid losing valuable classroom instructional time. Room facilities should be carefully planned in advance (i.e., electrical outlets, adaptors, seating, extension cords).
3. Materials should be carefully previewed before their utilization in the reading curriculum. Background information, including new vocabulary and concepts, should be provided to support the new ideas to be mastered.
4. Prior to its use, specific goals and purposes should be established to help students identify the objectives and expectations of the learning activity.
5. Content should be discussed and student knowledge evaluated and reviewed to assure understanding of the ideas and concepts presented.
6. The utilization of nonprint media should stimulate students toward a further expansion of literacy and lifelong skills in reading.

*Criteria recommended by the IRA Nonprint Media and Reading Committee and approved by the IRA Board of Directors, May 1984.

Questions teachers should ask the salesperson about computer based reading and language arts programs*

Each of the numbered requests listed is followed by additional questions. The purpose of these additional questions is to ensure that you get as much essential information about reading and language arts software as possible, as quickly as possible. A word of caution though; you might not get answers to many of your questions. Be persistent.

1. Tell me about the cost.
   Is the program copy protected?
   Is there an additional charge for backup copies?
   Is there an additional expense for supplemental or resource materials?
   Is there a single disk for the program or are multiple disks required?
   Is there a provision for refunds or returns?
   Is there a provision for upgrading the program if a new version is marketed?
2. Tell me which computer runs the program and if any special equipment is needed.
   Does the program need a color monitor?
   Does the program need two disk drives?
   Does the program need a student data disk?
   Does the program need a printer?
   Does the program need a speech synthesizer?
   Does the program need extra memory?
   Does the program need anything else?
3. Tell me where the program might fit into my curriculum.
   What grade level is appropriate?
   What types of students could use the program?
   What types of teaching styles would be compatible with the program?
   What types of reading and language arts materials are compatible?
   What time requirements are needed for the activities?
4. Tell me what the students read on screen or off screen.
   Do they read passages?
   Do they read sentences?
   Do they read individual words or phrases?
   Do they read questions?
   Do they recognize syllables?

---

*Based on Questions to ask about computer-based reading programs. *The Reading Teacher,* 1985, *39* (2), 250-252.

Do they recognize letters?
Do they read program or activity directions?
Do they read or recognize anything else?
5. Tell me about the program content.
   Are there instructional activities?
   Are there practice activities?
   Are there vocabulary activities?
   Are there comprehension activities?
   Are there study skills activities?
   Are there grammar activities?
   Are there syllable or alphabet activities?
   Are there game activities?
   Are there test activities?
   Are there other activities?
   Are there multiple activities on one disk?
6. Tell me about video presentations.
   Does the program present printed information with appropriate speed and legibility?
   Does the program present information appropriately spaced and sized?
   Does the program use graphics (with color)? What types? When? Why?
   Does the program use animation? When? Why?
   Does color interfere with print legibility?
7. Tell me about audio (and speech) presentations.
   Does the program use speech? When? Why? (synthesized speech — space-age voice or digitized speech — human voice)
   Does the program use nonspeech sound? When? why?
   Does the program allow me or the students to control or eliminate the volume?
8. Tell me about the program's stated reading and language arts objectives and goals.
   Are there objectives and goals for teachers (achievement, motivational, behaviorial, management)?
   Are there objectives and goals for students?
   Are there objectives and goals that meet my state or local educational requirements?
   Are there objectives and goals that meet or correlate with objectives and goals of tests?
   Are there objectives and goals for others, such as parents, administrators, or supervisors?

9. Tell me what prerequisite skills are needed.
   What computer literacy skills are needed?
   What keyboard skills are needed?
   What spelling skills are needed?
   What entry level reading skills are needed?
   What entry level background knowledge is needed?
   What other skills are needed?
10. Tell me about reinforcement in the program.
   What behaviors are reinforced? Why? When? How?
   What control do I have over the reinforcement?
11. Tell me about the operation of the program.
   Can the students use the program with little or no help from me?
   Can the students or I change the contents of activities?
   Can the students or I change the format of the activities?
   Can the students or I receive on screen prompts or help about questions involving the use of an activity or its content?
   Can the students or I make mistakes or accidents pressing the keys without ruining the activity?
   Can the students or I correct our entries?
   Can the students or I work on unfinished sections of an activity without repeating completed sections?
   Can the students or I reread previous screens easily without restarting the activity?
   Can the students or I reread questions and change answers easily without restarting the activity?
   Can the students or I use the activities without unloading and reloading the program disk? (Are multiple disks used for one activity?)
   Can the students or I use the activities if the program disk is removed from the disk drive?
   Can the program administer pretests or posttests over activity content?
   Can the activities be used with groups as well as with individual students?
12. Tell me about reviews of the program and field testing.
   Are critical and descriptive reviews of the program available?
   Are there any reports on field testing data?
13. Tell me about supplemental or resource materials.
   Are supplemental materials available that allow the students or me to examine the contents of the activities before using them with the computer?

Are supplemental materials available that allow the students or me to examine any background information relevant to the content of the activities?

Are supplemental materials available that allow the students or me to examine information about the instructional strategies used in the activities?

Are supplemental materials available about other educational resources?

14. Tell me about scoring and recordkeeping activities.

Does the program score or record activity performance or other information? How?

Does the program permit students as well as teachers an opportunity to see scoring or recordkeeping data?

Does the program store and allow the recall of information about students? What information is stored and why?

Does the computer score or record other information?

15. Tell me what reading and language arts educational opportunities this program offers my students that I cannot otherwise give them.

Chapter 3 provides references on software development and evaluation projects from local, state, and national sources; reading software evaluation guidelines; and suggestions on how to develop software.

References

1981

Kansky, B., Heck, W., and Johnston, J. Getting hard-nosed about software: Guidelines for evaluating computerized instructional materials. *Mathematics Teacher,* 1981, *74* (8), 600-604.

Kleinman, G., Humphrey, M., and Buskirk, T. Evaluating educational software. *Creative Computing,* 1981, *7* (10), 84-90.

Roblyer, M. When is it good courseware? Problems in developing standards for microcomputer courseware. *Educational Technology,* 1981, *21* (10), 47-54.

Discusses problems in trying to apply evaluation standards developed for mainframe software to microcomputer software. Suggests that evaluation systems be flexible enough to discern good quality regardless of the particular instructional vehicle. Divides software criteria into three categories: essential characteristics for instruction of any type, aesthetic characteristics, and characteristics dependent upon the learner and the objectives being taught. Argues that a review team rather than one individual should perform software evaluation.

1982

Anderson, R. Courseware deserves evaluation, including peer review. AEDS *Monitor,* 1982, *20* (10), 10.

Bingham, M. Software evaluation: A coordinated effort needed. *AEDS Monitor,* 1982, *20* (10), 11.

Cohen, V., and Blum L. *Evaluating instructional software for the microcomputer.* 1982. (ED 216 704)

Jostad, K. Search for software. *AEDS Monitor.* 1982, *20* (10), 25-27.

Kimmel, S. How to write a software review. *Creative Computing,* 1982, *8* (8), 242-244.

Lathrop, A. Microcomputer software for instructional use: Where are the critical reviews? *The Computing Teacher,* 1982, *9* (6), 22-26.

> Reports that less than 5 percent of the educational software has been reviewed critically. Also lists journals that review software.

Peters, H., and Hepler, M. Reflections on ten years of experience. *AEDS Monitor,* 1982, *20* (10), 12-15.

> Discusses the review process used by CONDUIT, which was incorporated in a later MicroSIFT evaluation form.

Wagner, W. The software evaluation dilemma. *AEDS Monitor,* 1982, *20* (10), 5-6.

> Suggests that instructional effectiveness, ease of use, and user acceptance should be considered in evaluating software.

1983

Hunter, B. A guide to selecting educational software. *Media & Methods,* 1983, *20* (1), 15-17, 41.

> Offers suggestions for software selection: correlate learning objectives with software, consider learning objectives with software, depend on dealer support, consider software produced by major publishers, review software evaluations, understand the copy protection limits, and consider student interests and abilities.

Jones, N., and Vaughan, L. (Eds.). *Evaluation of educational software: A guide to guides.* Chelmsford, MA: Northeast Regional Exchange, 1983.

Riordan, T. How to select software you can trust. *Classroom Computer News,* 1983, *3* (4), 56-61.

Sanders, R., and Sanders, M. Evaluating microcomputer software. *Computers, Reading and Language Arts,* 1983, *1* (1), 21-25.

> Presents a guideline for evaluating software and a Software Evaluation Checklist.

Smith J.D. Microcomputers in the reading curriculum. *Computers, Reading and Language Arts,* 1983, *1* (1), 39-40.

> Discusses the limitations and capabilities of reading software (circa 1983). The author believes the computer can provide enhanced instructional opportunities because it can motivate students and provide for individualization. Presents seventeen features of good reading software.

1984

Auten, A. *How to find good computer software in English and language arts.* 1984. (ED 250 692)

> Presents sources for software reviews and evaluations: subscription publications, online sources, specific guides, and the suggestion "identify and befriend an independent distributor of software."

Balajthy, E. Reinforcement and drilling by microcomputer. *The Reading Teacher,* 1984, *37* (6), 490-494.

Claims that some reading teachers are far more impressed by the computer's ability to provide drillwork than they are by its higher level activities. Discusses computer advantages in drillwork, types of computerized drillwork, characteristics of good drill programs, and using computer drills in the classroom.

Bialo, E., and Erickson, L. *Microcomputer courseware: Characteristics and designs.* 1984. (ED 244 606)

Describes strengths and weaknesses found in 163 computer programs evaluated by the Educational Products Information Exchange (EPIE). Strengths were accuracy in fact, spelling, and grammar; uncontroversial content; avoidance of stereotyping; and good warranties. Weaknesses were lack of field testing in phases of program development; limited documentation for learner objectives, support materials, and teaching strategies; ineffective delivery techniques; poor audio quality; limited use of management systems; and little evaluation of student learning.

Caissy, G. Evaluating educational software: A practitioner's guide. *Phi Delta Kappan,* 1984, *66* (4), 249-250.

Offers suggestions for software evaluation, including consideration of the program's objective, ability levels, instructional design, operating instructions, and appropriate reinforcement.

Caldwell, R. Evaluating microcomputer software in the English language arts. *English Education,* 1984, *16* (1), 14-21.

Discusses evaluation criteria for English education software, including a section on the implications of computers in English education.

Crovello, T. Evaluation of educational software. *The American Biology Teacher,* 1984, *46* (3), 173-175.

Provides methods and sources that assist in software evaluation.

Janello, P. *Software evaluation for the teacher of the English language arts.* 1984. (ED 250 697)

Gives strategies for selecting instructional software. Areas discussed include documentation, organization and structure, feedback, pedagogical issues, previewing, and dealing with software publishers.

Kamil, M. Software: Evaluation and decisions. *Computers, Reading and Language Arts,* 1984, *1* (4), 15-16, 26.

Presents evaluation criteria for selecting good reading and language arts software.

Lee, H. Ten tips for finding good reading software. *Computers, Reading and Language Arts,* 1984, *2* (1), 26-27.

Lists nine tips: Choose quality software first, then compatible hardware; look for innovative formats; preview before purchase; consider if the "create" feature is functional; evaluate the quality and types of learner reinforcement; check for computer-learner interaction; be aware of software that reinforces reading skills, such as word processors, a drawing program, study techniques, simulations and games; evaluate the teacher aids; and keep abreast of new materials through software catalogs, journal articles, and computer stores.

Mason, G. Finding software—how to look. *The Reading Teacher,* 1984, *37* (4), 440-441.

Tells how teachers can find information about software they wish to use with their students. They can read computer books and magazines, attend conferences or sessions on computers, and contact salespeople and distributors. Provides information about each of these sources.

Otte, R. Courseware for the 80s. *T.H.E. Journal,* 1984, *12* (3), 89-91.

Wepner, S. Motivation and computers: A real incentive for teachers. *The Reading Teacher,* 1984, *38* (3), 363-364.

Suggests that computers can interest even the most apathetic students, but only if the teacher chooses good software. Suggests guidelines for software that can motivate. Select software that fits the standards demanded from other materials, fits in the curriculum, is easy to use, has lots of options, promotes socialization, and allows for pre and postactivities.

Wiener, R. Evaluating courseware: You don't have to be computer literate to effectively select CAI materials. *Lifelong Learning,* 1984, *7* (7), 14, 16-17, 28.

Discusses the five types of CAI courseware: tutorials, drills and practice, demonstrations, simulations, and instructional games. Offers a checklist for evaluating program operation and content, desired student outcomes, and teaching/learning concerns.

1985

Muller, E. Application of experimental and quasi-experimental research designs to educational software evaluation. *Education Technology,* 1985, *25* (10), 27-31.

Whiteside, C. Software checklist: An evaluator's best tool. *Electronic Education,* 1985, *4* (6), 20-21.

Presents a one page software review evaluation checklist and describes the best way to use this checklist.

1986

Miller, L., and Burnett, J. Theoretical considerations in selecting language arts software. *Computers and Education,* 1986, *20,* 19-28.

Reinking, D., Kling, M., and Harper, M. Characteristics of computer software in reading: An empirical investigation. Unpublished manuscript, University of Georgia at Athens, 1986.

Reading software development project references

1981

Lubar, D. Another look at educational software and books. *Creative Computing,* 1981, *7* (1), 36, 38.

1982

Northwest Regional Educational Lab. *Comprehension power program. MicroSIFT couseware evaluation.* 1982. (ED 226 765)

Describes the Comprehension Power Program by MicroSIFT Courseware. Includes instructional purpose, techniques, objectives, prerequisite skills, potential uses, and major strengths. Includes an evaluative table that rates content, purpose, instructional delivery, ease of use, and reliability.

Parker, S. *A review of first grade software materials.* 1982. (ED 225 562)

Attempts to locate and evaluate software for use with the first grade curriculum. Author rates nine math and five language arts programs according to technical, educational, and management criteria. Includes names and addresses of fifty software vendors, including seventeen that have first grade materials.

1983

Bass, G.M., and Perkins, H.W. Software: Side by side – elementary critical reading packages. *Electronic Learning,* 1983, *3* (3), 86-87.

Compares six critical reading software packages: Critical Reading by Borg Warner; Our Weird and Wacky World – Critical Reading by Educational Activities; How to Read in the Content Areas – Social Studies/Literature/Sciences/Mathematics by Educational Activities; Our Wild and Crazy World – Critical Reading by Educational Activities; Comprehension Power D-E-F by Milliken; and Tutorial Comprehension by Random House.

Bitter, G. Computer software roundup. *Instructor and Teacher,* 1983, *93* (4), 94-96, 98, 100.

Describes twenty-five educational software programs published in 1983, including five language arts programs and software for social studies, computer literacy, science, math, and classroom management.

Fortier, G., Eisele, J., and Mason, G. A microcomputer program for the storage and retrieval of bibliographical references. *Computers, Reading and Language Arts,* 1983, *1* (3), 39-42.

Explains the SRBR program available through the University of Georgia. Reading references are entered into the program according to main descriptors and subdescriptors, suggesting ease of access for reference retrieval.

Henk, W. Supplementary reading skills courseware. *The Reading Teacher,* 1983, *37* (2), 215-216.

Reviews the Reading Skills Courseware Series from Scott, Foresman.

Hornberger, T., and Whitford, E. The language of computers can be fun and games. *Computers, Reading and Language Arts,* 1983, *1* (1), 41-43.

Presents four computer vocabulary activities: video attack match, vertical puzzle, video names, and unusual definitions.

Rubin, A. The computer confronts language arts: Cans and shoulds for education. In A.C. Wilkinson (Ed.), *Classroom computers and cognitive sciences.* New York: Academic Press, 1983.

Discusses four issues relevant to computer based reading/language arts programs as they relate to three computer activities – QUILL, HANGMAN, and STORY MAKER. The four issues are level of text, role of feedback, learning by doing, and social environment of the program.

Slesnick, T. Creative play: An alternative use of the computer in education. *Simulation & Games,* 1983, *14* (1), 11-20.

Discusses several word games used at the Lawrence Hall of Science at Berkeley: Hangman, George (Hangman in Spanish), Big Red (computer generated story based on Little Red Riding Hood), Password (guess a word from synonyms), Words (guess a word from letter clues), Snap (guess a word flashed quickly), and WFF (using letters in a logic game).

Wedman, J. Software – what's in it for reading? *Journal of Reading,* 1983, *26* (7), 642.

Reports a review of reading software that concluded word attack software is the most common, followed by comprehension and study skills.

Wheeler, F. The puzzler. . .an answer to the reading riddle? *Classroom Computer Learning,* 1983, *4* (4), 46-51.

> Identifies The Puzzler as fulfilling eight criteria for quality reading software: a reading theory basis, development of reading strategies, higher level thinking, quality literature, creation of original work, easy to use program design, transfer to other reading strategies, and use of computers' unique features.

1984

Candler, A., and Johnson, D. Software for teaching reading in special education. *Academic Therapy,* 1984, *19* (5), 607-612.

> Describes four software reading programs designed to assist special education students – Compu-Read, Critical Reading Lesson Series A-H, Reading Comprehension: What's Different? and Comprehension Power Program.

Chomsky, C. Finding the best language arts software. *Classroom Computer Learning,* 1984, *4* (6), 61-63.

> Identifies Suspect Sentences, Story Maker, M-ss-ng L-nks, and Jabbertalky as challenging, enjoyable software for language arts development.

Deboe, M. *Writing to Read in the Portland Public Schools: 1983-1984 evaluation report.* 1984. (ED 255 552)

> Evaluates the IBM Writing to Read program in the Portland Public Schools.

Devall, Y. Using the computer to strengthen reading. *The Computing Teacher,* 1984, *12,* (2), 19-22.

> Suggests drill and practice, tutorial, game, and word processing programs to improve student spelling skills. Highlights features that quality spelling software should possess.

Fredericks, A. Basals, computers, and the reading program. *The Reading Teacher,* 1984, *38* (3), 361-362.

> Describes several commercially available software programs that can accompany basal readers: Phi Beta Filer, Bank Street Writer, PAL Reading Curriculum, M-ss-ng L-nks, Comes First/Sequence, Meet the Computer – Beginning BASIC, Koala Pad, and Vocabulary Baseball.

Higgins, J. Reading and risk-taking: A role for the computer. *ELT Journal,* 1984, *38* (3), 192-198.

> Describes Close-Up, a program encouraging readers to take risks in order to develop better reading skills. As one word from a text is randomly chosen, students attempt to identify the text's topic, matching the word to one of the eight displayed titles. A scoring system structures the format, creating both a challenge and strategy for winning.

Ivers, P. Previewing software for language arts instruction. *Computers, Reading and Language Arts,* 1984, *1* (4), 17-19, 26.

> Reviews three language arts software programs as an illustration of what to look for in good and bad software. The programs are MECC, English Volume 1; English SAT 1; and Vocabulary Prompter.

Kahn, K. A prototype grammar kit in PROLOG. *Instructional Science,* 1984, *13* (1), 37-45.

> Describes computer based grammatical instruction kit written in PROLOG. Notes that PROLOG's semantic complexity makes program malfunctions difficult to deal with.

Klein, S. (Ed.). *Computer education: A catalog of projects sponsored by the United States Department of Education 1983.* Washington, DC: United States Department of Education, National Institute of Education, 1984.

Contains 275 abstracts of Department of Education discretionary computer education projects that were active during 1983. Many projects deal directly or indirectly with reading education. The catalog is divided into the following sections: developing student computer literacy, computers as instructional aids for students, computers for educators, research and evaluation, and multipurpose computer education projects.

Krause, K. Choosing computer software that works. *Journal of Reading,* 1984, *28* (1), 24-27.

Tells how a secondary reading lab instructor selected software for his remedial and developmental reading students. Includes a list of recommended software.

Marcus, S. GOSUB: POET: RETURN computers and the poetic muse. *Educational Technology,* 1984, *24* (8), 15-20.

Discusses the creation of poetry in noninstructional and instructional contexts, including discussions about Compupoem.

Mason, G. *The micro can connect home, school and community—but it must be read.* 1984. (ED 245 194)

Observes types of reading and writing CAI used in a variety of school settings. Illustrates the significant impact that home and community resources can make on CAI in education. Describes a number of word processing programs and simulations that appeal to both children and their parents.

Mason, G. Using teacher utility programs—moving toward the ideal. *The Reading Teacher,* 1984, *37* (8), 809-810.

Explains that microcomputer utility educational programs can be an asset to any classroom reading program if teachers know how to use them. Utilities allow teachers to develop tests, instructional activities, puzzles, reports, games, and bulletin board displays. Presents several examples of utility programs.

Murphy, D., and Derry, S. *Description of an introductory learning strategies course for the Job Skills Educational Program.* 1984. (ED 244 108)

Describes a basic skills computer assisted curriculum developed at Florida State University for the Army Research Institute. The five steps included in the program are setting goals and self-pacing, mood management, reading comprehension, developing skilled memory, and problem solving.

National Diffusion Network, Department of Education. *Technology Programs that Work.* Washington, DC: National Diffusion Network, 1984.

Describes Technology Programs that Work, a product of the Technology Diffusion Network Project. Several of the programs related to reading are Basic Literacy through Microcomputers, Salt Lake City; Computer Assisted Diagnostic Prescriptive Program in Reading and Mathematics, Dillwyn, Virginia; and Computer Assisted Instruction, Merrimack Education Center, Chelmsford, Massachussetts.

Partridge, S. *Writing to Read.* 1984. (ED 254 820)

Evaluates the IBM Writing to Read program in North Carolina schools during 1982-1984.

Rauch, M., and Wogen, D. *Comprehension: Mapping information, a program for the Apple computer.* 1984. (ED 244 231)

Focuses on the effectiveness of mapping for comprehension and retention of expository information. Describes a program where students see a mapped or framework display of the main subject/topic, subcategories/ideas, and the details of the selected passage.

Rosegrant, T. Using microcomputers to foster progress in reading and writing development. In S. Leggett (Ed.), *Microcomputers go to school.* Chicago: Teach'em, 1984.

Describes the talking screen textwriter (TST), which allows users to hear letter names, morphemes, and words used during and after they are typed into a computer. The speech comes from an ECHO II synthesizer. Provides several examples of the TST in use.

1985

Balajthy, E. *A public domain software library for reading and language arts.* 1985. (ED 259 306)

Free software for reading and language arts teachers.

Bialo, E., and Erickson, L. Microcomputer courseware: Characteristics and design trends. *AEDS Journal,* 1985, *18* (4), 227-236.

Discusses a 1984 study in which 163 microcomputer courseware programs were evaluated by the Educational Products Information Exchange (EPIE) Institute to identify strengths and weaknesses in design. Approximately 23 percent of the 163 programs involved language arts and reading software. Using these numbers as a reference, the evaluations revealed the following weaknesses: lack of field testing, lack of learner objectives, lack of goal/content match, lack of support materials, lack of warranty, lack of record-keeping, lack of a management system, and lack of evaluation of student learning. Provides additional information and program strengths.

Blanchard, J., and Mason, G. Using computers in content area reading instruction. *Journal of Reading,* 1985, *29* (2), 112-117.

Discusses five applications of computers for middle and high school students; utility programs, word processing, simulations, telecommunications/databases, and interactive fiction. Suggests that teachers must help students meet the reading demands of computer delivered text.

Chiang, B. Teaching reading: A review of software. *Computers, Reading and Language Arts,* 1985, *2* (2), 25-26.

Examines software designed for increasing word attack skills and reading comprehension.

Dickson, W.P. Thought-provoking software: Juxtaposing symbol systems. *Educational Researcher,* 1985, *14* (5), 30-37.

Describes though provoking software as any that allows the students to manipulate any two or more culturally valued symbol systems. Describes different types of thought provoking software: oral communication game, typing communication game, talking communication game, talking word processors, graphing equations, Turtle graphics and LOGO, Mathboxes, musical and spatial representation, Wizard of Where, and matrix sorting game.

Dudley-Marling, C. Microcomputers, reading, and writing: Alternatives to drill and practice. *The Reading Teacher,* 1985, *38* (4), 388-391.

Explains that commercially available software can be used to stimulate a student's interest in language. Directs the reader's attention to "participa-stories," such as Snooper Troops, Dragon's Keep, Window on Learning, and Deadline and suggests that teachers can create their own stories using an authoring language like SuperPILOT. Word processing and electronic mail are mentioned as other ways to stimulate language interest.

Pogrow, S. Helping students to become thinkers. *Electronic Learning*, 1985, *4* (7), 26-29.

Describes HOTS (higher order thinking skills), a project to help schools develop a computer based thinking skills curriculum. HOTS uses readily available software (e.g., Moptown Parade, Bumble Games, Crossword Magic, Creative Play) that can be adapted for use in helping develop higher order thinking skills.

Schreiner, R. The computer, an electronic flash card. *The Reading Teacher*, 1985, *39* (3), 378-380.

Presents two programs (with source code): controlled flash and speed flash. Both programs are used for vocabulary drill.

Shalvoy, M. Basic skills: Can computers head back to basics? *Electronic Learning*, 1985, *5* (2), 42-43.

Describes five National Diffusion Network technology programs that work. Four of the five programs emphasize reading instruction—all use both Apple and TRS-80 computers in their programs. Also tells how to get information about National Diffusion Network computer programs and a catalog of NIE sponsored computer projects.

Smith, J. Software side by side: Vocabulary. *Electronic Learning*, 1985, *5* (1), 52-53.

Reviews Vocabulary Builder, Vocabulary Grade 11, Word Attack with SAT data disk, Vocabulator, and PSAT Word Attack Skills.

Developing software references

1979

Kehrberg, K. Microcomputer software development: New strategies for new technology. *AEDS Journal*, 1979, *12* (1), 103-110.

1980

Garson, J. The case against multiple choice. *The Computing Teacher*, 1980, *7* (4), 29-34.

Discusses the strengths and weaknesses of drill and practice programs. States that more students should be involved in the development of software they will be using.

1981

Dean, J. What's holding up the show? *Today's Education*, 1981, *71* (2), 22-25.

Claims that lack of easy to use computer authoring languages is holding back the development of educational software.

Gagne, R., Wage, W., and Rojas, A. Planning and authoring computer assisted instruction lessons. *Educational Technology*, 1981, *21* (9), 7-26.

Suggests that the guidelines provided for the users of computerized authoring systems will be more effective if they are based around nine events of instruction: gaining attention, informing learner of the lesson objective, stimulating recall of prior learning, presenting stimuli with distinctive features, guiding learning, eliciting performance, providing informative feedback, assessing performance, and enhancing retention and learning transfer. Provides a set of CAI guidelines based on these learning events.

Jelden, D. The microcomputer as a multi-user interactive instructional system. *AEDS Journal*, 1981, *14* (4), 208-217.

Contains guidelines for software development.

Kingman, J. Designing good educational software. *Creative Computing*, 1981, *7* (10), 72-81.

Kurshan, B. Computer technology and instruction: Implications for instructional designers. *Educational Technology*, 1981, *21* (8), 28-30.

Olds, H. The making of software. *Classroom Computer News*, 1981, *1* (6), 20-21.

Roblyer, M. Instructional design versus authoring of courseware: Some crucial differences. *AEDS Journal*, 1981, *14* (4), 173-181.

1982

Henney, M. *Development of microcomputer reading programs.* 1982. (ED 215 302)

Says that microcomputer software development focuses on paraphrasing — deciding which sentences best describe the same idea.

Kidd, M., and Holmes, G. The computer and language remediation. *Programmed Learning & Educational Technology*, 1982, *19* (3), 235-239.

States that CAI offers remedial students a climate that fosters learning, specificity to individual needs, self-pacing, instructional clarity, and individual and immediate feedback.

Roblyer, M. Developing computer courseware must be easier than some things. *Educational Technology*, 1982, *22* (1), 33-35.

Provides a quick look at how to develop and evaluate software, offering several examples to show that developing and evaluating computer based programs are more difficult than other forms of instructional materials.

Visniesky, C., and Hocking, J. *Choosing a microcomputer for use as a teaching aid.* 1982. (ED 214 608)

1983

Benfort, A. Micros for reading, spelling and self-esteem. *Journal of Reading*, 1983, *26* (7), 638-639.

Explains that tachistoscopic reading activities are one way computers can help remedial reading instruction. Tells how completing tachistoscopic reading activities can help students gain a sense of accomplishment and self-worth.

Jarchow, E. Teaching literature with the help of the microcomputer. *The Computing Teacher*, 1983, *11* (4), 35-36.

Presents one teacher's attempt to design software that features higher order, open ended questions for literature classes.

Tyler, J. Your prescription for CAI success. *Instructional Innovator*, 1983, *28* (2), 25-27, 40.

Offers a process for developing CAI software. Steps include identification of student needs and instructional goals; preparation of materials to include learning objectives, criteria for mastery, instructional delivery techniques, and resource materials; and determination of procedures for evaluation and revision.

1984

Alessi, S. Designing effective computer assisted instruction. *The American Biology Teacher,* 1984, *46* (3), 146-151.

Lists three strategies that may assist in producing quality CAI software: a consideration of the total instructional process, application of sound pedagogical principles, and material evaluation and revision.

Chan, J., and Korostoff, M. *Teachers' guide to designing classroom software.* Beverly Hills: SAGE, 1984.

Edelsky, C. The content of language arts software: A criticism. *Computers, Reading and Language Arts,* 1984, *1* (4), 8-11.

Introduces some theoretical constructs that appear to exist in the acquisition of language as they relate to reading and language arts software development.

Harris, D. Selecting computer software for play, language, and thinking. *Australian Journal of Reading,* 1984, *7* (2), 98-101.

Calls for software that capitalizes on the student's imagination and interaction with other students and teachers. Insists that quality software is student controlled, self-paced, easily managed, and integrated across subject areas.

Modla, V. Writing a program to reinforce reading skills. *Computers, Reading and Language Arts,* 1984, *1* (4), 27-29.

Discusses how to write a software program that lets students practice using fact and opinion comprehension activities.

Neufeld, K. *Computer-competencies for reading teachers.* 1984. (ED 250 663)

Lists beginner competencies: basic computer literacy, software evaluation, and planning for CAI. The intermediate level involves competency in word processing and computer management systems. Advanced competency allows the teacher to create original software using an authoring system or BASIC.

Ohanian, S. How today's reading software can zap kid's desire to read. *Classroom Computer Learning,* 1984, *5* (4), 27-31.

Criticizes the premise of some software that "reading can be achieved by drilling students on discrete skills."

Waldrop, P. Behavior reinforcement strategies for computer-assisted instruction: Programming for success. *Educational Technology,* 1984, *24* (9), 38-41.

Wepner, S., and Kramer, S. *Designing your computer curriculum: A process approach.* 1984. (ED 247 900)

Offers a step-by-step strategy for integrating computer technology into a school district's reading curriculum. Describes needs assessment, planning, implementation, and evaluation.

1985

Hazen, M. Instructional software design principles. *Educational Technology,* 1985, *25* (11), 18-23.

Richgels, D. Five easy steps to microcomputer programming. *Computers, Reading and Language Arts,* 1985, *2* (2), 34-37.

Includes some ways teachers may help students learn to program: Designate key computer commands; develop a short (less than 25 lines) program; and review the interaction of commands in the program.

1987

Blanchard, J. Instructional design issues in computer-based reading: Reinforcement and objectives. *Computers in the Schools,* 1987, *4* (1), 18-26.

Focuses on paper and pencil research involving extrinsic and intrinsic reinforcement and instructional objectives that may be important for those designing, evaluating, and using reading software.

4

Computers in teaching reading and reading assessment research

C omputer based reading research is of at least three distinctly different types: examining ways to use computers to teach reading, examining ways to assess reading and reading processes, and examining psychological and physiological aspects of reading processes.

Using computers in teaching reading

Investigations using computers to teach reading and language arts were first undertaken at the Stanford University Institute for Mathematical Studies in the Social Sciences under the direction of Richard Atkinson and Patrick Suppes. Early results were encouraging but expensive. By the late 1970s expectations and interest about mainframe, time sharing reading instruction had diminished because of the cost of computing and the lack of instructional flexibility. Yet from the two decades (1959-1979) of mainframe, time sharing, computer based instructional research, a clear picture emerged that the computer can teach reading, can save instructional time, and can be an enjoyable way to learn. In computer literature, this picture has been referred to as the CAI phenomenon.

In a metaanalysis of computer based instruction in basic reading skills (Roblyer, 1985), the research cited consistently reported that students showed slight (one-third of a standard deviation) advantages in achievement gains, learned information in less time, and seemed to enjoy the activity more than when taught by more traditional approaches. It is important to note that the CAI phenomenon studies involved drill and practice programs (perhaps with limited tutorial elements) presented by mainframe, time sharing computers or minicomputers. Today's minicomputer based reading programs may or may not support the CAI phenomenon; it is too early to tell. But present research does not include an ongoing assessment of the phenomenon with varied microcomputer programs.

However, other forms of reading research with microcomputers continue. Readers are reminded that reports of research annotated in this chapter include many studies comparing computer based instructional methods, usually based on the assumption that computer based methods are preferable. Therefore, few readers should be surprised that computer based methods usually are reported to result in superior performance by experimental groups — a self-fulfilling prophecy.

Computers and the reading process

There are many researchers using computers to investigate the myriad of psychological and physiological processes involved in reading. Most of their reports are referenced in this chapter or earlier editions of *Computer Applications in Reading*. These reports are so diverse that using the term "computers and the reading process" seems the only way to categorize them.

Reading assessment research

Recent developments in technology have demonstrated the computer's potential to provide decision making capabilities for educational and psychological assessment. Reading is just one area of assessment that can profit — and needs to profit — from these developments. For many reasons, all areas of educational and psychological assessment need to profit from advances in computer technology. The most compelling reason is demand. The demand for reading assessment continues to grow while the time and resources teachers and other professionals can devote to assessment continue to decline.

A continuum

Any computer based assessment program (reading or otherwise) can be placed on a decisionmaking continuum bracketed by the terms *active* and *passive*. *Active* implies decisionmaking and *passive* implies lack of decisionmaking. Using the ends of the continuum as points for discussion, the active end suggests programs that duplicate assessment activities of teachers, diagnosticians, and measurement specialists — everything from test design to interpretation. The passive end suggests programs that only score tests — programs devoid of decisionmaking. In a sense, the movement toward active assessment features can be quantified by the breadth and depth of decision making available in the program.

It is the movement away from the passive end of the continuum and toward the active end that is of concern to today's reading educators. Despite attempts to use active features in computer based reading assessment programs, for the most part, today's programs are predominantly passive.

Forms of computer based reading assessment

There are many computer based reading assessment formats. Despite the passive nature of these programs, their diversity makes it difficult to decide just what is meant by computer based reading assessment. At least five plausible program categories are suggested: test scoring, test, test generator, instructional system, and instruction/practice.

Test scoring programs. Test scoring programs may process student reading test results, store the result, and produce reports containing the test results. Interpretations, analyses, and prescriptions are usually done by teachers.

These programs usually are not associated with any materials or approaches and are the most passive form of reading assessment. Examples of test scoring programs are Instructional Management System Plus (National Computer Systems), and Scan-Tron.

Test programs. Test programs may process student reading test results, store the results, produce reports containing the test results, and provide computer based tests. These programs may assess one reading skill or many. They also may provide a simple accounting of number right versus number wrong or complex interpretations of reading performance with suggested prescriptions containing instructional materials and techniques.

Test programs are not inherently associated with any reading materials or approaches. Generally, teachers have little control over what reading skills are measured or how reading skills are measured with these programs. Examples of test programs include Computer Based Reading Assessment Instrument (Kendall/Hunt), Reading Style Inventory (Learning Research Associates), and Diascriptive Reading (Educational Activities).

Test generator programs. Test generator programs may process student reading test results, store the results, produce reports containing the test results, and provide computer based tests. However, these features are available only if the test generator program permits the activities and if the teacher programs the activities. Quite simply, teachers write their own tests. These programs use a test shell—a menu based computer program that allows teachers to select the testing features. Teachers may develop any test format provided in the program. In addition, test generator programs usually provide several scoring options. However, interpretations, analyses, and prescriptions would be likely to be done by the teachers without computer assistance.

Test generator programs or teacher made tests are not inherently associated with any reading materials or approaches. A few examples of test generator programs include SuperPilot (Apple Computer), Tutorial Quiz Master (Random House), Exams II (Shenandoah Software), Create-A-Test (Cross Educational Software), Quizmaster (Logical Systems), and Quick-Tests (Seven Hills Software).

Instructional system programs. Instructional system programs are associated with materials and approaches. These programs accompany published materials (including all major basal reader series) and are often referred to as computer based management programs. Instructional system programs may process student reading test results, store the results, produce reports containing the test results, and provide computer based tests. However, the reading tests will probably not be presented on screen. The recording, analyzing, and prescribing aspects of the programs almost always are done by computer. Teachers usually have very little control over what reading skills are measured, how they are measured, or analyses and interpretations of reading performance. Examples of nonbasal instructional system programs include Scholastic Reading Comprehension (Scholastic), Tandy ESTC (Radio Shack), and CSR (Educational Software Products).

Instruction/practice programs. Instruction/practice programs are not specifically designed as reading assessment programs, but student performance is one component of the program. Evaluation of student performance, whether before, during, or after an activity, is more for the benefit of the student than for diagnostic needs of teachers. In a sense, any reading program that includes an evaluation or scoring component is using computer based reading assessment. Usually, only rudimentary scores (number right versus number wrong) are provided, and interpretations, analyses, and prescriptions are absent.

Research: Some issues and a few answers

Despite a paucity of research, some issues involving relationships between reading assessment and computer technology have been investigated. Obviously, these are not the only issues facing computer based reading assessment—just the first to be investigated.

A first issue concerns whether any portions of the assessment procedure should be off screen. For example, in at least one research study

(Heppner et al., 1985), text was presented on screen followed by the comprehension questions off screen. Strictly speaking, this is not computer based reading assessment; it is computer aided paper and pencil reading assessment. If assessment is totally computer based, another concern is whether text and questions should be presented on the same screen. If the questions are presented on the same screen as the text, reading comprehension assessment can become study skills assessment (i.e., find the answer to the question). While only one study (Schloss, Schloss, & Cartwright, 1984) has investigated this issue, results indicate that computer based reading assessment may be more effective when the text and the questions are not presented on the same screen.

A third issue is how to measure reading comprehension in a computer based environment. Of the available computer based reading assessment studies, most have measured comprehension in a text and comprehension question format. Most of these studies have used familiar types of questions (such as multiple choice) plus a few examples of less familiar formats (sentence arrangement, fill in the blank). The predominant forms of computer based reading assessment are likely to continue to be passages and questions, but other assessment formats also will be required.

The fourth and fifth issues concern the relationship between on screen reading comprehension performance and reading rate. With regard to on screen reading and comprehension performance, Askwall (1985); Blank, Murphy, and Schneiderman (1986); Hansen, Doring, & Whitlock (1978); Hepner et al. (1985); Muter et al. (1982); and Olsen et al. (1986) present research suggesting that on screen reading does not result in much different comprehension performance than does off screen. At this point in the development of computer based reading assessment, we can tentatively conclude that on screen reading of text will not affect reading comprehension performance, either positively or negatively..

Concerning the relationship between on screen reading and reading rate, Hansen, Doring, and Whitlock, Heppner et al., and Muter et al. report research indicating reading rates that are substantially decreased for on screen reading. However, Askwall and Olsen et al. suggest that less time is needed for on screen reading. Some of these contradictory findings concerning comprehension performance and reading rate can be explained by the different research paradigms and computer technologies used in these studies.

A sixth issue concerns student attitudes toward computer based reading assessment. Unfortunately, no research directly relates to reading assessment. However, psychological assessment does provide some guidance. Based on the research of Burke and Normand (1986), Cliffe (1985), Klingler et al. (1977), and Schmidt, Urry, and Gugel (1978), it appears that teachers can anticipate few negative reactions to computer based reading assessment in either reading clinic or classroom settings.

It is important to note that these and other similar issues relate not only to reading assessment but also to the general reading requirements of computer use. A person either does or does not understand the textual dialogue of the computer. A computer you can converse with is still in the realm of science fiction. In today's computer reading environment, the computer assumes almost total understanding by the user; few programs provide clarification when misunderstandings occur.

Advantages and disadvantages of computer based assessment
Common sense tells us there are advantages and disadvantages in using computers in reading assessment. Currently, we can only hope the advantages outweigh the disadvantages, but continued development of computer based reading assessment should justify greater optimism.

Advantages
- Unlimited patience
  Computers are never tired. For example, assessment can proceed at any pace determined by the teacher and student (Duthie, 1984; Madsen, 1986; Space, 1981).
- Unlimited ability to store and recall test results and interpretations
  Computer based reading assessment results, interpretations, and prescriptions can be readily available in narrative as well as graphic formats. Storage and recall of results can be important for diagnosis, particularly if a perplexing problem surfaces that is not common to most assessment situations. In these cases, previous results, interpretations, and prescriptions can be quickly consulted to help decisionmaking (Madsen, 1986; Space, 1981).
- Limited examiner bias.
  The negative effects of poorly trained test administrators should be reduced with computer based reading assessment. The computer follows its program; divergence is impossible. This effectively ensures standardization and reduces examiner bias (Angle, 1981; Elithorn, Mornington, & Stavrou, 1982; Herr & Best, 1984; Sampson & Pyle, 1983; Space, 1981).
- Limited response bias
  Psychological assessment studies indicate that people react favorably to computer based assessment. Response accuracy can be improved over

conventional testing procedures. This should be true of computer based reading assessment. In addition, readers using computer based counterparts of paper and pencil tests should have little trouble acclimating to the computer testing environment (Angle et al., 1977; Duthie, 1984; Greist & Klein, 1980; Harrell & Lombardo, 1984; Lushene, O'Neil, & Dunn, 1974; Moore, Summer, & Bloor, 1984; Rumelhart & Norman, 1980; Sanders, 1985; Schmidt, Urry, & Gugel, 1978; Slack & Slack, 1977; Space, 1981).

- Limited assessment demands on professionals
  Computer based reading assessment should save time and money and eliminate many mechanical tasks for reading professionals. It also generates more information from fewer questions (Byers, 1981; Gedye & Miller, 1969; Space, 1981; Stout, 1981).
- Unlimited use of paraprofessionals in assessment
  Under the direction of professionals, and with proper training, paraprofessionals can assume many computer based reading assessment tasks.
- Unlimited use of peripheral assessment devices
  As an example, computer based assessment devices could almost automatically measure variables such as reaction and response times (Dunn, Lushene, & O'Neil, 1972; Madsen, 1986; Space, 1981).
- Unlimited adaptability
  Computer based assessment can lead to easier individualized testing, an especially important feature for students with special assessment problems such as cerebral palsy(Beaumont, 1982; Evan & Miller, 1969; Katz & Dolby, 1981; Kelley & Tuggle, 1981; Lucas et al., 1977; Meier & Geiger, 1986; Stout, 1981).
- Unlimited use of assessment procedures in research
  Computer based reading assessment can lead to easier collection, organization, scoring, and analysis of data in all forms of reading research (Space, 1981).
- Unlimited use of graphics for assessment
  The use of computer based graphics (including animation and film) should enhance reading assessment capabilities, particularly for young or poor readers.

Disadvantages

- Dehumanization and depersonalization
  This can be a problem for both students and teachers because of the limited human relationships inherent in computer based reading assessment. For example, the teacher may feel a loss of control or understanding during assessment (Hirsch, 1981; Space, 1981).

Computer applications in reading

- Costs of hardware and software
  Costs are high for computer based reading assessment. Costs to users usually can compensate for expenses by reductions in time and expenses for professional services. However, costs will remain high for developers (Lesse, 1983; Space, 1981).
- Computer literacy requirements
  Students and teachers using computer based reading assessment must learn to use the computer, its software, and its supporting peripheral devices.
- Mechanical failures
  Computer based reading assessment can be halted by malfunctions and breakdowns in hardware, software, and peripherals.
- Limited computer based assessment research
  As computer based assessment continues, research is needed to answer questions about differences between conventional and computer based assessment.
- Confidentiality and right of privacy
  Computer based assessment might be more vulnerable to breaches of confidentiality than conventional testing because results are often stored on memory devices such as floppy disk or hard disk where many may have access (Herr & Best, 1984; Meier & Geiger, 1986; Sampson & Pyle, 1983).
- On screen presentation of text and questions
  There are many problems relating to the presentation of reading tests on screen, including rereading text, reading questions and answers, changing questions and answers, and text presentation rate. In addition, ergonomic variables such as screen size, legibility, and lighting can affect the presentation of text and questions (Bevan, 1984; Blank, Murphy, & Schneiderman, 1986).
- Resistance by professionals and others
  Professionals and paraprofessions must be trained in the proper use and application of computer based reading assessment, including problems of overdependency and misuse (Butcher, 1978; Byrnes & Johnson, 1981; Loesch, 1986; Matarazzo, 1983; Meier & Geiger, 1986; Space, 1981).
- Limited decisionmaking features
  Computer based assessment instruments are simply computerized versions of existing instruments; they do not fully exploit the power of the computer. The strength of an assessment program should lie in the depth and breadth of computer based decisionmaking.
- Nonexpert based interpretations
  Computer based interpretations, analyses, and prescriptions are only as

good as the programer who wrote them. Teachers using this information must always question its validity. If incorrect information and algorithms are used, the interpretations, analyses, and prescriptions may be of little value (Madsen, 1986; Space, 1981).

Computers and the reading process

Using computers to investigate the psychological and physiological processes in reading is becoming commonplace, particularly in physiological research. However, the number of research studies presently available is limited. Most of the available research is listed in the references of this chapter, chapter 10, or the references in earlier editions of *Computer Applications in Reading.*

While the research may be limited, the psychological and physiological processes under investigation are quite diverse. The leader in microcomputer based research has been the Center for the Study of Reading at the University of Illinois. (For a complete list of the Center's Technical Reports and Reading Education Reports, write to the Center for the Study of Reading, 51 Gerty Drive, Champaign, Illinois 61820.)

The references in this chapter are divided into four sections: computer assisted instruction in reading, psychological and physiological research, reviews of reading research, and reading assessment. Readers interested in additional references on psychological and physiological processes in reading references that apply directly to legibility should consult chapter 10.

Computer assisted instruction in reading references

1970

Mathis, A., Smith, T., and Hansen, D. College students' attitudes toward computer assisted instruction. *Journal of Educational Psychology,* 1970, *61,* 46-51.
> Describes a study in which college students were pretested on attitudes toward CAI, then assigned either outside reading or 45 minutes of computer assisted instructon. Students had more positive attitudes toward CAI than outside reading, particularly if they had few errors during CAI instruction.

1972

Thompson, B. Effect of CAI on the language arts achievement of elementary school children. *Dissertation Abstracts International,* 1972, *33* (8), 4077A.
> Compres language arts achievement of 200 intermediate students, half of whom received daily CAI in word meaning, spelling, and general language usage. Achievement posttests at a lower level of abstraction (paragraph meaning and general language usage) showed significant gains as compared to spelling and word meaning posttests having a higher level of abstraction.

1973

Caldwell, R. *A comparison of a programmed text and a computer based display unit to teach reading skills to semiliterate adults.* Unpublished doctoral dissertation, Pennsylvania State University, 1973.

Indicates that young adults spent more time at computer terminals than a comparable group spent with programed reading texts. Attitudes toward CAI reading were more positive than those of the group taught with programed texts. However, there were no significant differences in reading achievement between the two groups.

1974

Anderson, T., Anderson, R., Dalgaard, B., Biddle, W., Surber, J., and Alessi, S. An experimental evaluation of a computer based study management system. *Educational Psychologist,* 1974, *11,* 184-190.

Fitzgerald, B. An analysis of computer assisted instruction in the reading program at Carl Hayden High School. *Dissertation Abstracts International,* 1974, *35,* 4069A.

1975

Strang, H. The automated instruction of practical reading skills to disadvantaged sixth grade children. *Improving Human Performance,* 1975, *4,* 43-52.

Describes how sixth graders were pretested on reading skills such as using a telephone directory and locating topics in an encyclopedia. Experimental group students then received CAI covering the reading skills and control group students received nonCAI instruction. Results favored the CAI group.

1976

Okey, J., and Majer, K. Individual and small group learning with computer assisted instruction. *AV Communication Review,* 1976, *24,* 79-86.

Tells how undergraduate students studied Bloom's mastery learning strategy at the PLATO IV terminal. Some studied alone and some studied in groups of two, three, or four. Groups selected one of their number to respond by using the keyboard. There were no differences in achievement, but the pairs took more computer time than single students or groups of three or four. This time seemed to have been used for discussion of concepts presented.

Robbins, W., and Tharp, A. A natural language computerized instruction system for elementary education. *Educational Technology,* 1976, *13* (3), 32-35.

Discusses CAI geography and history lessons that incorporated some aspects of tutorial/dialogue instruction.

1977

Anelli, C. Computer-assisted instruciton and reading achievement of urban third and fourth graders. *Dissertation Abstracts International,* 1977, *38* (11), 6662A.

Describes a study of 121 third and fourth grade students who received computer assisted reading instruction in twenty or forty minute time periods. Suggests that total CAI time, session length, or session frequency do not affect posttest reading achievement scores.

Litman, G. Relation between CAI and reading achievement among fourth, fifth, and sixth grade students. *Dissertation Abstracts International,* 1977, *83* (4), 2003A.

Suggests the effectiveness of CAI as a practicable instructional technique in reading achievement. Followup studies indicated a positive correlation between achievement and CAI two years after the year of instruction.

Steinberg, E. Review of student control in computer-assisted instruction. *Journal of Computer Based Instruction,* 1977, *3,* 84-90.

1978

Sturges, P. Delay of information feedback in computer assisted testing. *Journal of Educational Psychology,* 1978, *70,* 378-387.

Studies the effect of delayed feedback on retention in computer assisted reading. One hundred twelve college students took a 30 minute, multiple choice, computer assisted test and received the correct answers either immediately after each item, at the end of the test, 24 hours later, or not at all. Delayed feedback was better than immediate feedback on comprehension performance.

1979

Bath Elementary School Staff. *Results of computer assisted instruction at Bath Elementary School.* 1979. (ED 195 245)

Describes a pilot project in which excellent gains in reading resulted from 20 minutes spent daily at the computer by 100 sixth graders. The displays appeared one letter at a time and seemed to speed up the slower readers.

Caldwell, R., and Rizza, P. A computer based system of reading instruction for adult nonreaders. *AEDS Journal,* 1979, *12* (4), 155-162.

Reports that "initial performance data from eight demonstration projects in adult basic education centers indicated that learners gained on the average one entire year in reading after less than 12 hours of instruction." Dropout rates of only 5 percent were reported.

1980

Argento, B.J. *Alternative education models—preliminary findings of the Job Corps educational improvement effort.* 1980. (ED 206 868)

Provides a detailed treatment of the Job Corps Educational Improvement Effort targeting the basic education program. Discusses both traditional and innovative approaches, including a limited discussion of CAI and CMI and their places in an educational delivery system.

Diem, R., and Fairweather, P. An evaluation of a computer assisted education system in an untraditional academic setting—a county jail. *AEDS Journal,* 1980, *13* (3), 204-213.

Describes use of the CDC PLATO Basic Skills Reading Program in Bexar County, Texas. The program made gains in math but not in reading. Suggested that reading materials were not adult enough and that tutors should work at terminals with tutees.

Feldman, S., Alne, D., and Seltzer, J. *Use of a simulation program for teaching diagnostic skills.* 1980. (ED 196 428)

Reports positive cognitive and affective gains in teachers from a computer simulation of reading diagnosis.

Gifford, R. The rate of mastery learning of CAI lessons in basic reading and mathematics. *Dissertation Abstracts Internaitonal,* 1980, *41* (4), 1553A.

Explains how research data from 88 third to eighth grade students receiving PLATO instruction in reading and math were used to predict overall changes in the rate of student learning, the effects of entry level variables, and the frequency of mastery learning test failure. Provides technical data.

Computer applications in reading

L'Allier, J. *An evaluation study of a computer-based lesson that adjusts reading level by monitoring on task reader characteristics.* Unpublished doctoral dissertation, University of Minnesota, 1980.

Mravetz, P. The effects of computer-assisted instruction on student self-çoncept, locus of control, level of aspiration, and reading achievement. *Dissertation Abstracts International,* 1980, *41* (3), 994A.

> Reports a study of 30 junior high school students that suggests CAI had a positive effect on reading achievement. In addition, CAI's impact may encourage attitudes of responsibility and realistic decisionmaking in the learning process.

Smith, E. The effect of CAI on academic achievement, school daily attendance and school library usage at Margaret Murray Washington Career Center. *Dissertation Abstracts International,* 1980, *41* (6) 2431A.

> Describes an investigation of the relationship among CAI and school attendance, achievement, and library use. Data for 154 students suggest no significant correlation between reading achievement and CAI.

1981

Carver, R., and Hoffman, J. The effect of practice through repeated reading on gain in reading ability using a computer based instructional system. *Reading Research Quarterly,* 1981, *16* (3), 375-390.

> Tells how programed prose, a computer program for the PLATO IV terminal connected to ERL by phone line, generated Bormuth's passages for repeated reading and various cloze deletions. Students were tested on passages with a two choice maze activity for each deletion. Results were favorable for fluency, but not for other skills.

Griswold, P. An evaluation of Bloom's theory of school learning in a computer-assisted instruction curriculum. *Dissertation Abstracts International,* 1981, *43* (5), 1477A.

> Poses two questions: How well did intermediate students achieve in a CAI curriculum and was their achievement predictable using Bloom's theory of school learning? Achievement data indicated Blacks and Hispanics experienced greater reading achievement gains than Whites, while Blacks exhibited more positive attitudes than either Whites or Hispanics. Indicates cognitive entry behavior as a factor in predicting later performance. Statistical data are used to explain achievement variation.

Kelly, H. Simultaneous computer delivered audiovisual word cuing: Same vs. different target-related cues with two levels of cloze redundancy. *Dissertation Abstracts International,* 1981, *42* (4), 1448A.

> Consists of a technical report recommending visual cuing treatment for general practice in computer assisted instruction. In reading cloze tasks, data indicated the superiority of visual cuing to both audiovisual same word (AVS) and audiovisual different word (AVD) cues.

1982

Alessi, S., Siegel, M., Silver, D., and Barnes, H. Effectiveness of a computer-based reading comprehension program for adults. *Journal of Educational Technology Systems,* 1982, *11* (1), 43-57.

> Describes the PLATO Corrections Project, begun in 1975, which was designed to offer computer based instruction to adult correctional centers in

Illinois. Suggests that instructional formats in paraphrasing and finding information are effective, with evidence of retention over an extended period.

Ballas, M. Computer drill and practice make the grade. ETS *Developments*, 1982, *28* (1), 5-8.

> Describes a four year longitudinal study of students who received regular drill and practice instruction with materials prepared by the Educational Testing Service in one of four Computer Assisted Instruction (CAI) curricula: mathematics (grades 1-6); reading (grades 3-6); language arts (grades 3-6); and reading for comprehension (final year only). The focus was on how CAI drill and practice, which reinforced classroom work, helped the weaker students learn the basic skills.

Blohm, P. Computer-aided glossing and faciliated learning in prose recall. In J. Niles and L. Harris (Eds.), *New inquiries in reading research and instruction*. Thirty-First Yearbook of the National Reading Conference. Rochester, NY: National Reading Conference, 1982.

Easterling, B. The effects of computer assisted instruction as a supplement to classroom instruction in reading comprehension and arithmetic. *Dissertation Abstracts International*, 1982, *43* (7), 2231A.

> Concludes that supplementary computer assisted instruction, used twice weekly in 15 minute sessions for 16 weeks, does not significantly improve total reading and math comprehension of fifth graders as measured by the California Achievement Test.

Edyburn, D. *The effects of two levels of microcomputer graphics on reading comprehension*. 1982. (ED 218 593)

> Explains that computer graphics (TRS-80 color) "did not appear to increase the general reading comprehension of seventh graders on a programmed textual selection." Computer graphics did have a positive effect on attitude toward CAI. Reviews the literature on the relationship between comprehension and graphics.

Gadzella, B. Computer-assisted instruction in study skills. *Journal of Experimental Education*, 1982, *50* (2), 122-126.

Kester, D. *Is microcomputer assisted basic skills instruction good for black, disadvantaged community college students from Watts and similar communities?* 1982. (ED 219 111)

> Investigates the effectiveness of CAI at Los Angeles Southwest College. Technical data suggest that students who received computer based supplementary basic skills instruction experienced significant gains in reading. Urges further research to determine CAI's effectiveness with particular student populations.

Mayles, L., and Newell, J. Microcomputers in postsecondary curriculum. *Academic Therapy*, 1982, *18* (2), 149-155.

> Describes the implementation of a computer assisted basic skills program at Cabrillo College, California. Includes a number of resources that might assist others in such a process.

Merritt, R. Achievement with and without computer-assisted instruction in the middle school. *Dissertation Abstracts International*, 1982, *44* (1), 34A.

> Describes a study designed to compare the differences in students receiving traditional instruction and computer assisted instruction. Variables surveyed

include achievement, anxiety, self-concept, attitude toward teacher, and attitude toward school. Data indicated significant reading and mathematics achievement gains by the experimental groups, although only one of the four computer assisted groups gained significantly in the other variables.

Portland Public Schools. *Evaluation report on three new instruction programs: Help one student to succeed, prescription learning, and computer assisted instruction.* 1982. (ED 234 088)

> Evaluates three instructional programs used by Portland Public Schools in 1981-1982 with Chapter I populations: HOSTS (Help One Student to Succeed), a person to person structured tutorial program; Prescription Learning, a multimedia management program using computer instruction; and CAI, targeting reading and mathematics. Provides detailed results profiling each program.

Weaver, P. *Perceptual units training for improving analysis skills.* 1982. (ED 219 739)

> Describes a computer based training program designed to instruct students in the detection of a target multiletter unit as it appears in a series of stimulus words. Notes performance gains in this task and transfer to other tasks related to word recognition.

1983

Bright, G. Explaining the efficiency of computer assisted instruction. *AEDS Journal,* 1983, *16* (3), 144-152.

> Discusses the CAI phenomenon—CAI versus control group research will result in findings that indicate slight achievement gains for the CAI group over control counterparts. Points to research evidence for the phenomenon's existence. Also explains the implications of the phenomenon for CAI development.

Frederiksen, J. *A componential approach to training reading skills.* 1983. (ED 229 727)

> Describes three computer systems that target key processing components involving word analysis and contextual understanding. Significant improvement was noted in the target skills, with evidence of transfer to related reading processes.

Frederickson, J., Weaver, P., Warren, B., Gillotte, H., Rosebery, A., Freeman, B., and Goodman, L. *A componential approach to training reading skills.* Report No. 5295. Cambridge, MA: Bolt, Beranek and Newman, 1983.

> Tells how three computer games were used in this study for the training of component reading skills—Speed Game, Racer Game, and Ski Jump Game.

Goddard, C. *Computer-based learning and postsecondary education: Some experimental projects and a learning model.* 1983. (ED 248 841)

> Looks at some PLATO and TICCIT education projects.

Hunter, S. *The impact of the microcomputer labs, 1983 January to June.* 1983. (ED 248 875)

> Discusses two computer labs, one in a high school and the other in an elementary school.

Kearsley, G., Hunter, B., and Seidel, R. Two decades of computer based instruction projects: What have we learned? *T.H.E. Journal,* 1983, *10* (4), 90-96. Part two.

Describes the effectiveness of CBI on cognitive and affective student outcomes.

Lundgren, C. An experimental study of the effects of two methods of teaching English grammar on achievement and attitudes. *Dissertation Abstracts International,* 1983, *44* (6), 1672A.

Compares effectiveness of programed text instruction and CAI in English grammar skills and attitudes toward subject matter. Results indicate programed instruction was more effective than CAI in grammar skills achievement, while no significant difference in attitudes was apparent between the two groups.

Marsh, M. Computer assisted instruction in reading. *Journal of Reading,* 1983, *26* (8), 697-701.

Summarizes a few of the more salient research efforts on CAI in reading and suggests that a knowledge of the history of CAI research can help teachers avoid many of today's CAI problems. Cites several examples of earlier CAI research.

Newman, J. A comparison of traditional, classroom, computer and programed instruction. *Dissertation Abstracts International,* 1983, *44* (4), 976A.

Describes a study of 55 eleventh grade students that suggests traditional, programed, and computer assisted instruction are effective ways to teach usage of reference materials in high school. Also indicates that programed instruction produces more homogeneous performance results than the other methods used.

Noda, P. Exploratory study of the impact of computer assisted instruction on the English language reading achievement of LEP Arabic and Chaldean middle school students. *Dissertation Abstracts International,* 1983, *44* (12), 3590A.

Tells how 101 LEP Iraqi-Chaldean middle school pupils participated in this exploratory study designed to measure the effectiveness of computer assisted language instruction. Significant gains in English language reading achievement were made by students receiving computer assisted and individualized instruction, when compared to pupils receiving traditional group instruction.

Ortmann, L. The effectiveness of supplementary computer-assisted instruction in reading at the 4-6 grade level. *Dissertation Abstracts International,* 1983, *45* (1), 140A.

Analyzes pre and posttest reading scores of 340 Chapter 1 pupils to determine the effectiveness of supplementary computer assisted instruction. Suggests this instructional mode may contribute to increased reading achievement for some students. In addition, research revealed ethnicity and sex are not reliable predictors of achievement in reading.

Pitts, M. *Monitoring: Longitudinal unobtrusive measurement with computers.* 1983. (ED 233 309)

Describes a project designed to measure the effectiveness of computer based comprehension strategies for passages with "embedded comprehension obstacles." Posttest results revealed no significant difference in scores of control and experimental groups, although those receiving CAI tended to use a wider variety of comprehension strategies.

Poplin, R., and Vinsonhaler, J. *Computer-based simulated cases as a tool for teaching reading diagnosis.* 1983. (ED 233 303)

Porinchak, P. Computer-assisted instruction in secondary school reading: Interaction of cognitive and affective factors. *Dissertation Abstracts International,* 1983, *45* (2), 478A.

> Reports findings of study to determine the impact of CAI on students' reading achievement and attitudes toward reading; students' preferred mode of instruction; and responsiveness of CAI to students' intelligence levels. Based on research data, CAI and traditional methods seem equally effective with average students while below average students might benefit more from CAI.

Pulver, C. The effects of small group and computer assisted inference training programs on fifth-grade students' comprehension of implicit causal relationships. *Dissertation Abstracts International,* 1983, *44* (12), 3640A.

> Suggests that both small group and computer assisted instruction aid fifth grade students in comprehension of implicitly stated causal relationships.

Stevens, R. Strategies for identifying the main idea of expository passges: An experimental study. *Dissertation Abstracts International,* 1983, *45* (1), 75A.

> Researches effectiveness of CAI in identification of the main idea of expository passages. Explains interventions used with remedial reading students including strategy training and classification skills. Technical data recommend these techniques as being both effective and useful in reading instruction.

Taylor, V. Achievement effects on vocabulary, comprehension and total reading of college students enrolled in a developmental reading program using the drill and practice mode of computer assisted instruction. *Dissertation Abstracts International,* 1983, *44* (8), 2347-2348A.

> Assess the effectiveness of traditional instruction and CAI in a developmental reading class for entry level college students. Control groups received traditional instruction only while experimental groups received a combination of computer assisted instruction and traditional instruction. Nelson-Denny Reading Test scores indicated that CAI groups rated higher in comprehension and total reading than did control students. In contrast, control students rated higher in vocabulary scores.

Turner, G. A comparison of computer assisted instruction and a programed instructional booklet in teaching preselected phonics skills to preservice teachers. *Dissertation Abstracts International,* 1983, *33* (8), 4077A.

> Concludes that both computer assisted instruction and programed instruction are effective techniques for improving phonics achievement of preservice teachers. Teacher attitudes associated with phonics instruction were more positively affected by CAI.

Wilkinson, A. Learning to read in real time. In A. Wilkinson (Ed.), *Classroom computers and cognitive science.* New York: Academic Press, 1983.

> Reviews a computer program entitled READINTIME, looking at three criteria: technological novelty, psychological design, and pedagogical importance. Discusses types of activities in READINTIME—individual word games and various text reading formats.

1984

Abram, S. The effect of computer assisted instruction on first grade phonics and mathematics achievement computation. *Dissertation Abstracts International,* 1984, *45* (4), 1032A.

Summarizes study of 103 first grade students who received traditional as well as computer assisted reading instruction. Pretests and posttests in word analysis revealed no significant differences in achievement between the CAI and the control group.

Ashmore, T. *Evaluating CAI material for the microcomputer.* 1984. (ED 252 180)

Bass, G., and Perkins, H. Teaching critical thinking skills with CAI. *Electronic Learning*, 1984, *4* (2), 32, 34, 96.

Explains that seventh graders received a special critical thinking curriculum made up of the following software: Rocky's Boots, Inference and Prediction (teaching logical reasoning), Analogies, Word Analogies (teaching verbal analogies), Snooper Troops, Critical Reading (teaching inductive/deductive reasoning), and Problem Solving Strategies (teaching problem analysis). The curriculum appears to have had a positive impact on the development of critical thinking skills.

Bradley, V. Reading comprehension instruction in microcomputer reading programs. *Dissertation Abstracts International*, 1984, *44* (10), 3023A.

Reviews 38 reading comprehension lessons from Basic Learning Systems Tutorcourses, the Control Data Basic Reading Series, the Random House Tutorial Comprehension Series, and the Scott, Foresman Reading Skills Courseware Series, revealing that the Random House and BLS programs had the most comprehension instruction, while the Scott, Foresman program had the least. Surface features, including documentation and instructional design, were present in the four programs, with Scott, Foresman having significantly more features than the other three programs.

Bryg, V. The effect of computer-assisted instruction upon reading achievement with selected fourth-grade children. *Dissertation Abstracts International*, 1984, *45* (9), 2817A.

Compares the reading achievement levels of 132 fourth grade students who received either traditional or computer assisted reading instruction for a fifteen week period. Indicates significant gains made by the experimental group. Recommends matching appropriate software to reading curriculum objectives.

Burnett, J., and Miller, L. Computer-assisted learning and reading: Developing the product or fostering the process? *Computer Education*, 1984, *8*, 145-150.

Cortez, M., and Hotard, S. *Loss of achievement gains over summer vacation.* 1984. (ED 251 495)

Focuses on summer vacation regression. May and September math and reading achievement scores for Chapter 1 remedial students receiving CAI indicated a half year regression in mathematics skills but observed no significant skill loss in reading. Suggests that reading comprehension techniques have more carryover compared to computational skills used in mathematics.

Cuppett, T. An analysis of community college reading programs since the passage of CLAST legislation in Florida. *Dissertation Abstracts International*, 1984, *45* (9), 2819A.

Examines the effects of the state mandated College Level Academic Skills Test on community college reading programs in Florida. Recommends a variety of strategies for increasing student reading achievement levels, including heightened use of computer assisted instruction.

Enochs, J. *The relationship of learning style, reading vocabulary, reading comprehension, and aptitude for learning to achievement in the self-paced and computer-assisted instructional modes of the Yeoman "A" School at the Naval Technical Training Center, Meridian, Mississippi.* 1984. (ED 250 550)

Indicates the need for correlating instructional patterns with student learning styles and aptitudes. Technical data showed those students who learned best through CAI were concerned with abstractions rather than concreteness and were more oriented to objects or things, with less orientation to people.

Ewing, R. Computer-assisted Chapter 1 instruction. *Dissertation Abstracts International,* 1984, *45* (7), 1934A.

Tells how 257 low achieving Chapter 1 sixth grade students received supplemental CAI in reading and language arts. An equal number of moderate and high achieving students received similar instruction without CAI. Results indicate gains for the CAI group as compared to the predicted gains for the nonCAI group.

Fiedorowicz, C. Component reading skills training with different types of reading disabilities. *Dissertation Abstracts International,* 1984, *44* (9), 2921B.

Describes a study involving reading disabled students who received computer assisted training in their skill deficit. Emphasis on accuracy and speed in letter, syllable, and word recognition. Concludes CAI is effective in reading skill improvement and training can transfer to other achievement measures.

Glidden, W. *The Coast Guard's CAI approach to basic math and reading skills.* 1984. (ED 249 365)

Explains that with the philosophy that career opportunities could be provided for all recruits, the Coast Guard developed BEEP (Basic Educational Enrichment Program). Designed to provide remediation, this program uses PLATO's basic skills curriculum integrated with Navy developed conventional materials. Thus, far, BEEP graduates have demonstrated significant increases on the Armed Services Vocational Aptitude Battery (ASVAB) verbal and arithmetic sections.

Griwsold, P. Elementary students' attitudes during 2 years of computer-assisted instruction. *American Educational Research Journal,* 1984, *21* (4), 737-754.

Describes a program in which fourth and fifth graders completed the drill and practice curriculum of Computer Curriculum Corporation (CCC) covering reading and language arts—grades three to six. Among other things, the researchers investigated the effects of CAI on students' attitudes; many of the students were "disadvantaged." Selected results indicate that "two years participation in CAI by educationally disadvantaged students was associated with greater levels of attributing their success internally and viewing themselves as good readers who do well in school." Includes other results about CAI reading and CAI math results.

Harper, D. Using computer-assisted learning for teacher training in Malaysia. *Dissertation Abstracts International,* 1984, *45* (9), 2841A.

Focuses on the requisite conditions for successful computer use in Malaysia's teacher education program. English comprehension skills, mathematics skills, and spatial abilities are significant predictors of success for those who might use PILOT and LOGO languages.

Hoffman, J. Reading achievement and attitude toward reading of elementary students receiving supplementary computer assisted instruction compared with students receiving supplementary traditional instruction. *Dissertation Abstracts International*, 1984, *45* (7), 2050A.

> Provides conclusions based on pre and posttests: gender contributed to student attitude toward reading; CAI was more effective with males, while traditional supplementary vocabulary and comprehension instruction was more effective for females; both traditional and computer assisted instruction were effective in supplemental vocabulary and comprehension instruction; males receiving supplemental CAI in vocabulary and comprehension performed significantly better than males receiving supplemental traditional instruction; and females receiving supplemental traditional instruction achieved statistically significant gains.

Leton, D., and Pertz, D. The use of computer-automated reading in reading instruction. *Psychology in the Schools*, 1984, *21* (4), 512-515.

> Describes a program in which beginning level reading books were used to generate teacher produced, computer based reading programs. Twenty first and second grade compensatory education students received reading instruction via traditional or experimental format. Notes significant gains made by the second grade experimental group. Explores the school psychologist's role in assisting with CAI.

Levin, H. *Cost-effectiveness of four educational interventions.* 1984. (ED 246 533)

> Claims that of the four interventions presented, peer and adult tutoring is the most cost effective approach for improving mathematics and reading performances by elementary students. Least cost effective interventions include reducing class size and increasing the school day's length. Computer related costs place this instructional approach second to cross age tutoring in cost effectiveness.

Levin, H., Glass, G., and Meister, G. *Cost-effectiveness of four educational interventions.* Project Report No. 84-A11. Stanford, CA: Stanford University, School of Education, 1984.

> Explains that four methods of educational intervention were used to improve reading performance in the most cost effective manner: reducing class size, increasing length of the school day, computer assisted instruction, and peer and adult tutoring. Adult tutoring was the most effective means of improving reading performance, but also the most expensive. The least costly method was peer tutoring, followed by CAI.

Levy, C. A comparative study of the reading achievement of pupils exposed to computer-assisted reading instruction, prescriptive reading instruction, and traditional reading instruction. *Dissertation Abstracts International*, 1984, *44* (10), 2970A.

> Compares reading achievement of 300 randomly selected elementary students who received CAI, traditional reading instruction, and prescriptive reading instruction. Suggests traditional methods are more efficient in increasing total reading and vocabulary scores of fourth and fifth grade students, while traditional and computer assisted methods are more efficient for increasing reading comprehension scores. Includes technical data.

Martin, J. An eclectic approach to reading. *The School Administrator,* 1984, *41* (2), 18-19.

> Provides results of a study to determine the effectiveness of IBM's Writing to Read system. Data revealed strong positive reaction to the program by both teachers and parents, that kindergartners and first graders developed skill at independent sentence writing, and that kindergartners performed well on standardized reading tests.

Merrell, L. The effects of computer-assisted instruction on the cognitive ability gain of third, fourth, and fifth grade students. *Dissertation Abstracts International,* 1984, *45* (12), 3502A.

> Attempts to determine the impact of CAI on traditional reading and mathematics instruction. Students received either direct computer assisted reading and mathematics instruction, computer experience, or no computer instruction. While math posttest scores showed significant improvement for computer groups, data suggested the need for further research in determining the effectiveness of computer assisted reading instruction.

Merrill, P., and Salisbury, D. Research on drill and practice strategies. *Journal of Computer-Based Instruction,* 1984, *11* (1), 19-21.

> Describes effective drill and practice strategies with reference to reading skills instruction.

Moskowitz, C. Reading teachers' reactions to a field test of a computer assisted instruction reading program in a microcomputer laboratory setting in a middle school. *Dissertation Abstracts International,* 1984, *45* (10), 3118A.

> Uses interviews, questionnaires, and observations to determine teachers' perceptions of microcomputer assisted instruction in a developmental reading program. Reactions attest to the computer's versatility in instruction and management, as well as indicating a need for heightened awareness of teachers' new role as coinstructors with the computer.

Pressman, I., and Rosenbloom, B. CAI: Its cost and its role. *Journal of Educational Technology Systems,* 1984, *12* (3), 183-208.

> Provides a thorough treatment of system costs for CAI implementation. Concludes "CAI can be viewed more in terms of an investment yielding real returns."

Roth, S., and Beck, I. *Research and instructional issues related to the enhancement of children's decoding skills through a microcomputer program.* 1984. (ED 248 461)

> Examines the software program Construct a Word, which emphasizes decoding and word recognition skills. Discussion includes theory and research behind the program, instructional goals, program components, and field test results.

Sedlacek, C. A study comparing achievement and attitude differences in fifth-grade remedial reading students taught using computer-assisted instruction and conventional management programs. *Dissertation Abstracts International,* 1984, *45* (7), 1980A.

> Explains that three groups of fifth grade students received reading instruction using CAI or a traditional format for twelve weeks. All groups made significant increases in vocabulry, comprehension, and attitude. However, the increase did not result in significant differences between the groups.

Self, C., Self, M., and Rahaim, C. Computers in audio-tutorial biology. *The American Biology Teacher*, 1984, *46* (3), 168-172.

> Describes a computer based reading program for freshman biology students at Bunker Hill Community College in Massachusetts. Possible areas of weakness in the content area were revealed by a pretest. Remediation occurred via the computer. A posttest signaled mastery or the need for further study. Significant improvements in comprehension and understanding were noted in students receiving CAI.

Siegel, M., and Misselt, A. Adaptive feedback and review paradigm for computer-based drills. *Journal of Educational Psychology*, 1984, *76* (2), 310-317.

> Contains valuable information for anyone interested in designing good drill and practice software, including reading and language arts software.

Silfen, R., and Howes, A. A summer school reading program. *Computers, Reading and Language Arts*, 1984, *1* (4), 20-22.

> Tells how CAI in reading and language arts was used in a summer remedial program. Results were positive in both achievement and attitude.

Williams, G. The effectiveness of computer-assisted instruction and its relationship to selected learning style elements. *Dissertation Abstracts International*, 1984, *45* (7), 1986A.

> Reports results of a study involving 300 fourth graders demonstrating the effectiveness of CAI in math and suggesting the need for further research in determining the computer's role in reading instruction. Indicates CAI did not produce significant correlation between achievement and the elements of student selected learning style.

Zsiray, S. A comparison of three instructional approaches in teaching the use of the abridged Reader's Guide to Periodical Literature. *Journal of Educational Technology Systems*, 1984, *12* (3), 241-247.

> Tells how eighth grade students received instruction in library media skills via lecture, independent reading, or computer based courseware. Statistical analysis revealed CAI and lecture produced identical student reading achievement, surpassing those results gained through independent reading.

1985

Alfano, J. *Seventh grade vocabulary computer instruction versus classroom instruction*. Unpublished master's thesis, Kean College, 1985.

> Tells how low achieving seventh graders learned vocabulary words in computer versus direct instruction treatments. The computer group did not outperform the direct instruction group on vocabulary measures.

Copperman, K. An experimental study to compare the effectiveness of a regular classroom reading program with a computer-assisted instruction program in reading comprehension skills in grades two through four. *Dissertation Abstracts International*, 1985, *46* (5), 1234A.

> Finds no significant difference between student performance on reading measures in CAI reading instruction versus normal classroom reading instruction procedures.

Douglas, E., and Bryant, D. Implementing computer assisted instruction: The Garland way. *T.H.E. Journal*, 1985, *13* (2), 86-91.

> Explains that WICAT Systems hardware and software were selected for use in the Garland, Texas, Independent School District. WICAT uses a minicompu-

ter that drives 30 terminals. Discusses the first year the school district used the WICAT materials. In reading, elementary students used the computers twice a week for 20 minutes a day. After a year, ITBS reading scores increased 9 percent in grade three and 6 percent in grade five.

Gadzella, B.M. Study skills presented through computer-assisted instruction to high school students. *Texas Tech Journal of Education,* 1985, *12* (1), 47-50.

Describes how high school students in two studies used researcher developed materials to learn about study skills (CAI Study Skills Modules). The materials covered time management, memory improvement, note taking, textbook reading, examination taking, report writing, oral reporting, scholastic motivation, interpersonal relationships, and improvement of concentration. In the CAI portion of the study skills instruction, the computer presented the text. Both studies showed that researcher developed materials improved students' knowledge of study skills as presented in the modules.

Geller, D., and Shugoll, M. The impact of computer-assisted instruction on disadvantaged young adults in a non-traditional educational environment. *EADS Journal,* 1985, *19 (1), 49-65.*

Describes the Job Corps Comprehensive Computer Program. The program uses mostly PLATO software in reading and math remedial efforts with eighteen year olds reading at the sixth grade level. Initial results at one site indicate that the computer program enhanced achievement by as much as one reading grade level, as opposed to noncomputer remediation. Reviews previous CAI research with educationally/economically disadvantaged students.

Levy, M. An evaluation of computer assisted instruction upon the achievement of fifth grade students as measured by standardized tests. *Dissertation Abstracts International,* 1985, *46* (4), 860A.

Explains that CAI is an effective means of teaching reading to fifth graders. Students in the CAI groups spent more time on task than students in non-CAI groups.

Reed, S. Effect of computer graphics on improving estimates to algebra word problems. *Journal of Educational Psychology,* 1985, *77* (3), 285-298.

Computer based simulations were used to improve learning in algebra word problems involving average speed, volume, and mixture. The researcher found that the level of complexity of the simulation had an effect on learning. In particular, learning by coaching simulations were best, followed by learning by doing and learning by viewing. Includes other possible applications of simulations to text comprehension.

Reinking, D., and Schreiner, R. The effects of computer-mediated text on measures of reading comprehension and reading behavior. *Reading Research Quarterly,* 1985, *20* (5), 536-552.

Investigates the effects of computer mediated text on comprehension processes using expository text with fifth and sixth grade students. The computer based manipulation schemes involved reading text on-line and providing definitions of key words, simpler versions of a text, background information, and main ideas. Teachers supplied the definitions, main ideas, background information, and simpler version of the texts. The computer delivered the teachers' information to the students upon request. Authors found that "computer mediated text can influence reading comprehension. . . ."

Schloss, P., Schloss, C., and Cartwright, P. Questions and highlights in CAI modules. *The Computing Teacher,* 1985, *12* (6), 14-15.

>Describes three studies involving university students, finding that student performance is positively affected by questions and highlights in CAI modules; student mastery is heightened when questions address specific concepts; while questions seem more productive, highlighting is preferred over questioning and appears to produce higher motivation; and questions and highlighting are more effective when they occur on a separate screen from the information.

Sudia, D. *The computer's effect on the learning of new words.* Unpublished master's thesis, Kean College, 1985.

>Tells how first graders were taught sight words with and without a computer. The students who followed normal classroom procedures learned more words than the students using the computer.

Tennyson, R., Park, O., and Christensen, D. Adaptive control of learning time and content sequence in concept learning using computer-based instruction. *Journal of Educational Psychology,* 1985, *77* (4), 481-491.

>Tells how eleventh graders studied social science/psychology content through interrogative statements requiring answers. Learning time means "wait time," how long the student was permitted to wait before selecting an answer to a question or having an answer/example provided. Content sequence means whether review/reinforcement included interrogative statements previously identified correctly or incorrectly. Concludes that, for immediate or delayed recall, learning time and content sequence are important variables.

Watkins, M., and Abram, S. Reading CAI with first grade students. *The Computing Teacher,* 1985, *12* (7), 43-45.

>Describes how researchers used drill and practice phonics software (The Reading Machine) to determine if the instruction led to gains over noncomputer groups. First graders in the experimental group used the software 45 minutes a week along with the Addison-Wesley Basal Reading Program. Control groups followed the phonics instruction in the Basal. Results indicated a one-third standard deviation increase for the experimental group over the control group in phonics knowledge.

1986

Blanchard, J., Chang, F., Logan, J., and Smith, K. An investigation of computer-based mathemagenic activities. *Texas Tech Journal of Education,* 1986, *12* (3), 159-174.

>Describes three experiments designed to test the appropriateness of microcomputers as aids to learning and studying. Finds that computer based underlining activities and a computer generated lexicon made available during a test can help to curb the deterioration of information; that the subjects' performance (both immediate and delayed recall) was influenced positively by the extent to which the passage contained redundant information; and that although the subjects using computers clearly outperformed the noncomputer using group, the cloze procedure seemed to be less useful than the other study procedures in aiding college age subjects to recall expository factual prose.

Diem, R. Microcomputer technology in educational environments: Three case studies. *Journal of Educational Research,* 1986, *80* (2), 93-98.

Case studies of microcomputer applications in an elementary school bilingual classroom, secondary special education classroom, and adult literacy classroom. All classrooms used reading and language arts software for instruction and practice. A discussion of the findings focused on problems related to software, teachers, and students.

Icabone, D., and Hannaford, A. A comparison of two methods of teaching unknown reading words to fourth graders: Microcomputer and tutor. *Educational Technology,* 1986, *26* (2), 36-39.

Finds no difference in performance outcomes between using a tutor or a microcomputer equipped with a speech synthesizer to teach words.

Johnson, R., Johnson, D., and Stanne, M. Comparison of computer-assisted cooperative, competitive, and individualistic learning. *American Educational Research Journal,* 1986, *23* (3), 382-392.

Explains that computer assisted cooperative instruction (using a simulation entitled Geography Search) was superior, in quality and quantity of student performance, to computer assisted competitive and individual instruction.

Psychological and physiological research references

1970

Leton, D. *Computer program to convert word orthography to phoneme equivalents.* 1970. (ED 038 266)

Describes computer simulation of reading skill acquisition. The research aim was to convert orthography of English words to phoneme equivalents for computer programing. The conversion was done at the preprimer and primer levels of the Lippincott basal readers.

1972

Collins, A., and Quillian, M. Experiments on semantic memory and language comprehension. In L. Gregg (Ed.), *Cognition in learning and memory.* New York: John Wiley and Sons, 1972.

Describes a computer program that comprehends printed text by comparing it to a memory bank of stored factual semantic information.

1973

Reder, S. On-line monitoring of eye-position signals in contingent and noncontingent paradigms. *Behavioral Research Methods & Instrumentation,* 1973, *5* (2), 218-228.

Hawley, I., Stern, J., and Chen, S. Computer analysis of eye movements during reading. *Reading World,* 1974, *13,* 307-317.

Describes computer analysis of electrically recorded eye movements during reading.

Leton, D. Computer simulation of reading: A progress report. *Journal of Reading Behavior,* 1974, *6* (2), 131-141.

Describes SIMUREAD, a computer program designed to aid in reading research.

Pennock, C. Quick word lists for Canadian readers. *Alberta Journal of Educational Research,* 1974, *20,* 8-14.

Describes computer processed word lists that might be used to supplement or replace other word lists.

1975

Behavior Research Laboratory, Washington University, St. Louis. *Visual search activity: A tool for the evaluation and development of computer assisted reading instructional programs.* 1975. (ED 112 362)

Describes how eye movements of readers using the plasma panel of the PLATO terminal were analyzed by computer. Competent readers made fewer saccadic movements per line and had shorter fixation times. When reading for detail, competent readers changed only by increasing their fixation times. Less competent readers made more fixations when reading for detail.

Goltz, R. *Comparison of the eye movements of skilled and less skilled readers.* Unpublished doctoral dissertation, Washington University, 1975.

Claims that good readers made longer fixation pauses when reading to generalize than when reading for detail. Poor readers did not.

O'Regan, J. *Structural and contextual constraints on eye movements in reading.* Unpublished doctoral dissertation, University of Cambridge, 1975.

Tells how the author replaced letters in the visual periphery with *X*s and found that little information is gained from peripheral vision.

1976

Aaronson, D., and Scarborough, H. Performance theories for sentence coding: Some quantitative evidence. *Journal of Experimental Psychology: Human Perception and Performance,* 1976, *2,* 56-70.

Explains that computer recordings of word by word reading times showed prolonged pauses at phrase boundaries for subjects reading for delayed recall, but not for subjects reading for immediate recall.

Martin, J., and Meltzer, R. Visual rhythms: Report on a method for facilitating the teaching of reading. *Journal of Reading Behavior,* 1976, *8,* 153-160.

Reports on an experimental program that uses the video presentation of printed syllables simultaneously with an oral presentation of the syllables. Suggests applications.

McConkie, G., and Rayner, K. Asymmetry of the perceptual span in reading. *Bulletin of the Psychonomic Society,* 1976, *8* (5), 365-368.

Tells how, using computer controlled text displays, the authors found visual information to be derived from no more than four letter positions to the left of the fixation during reading by high school students. However, the students derived information from more than four letter positions to the right of the fixation.

1977

Rayner, K. Visual attention in reading: Eye movements reflect cognitive processes. *Memory and Cognition,* 1977, *5* (4), 443-448.

Finds that the fixations for main verbs are longer than for other words in the sentences.

Computer applications in reading

1978

Hansen, W., Doring, R., and Whitlock, L. Why an examination was slower on-line than on paper. *International Journal of Man-Machine Studies*, 1978, *10*, 507-519.

McConkie, G., Zola, D., Wolverton, G., and Burns, D. Eye movement contingent display control in studying reading. *Behavior Research Methods & Instrumentation*, 1978, *10* (2), 154-166.

Stern, J. Eye movements, reading and cognition. In J. Sanders, D. Fisher, and R. Monty (Eds.), *Eye movements and the higher psychological functions*. Hillsdale, NJ: Erlbaum, 1978.

Taylor, G., Klitze, D., and Massaro, D. A visual display system for reading and visual perception research. *Behavioral Research Methods & Instrumentation*, 1978, *10* (2), 148-153.

1979

DeJong, G. Prediction and substantiation: A new approach to natural language processing. *Cognitive Science*, 1979, *3*, 251-273.

Presents a computer program called FRUMP (Fast Reading Understanding and Memory Program) that mimics human skimming processes.

Mandel, T. Eye movement research on the propositional structure of short texts. *Behavior Research Methods & Instrumentation*, 1979, *11* (2), 180-187.

Rayner, K. Eye movements and cognitive psychology: On-line computer approaches to studying visual information processing. *Behavior Research Methods and Instrumentation*, 1979, *11* (2), 164-171.

Reynolds, R., Standiford, S., and Anderson, R. Distribution of reading time when questions are asked about a restricted category of text information. *Journal of Educational Psychology*, 1979, *71* (2), 183-190.

Russo, J. A software system for the collection of retrospective protocols prompted by eye fixations. *Behavior Research Methods & Instrumentation*, 1979, *11* (2), 177-179.

1980

Malone, T. *What makes things fun to learn? A study of intrinsically motivating computer games.* Cognitive and Instructional Sciences Series CIS-7. Palo Alto, CA: Xerox, Palo Alto Research Center, 1980.

Consists of an early and seminal work on what aspects of computer games are intrinsically motivating. Many parts of this report would be of interest to reading professionals.

1981

Den Buurman, R., Roersema, T., and Gerrissen, J. Eye movements and the perceptual span in reading. *Reading Research Quarterly*, 1981, *16* (2), 227-233.

Tells how computer controlled text displays helped identify the text area from which information is drawn during reading. The spans found consisted of twelve to fifteen letters to the right and left of the fixation center.

Epstein, K. The road to literacy: Teaching a sixteen year old to read. *Journal of Reading*, 1981, *24* (6), 497-502.

Describes a case study in which a clinician used Speak N Spell to teach remedial reading.

Kliegl, R. Automated and interactive analysis of eye fixation data in reading. *Behavior Research Methods & Instrumentation*, 1981, *13* (2), 115-120.

Rayner, K., Inhoff, A., Morrison, R., Slowiaczek, M., and Bertera, J. Masking of foveal and parafoveal vision during eye fixations in reading. *Journal of Experimental Psychology: Human Perceptions and Performance*, 1981, 7 (1), 167-179.

>Finds that most of the visual information required for reading is acquired during the first 50 milliseconds of a fixation.

1982

Blohm, P. *I use the computer to ADVANCE advances in comprehension-strategy research*. 1982. (ED 216 330)

Bruce, B. *HWIN: A computer model of language comprehension and production*. Technical Report No. 236. Urbana, IL: University of Illinois, Center for the Study of Reading, 1982.

>Discusses the role of plan recognition and generation in relation to artificial intelligence.

Johnson, G.W. Microcomputer-administered research: What it means for educational researchers. *Educational Researcher*, 1982, *11* (3), 12-16.

>Discusses the advantages of microcomputer-administered research.

McConkie, G. *Studying the reader's perceptual processes by computer*. Reading Education Report No. 34. Urbana, IL: University of Illinois, Center for the Study of Reading, 1982.

>Suggests that computer controlled text manipulation with simultaneous recording of eye movements may enable reading diagnosticians to determine whether specific reading skills are developing normally and, if not, what deviations may need remediation.

Muter, P., Latremouille, S., Treurniet, W., and Beam, P. Extended reading of continuous text on television screens. *Human Factors*, 1982, *24* (5), 501-508.

Reiser, R., and Gagne, R. Characteristics of media selection models. *Review of Educational Research*, 1982, *52* (4), 499-512.

>Discusses ten features of media selection models, including display formats, learner characteristics, settings, and task demands.

Weyer, S. The design of a dynamic book for information search. *International Journal of Man-Machine Studies*, 1982, 7 (1), 87-107.

>Focuses on research involving dynamic books. Dynamic books provide "electronic transformation of information that could potentially offer multiple paths through complex information and help us actively in searching." A prototype dynamic book was tested with students with favorable results.

1983

Gerrell, H., and Mason, G. Computer-chunked and traditional text. *Reading World*, 1983, *22* (3), 241-246.

>Investigates the impact of computer displayed text and traditional printed text on student performance. Examines the effects of chunking (breaking text into meaning units), which seems to contribute to improved reading rate and comprehension. Suggests the display device makes no difference in student performance.

Henney, M. The effect of all-capital versus regular mixed print, as presented on a computer screen, on reading rate and accuracy. *AEDS Journal*, 1983, *16* (4), 205-217.

Reports two studies, one with college students and the other with sixth graders, on the effect of all capital versus mixed capital print on reading rate and accuracy. Results indicated that college students read mixed print significantly faster, but all capitals more accurately. However, for sixth graders, the type of print did not affect rate or accuracy.

Sheingold, K., Kane, J., and Endreweit, M. Microcomputer use in schools: Developing a research agenda. *Harvard Educational Review*, 1983, *53* (4), 412-432.

Thomas, O. The alphabet and the computer: Artificial intelligence and syllable recognition. *Computers, Reading and Language Arts*, 1983, *1* (2), 23-26.

Describes project where essential word attack skills were identified through a computer program designed to recognize and tally English word syllables. Indicates the cruciality of word attack skill instruction for children.

Waern, Y., and Rollenhagen, C. Reading text from visual display units. *International Journal of Man-Machine Studies*, 1983, *18* (5), 441-465.

1984

Glock, M. *Understanding picture-text instruction.* 1984. (ED 241 911)

Explores how procedural information is perceived, understood, and acted upon. By combining a computer based delivery system with "hypertext" (user receives additional information with a touch of the screen), errors in processing were reduced dramatically.

Grabinger, R. CRT text design: Psychological attributes underlying the evaluation of models of CRT text displays. *Journal of Visual/Verbal Languaging*, 1984, *4* (1), 17-39.

Examines the impact of graphic design and layout on computer displayed text legibility.

Grabowski, B., and Aggen, W. Computers for interactive learning. *Instructional Innovator*, 1984, *29* (2), 27-30.

Discusses the computer's role in accessing sensory, short term, and long term memory. Includes distinct features and outcomes of computer based interactive video (CCBIV).

Hathaway, M. Variables of computer screen display and how they affect learning. *Educational Technology*, 1984, *24* (1), 7-11.

Considers the impact of computer displayed text on learners' attention, retention, and response accuracy. Viewer fatigue is noted after prolonged reading periods using the CRT. Additional studies investigate effects of text density, scrolling (movement of text across the screen), letter size, uppercase versus lowercase letters, and graphic displays.

Monk, A. Reading continuous text from a one-line visual display. *International Journal of Man-Machine Studies*, 1984, *21* (3), 269-277.

Investigates effects of LCD (line only text) versus CRT (multiple line text) formats. Reading was not a problem with either, but the author suggests that the reason for reading could influence performance with LCDs.

1985

Askwall, S. Computer supported reading versus reading text on paper: A comparison of two reading situations. *International Journal of Man-Machine Studies*, 1985, *22* (3), 425-439.

Compares reading on a CRT using a forty column display versus reading text on paper. Reading times were almost identical for CRT versus paper, and comprehension appeared unaffected.

Gould, J. *Reading is slower from* CRT *displays than from paper: Some experiments that fail to explain why.* Yorktown Heights, NY: IBM Research Center, 1985.

Suggests some reasons why CRT based reading is slower than non-CRT based reading.

McNinch, G., and Creamer, M. *Reading comprehension under three forms of display: Computer, film projection, and typed.* Paper presented at the annual conference of the College Reading Association, Pittsburgh, Pennsylvania, October 1985.

Finds that fifth graders did not have significant comprehension performance differences when reading "typed" text, "tachistoscopic" (with computer display) presented text, or "film" presented text.

Thompson, M. Beyond the computer: Reading as a process of intellectual development. *Computers, Reading and Language Arts,* 1985, *2* (2), 13-15, 43.

Speculates on the consequences and contributions of computers in the study of the reading process.

Wollen, K., Cone, R., Margres, M., and Wollen, B. Computer programs to facilitate detailed analysis of how people study text passages. *Behavior Research Methods, Instruments, & Computers,* 1985, *17* (3), 371-378.

Describes a program that permits investigators (using an IBM PC with light pen and real time clock) to analyze many features of how people study text passages.

Reviews of reading research references

1980

Thompson, B. Computers in reading: A review of applications and implications. *Educational Technology,* 1980, *20* (8), 38-41.

Reviews computers for reading instruction and modes of CAI: drill and practice, tutorial, problem solving, games, and simulations. Describes several CAI systems and reviews CAI effectiveness research.

1982

Bracey, G.W. Computers in education: What the research shows. *Electronic Learning,* 1982, *2* (3), 51-54.

Addresses several questions about computer assisted instruction in classroom settings: achievement outcomes, affective/motivational outcomes, social outcomes, what the research can't say, and what the research should say.

1983

Bell, T. My computer, my teacher. *Personal Computing,* June 1983, 118-127.

Reviews recent studies on how computers can help students learn.

Clark, R. Reconsidering research on learning from media. *Review of Educational Research,* 1983, *53* (4), 445-459.

Argues that reviews of research (including computer applications) indicate that various forms of media do not influence learning under any conditions. Should interest reading educators concerned with the variables surrounding uses of computers in education.

Fisher, G. Where CAI is effective: A summary of the research. *Electronic Learning,* 1983, *3* (3), 82, 84.

Says that CAI appears to have the most chance of being effective in reading and language arts when it is used with specific types of students, is fully integrated into the classroom curriculum, and is used in a proper setting with appropriate scheduling.

Kearsley, G., Hunter, B., and Seidel, R. Two decades of computer based instruction projects: What have we learned? *T.H.E. Journal*, 1983, *10* (3), 90-94.
Reviews over fifty major CBI projects in education.

Kearsley, G., Hunter, B., and Seidel, R. *Two decades of CBI research.* HumRRO-PP-3-83. Alexandria, VA: Human Resources Research Organization, 1983.
Summarizes major CBI research projects (1959-1982), including several reading research projects.

Orlansky, J. Effectiveness of CAI: A different finding. *Electronic Learning,* 1983, *3* (1), 58, 60.
Explains that, in military training, including reading to understand technical content, computer assisted drill and practice instruction has been unable to demonstrate superior gains in achievement over noncomputer groups. However, CAI appears to have been a cheaper way to provide drill and practice activities.

Zuberman, L. *The foundation and development of computer assisted instruction in the field of reading from its inception to the present.* 1983. (ED 252 183)
Reviews seventeen research studies and four surveys in seeking answers to common computer based reading questions.

1984

Tanner, D. Horses, carts, and computers in reading: A review of research. *Computers, Reading and Language Arts,* 1984, *2* (1), 35-38.
Reviews seven reading and research journals for a fourteen year period, then notes major computer related issues, including motivation, CMI, student performance, and individualized instruction. Suggests a "dearth of empirical information" concerning the degree to which computers can significantly affect the instructional delivery system.

Thompson, R. *Computer assisted reading instruction research.* 1984. (ED 243 091)
Offers five implications of CAI for teaching: computers can be useful in computer assisted reading instruction; CAI will not replace the teacher, but will assist in performing teacher instructional tasks; CAI can affect reading achievement as much as teacher directed instruction; poorly designed CAI can have the same negative effects as lacklustre teacher prepared lessons; and with widespread computer use in education, computers are no longer just for experts—classroom teachers must be involved.

Tolman, M., and Allred, R. *The computer and education. What research says to the teacher.* 1984. (ED 252 173)
Focuses on the computer's impact in education and the opportunities offered by its use. Explores classroom applications (CAI, CMI, testing/recordkeeping, instructional games) and curricular applications (social studies, language arts, mathematics, science). Includes the computer as a motivational tool and shows positive effects of CAI with exceptional students.

Zuberman, L. On reading and CAI: A review. 1984. (ED 252 183)

1985

Roblyer, M. *Measuring the impact of computers in instruction: A non-technical review of research for educators.* Washington, DC: Association for Educational Data Systems, 1985.

> Provides a two part text on research in computer based education. The first part reviews premetaanalysis and metaanalysis of research studies. Recommendations for future research are included. The second part of the text includes the reference lists for each of the studies reviewed and the references used by the author in text comments.

1986

Salomon, G., and Gardner, H. *Educational Researcher,* 1986, *15* (1), 13-19.

> Reviews the research on the problems that plagued TV based learning studies and discusses how to avoid similar problems with computer based learning studies.

Reading assessment references

1967

Williams, G. Use of the computer for testing and programing in adult reading. In G. Schick and H. Merrill (Eds.), *Junior college and adult reading.* Sixteenth Yearbook of the National Reading Conference. Rochester, NY: National Reading Conference, 1967.

1969

Evan, W., and Miller, J. Differential effects on response bias of computers versus conventional administration of a social science questionnaire: an exploratory methodological experiment. *Behavioral Sciences,* 1969, *14,* 216-227.

Gedye, J., and Miller, E. The automation of psychological assessment. *International Journal of Man-Machine Studies,* 1969, *1,* 237-262.

1972

Dunn, T., Lushene, R., and O'Neil, H. Complete automation of the MMPI and a study of its response in latencies. *Journal of Consulting and Clinical Psychology,* 1972, *39,* 381-387.

1974

Lushene, R., O'Neil, H., and Dunn, T. Equivalent validity of a completely computerized MMPI. *Journal of Personality Assessment,* 1974, *38,* 353-361.

1977

Angle, H., Hay, W., Hay, L., and Ellinwood, E. Computer-aided interviewing in comprehensive behavioral assessment. *Behavior Therapy,* 1977, *8,* 747-754.

Klingler, D., Miller, D., Johnson, J., and Williams, T. Process evaluation of an online computer-assisted unit for intake assessment of mental health patients. *Behavior Research Methods & Instrumentation,* 1977, *9,* 110-116.

Lucas, R., Mullin, P., Luna, C., and McInroy, D. Psychiatrists and a computer as interrogators of patients with alcohol related illnesses: A comparison. *British Journal of Psychiatry,* 1977, *131,* 160-167.

Slack, W., and Slack, C. Talking to a computer about emotional problems: A comparative study. *Psychotherapy: Theory, Research and Practice,* 1977, *14,* 156-164.

1978

Butcher, J. MMPI computer scoring and interpreting services. In O. Buros (Ed.), *The eighth mental measurements yearbook.* Highland Park, NJ: Gryphon Press, 1978.

Hansen, W., Doring, R., and Whitlock, L. Why an examination was slower on-line than on paper. *International Journal of Man-Machine Studies,* 1978, *10,* 507-519.

Howze, G. An interactive software system for computer assisted testing. *AEDS Journal,* 1978, *11* (2), 31-37.

Millman, J., and Outlaw, W. Testing by computer. *AEDS Journal,* 1978, *11* (3), 57-72.

Describes a minicomputer program that creates tests.

Schmidt, F., Urry, V., and Gugel, J. Computer assisted tailored testing: Examinee reactions and evaluations. *Educational and Psychological Measurement,* 1978, *38,* 265-273.

1979

Henney, M., and Boysen, V. Effect of computer simulation training on ability to administer an informal reading inventory. *Journal of Educational Research,* 1979, *72,* 265-270.

Nicastro, A. Exam time: Reading and comprehension tests for language arts. *Creative Computing,* 1979, *5* (5), 62.

Describes a minicomputer program that helps teachers create reading tests.

1980

Griest, J., and Klein, M. Computer programs for patients, clinicians, and researchers in psychiatry. In J. Sidowski, J. Johnson, and T. Williams (Eds.), *Technology in mental health care delivery systems.* Norword, NJ: Ablex, 1980.

Rumelhart, D., and Norman, D. *Analogical processes in learning.* Center for Human Information Processing Report No. 97. San Diego, CA: University of California, 1980.

1981

Angle, H. The interviewing computer: A technology for gathering comprehensive treatment information. *Behavior Research Methods & Instrumentation,* 1981, *13,* 607-612.

Byers, A. Psychological evaluation by means of an on-line computer. *Behavior Research Methods & Instrumentation,* 1981, *13,* 585-587.

Byrnes, E., and Johnson, J. Change technology and the implementation of automation in mental health care settings. *Behavior Research Methods & Instrumentation,* 1981, *13,* 573-580.

Hirsch, R. Procedures of the Human Factors Center at San Jose. *IBM Systems Journal,* 1981, *29,* 123-171.

Katz, L., and Dolby, J. Computer and manual administration of the Eyesenck Personality Inventory. *Journal of Clinical Psychology,* 1981, *37,* 586-588.

Kelley, R., and Tuggle, F. In the blink of an electronic eye: A prospectus. *Behavior Research Methods & Instrumentation,* 1981, *13,* 434-435.

Space, L. The computer as psychometrician. *Behavior Research Methods & Instrumentation,* 1981, *13,* 595-606.

Stout, R. New approaches to the design of computerized interviewing and testing systems. *Behavior Research Methods & Instrumentation,* 1981, *13,* 436-442.

1982

Andolina, M. Reading tests: Traditional versus computerized. *Classroom Computer News*, 1982, *2* (5), 39-40.

Finds favorable test results between paper and pencil versus computer delivery.

Beaumont, J. System requirements for interactive testing. *International Journal of Man-Machine Studies*, 1982, *17*, 311-320.

Brown, B. Automated tests and quiz production. *Classroom Computer News*, 1982, *2* (4), 33-35.

Cicciarella, C. Test writer. *Classroom Computer News*, 1982, *2* (4), 36-37.

Elithorn, A., Mornington, S., and Stavrou, A. Automated psychological testing: Some principles and practice. *International Journal of Man-Machine Studies*, 1982, *17*, 247-263.

Jelden, D. Computer generated testing. *AEDS Monitor*, 1982, *20*, 32-35.

Muter, P., Latremouille, S., Treurniet, W., and Beam, P. Extended reading of continuous text on televisions. *Human Factors*, 1982, *24*, 501-508.

Odor, P. Microcomputers and disabled people. *International Journal of Man-Machine Studies*, 1982, *17*, 51-58.

1983

Lesse, S. A cybernated health-science diagnostic system: An urgent imperative. *American Journal of Psychotherapy*, 1983, *37*, 451-455.

Matarazzo, J. Computerized psychological testing. *Science*, 1983, *221*, 323.

Sampson, J., and Pyle, K. Ethical issues involved with the use of computer administered counseling, testing and guidance systems. *Personnel and Guidance Journal*, 1983, *61*, 283-287.

1984

Bevan, N. Is there an optimum speed for presenting text on a VDT? *International Journal of Man-Machine Studies*, 1984, *14*, 59-76.

Duthie, B. A critical examination of computer-administered psychological tests. In M. Schwartz (Ed.), *Using computers in clinical practice: psychotherapy and mental health applications*. New York: Haworth Press, 1984.

Harrell, T., and Lombardo, T. Validation of an automated 16 PF administration procedure. *Journal of Personality Assessment*, 1984, *48*, 638-542.

Herr, E., and Best, P. Computer technology and counseling: The role of the profession. *Journal of Counseling and Development*, 1984, *63*, 192-195.

Moore, N., Summer, K., and Bloor, R. Do patients like psychometric testing by computer? *Journal of Clinical Psychology*, 1984, *40*, 875-877.

Schloss, P., Schloss, C., and Cartwright, G. Location of questions and highlights in the same page or a following page as a variable in computer assisted instruction. *AEDS Journal*, 1984, *11*, 113-122.

1985

Askwall, S. Computer supported reading versus reading text on paper: A comparison of two reading situations. *International Journal of Man-Machine Studies*, 1985, *22*, 425-439.

Cliffe, M. Microcomputer implementation of an idiographic psychological instrument. *International Journal of Man-Machine Studies*, 1985, *23*, 89-96.

Heppner, F., Anderson, J., Farstrup, A., and Weiderman, N. Reading performance on a standardized test is better from print than from computer display. *Journal of Reading*, 1985, *28*, 321-325.

Sanders, R. Computer-administered individual psychological testing: A feasibility study. *International Journal of Man-Machine Studies*, 1985, *23*, 197-213.

1986

Blank, D., Murphy, P., and Schneiderman, B. A comparison of children's reading comprehension and reading rates at three text presentation speeds on a CRT. *Journal of Computer-Based Instruction*, 1986, *13*, 84-87.

Burke, M., and Normand, J. *Examinee attitudes toward computer-administered psychological testing: A path analytic approach.* Paper presented at the annual meeting of the American Educational Research Association, San Francisco, California, April 1986.

Loesch, L. Computer assisted assessment: A reaction to Meier and Geiger. *Measurement and Evaluation in Counseling and Development*, 1986, *19*, 35-37.

Madsen, D. Computer applications for test administration and scoring. *Measurement and Evaluation in Counseling and Development*, 1986, *19*, 6-17.

McKenna, M. CARA: New tool for reading assessment. *The Computing Teacher*, 1986, *13* (5), 16-19.

> Describes the CARA diagnostic program, which asks questions about variables related to reading performance (e.g., language background, attendance) of a student. The program presents conclusions based on the information gathered through the diagnostic questions.

Meier, S., and Geiger, S. Implications of computer-assisted testing and assessment for professional practice and training. *Measurement and Evaluation in Counseling and Development*, 1986, *19*, 29-34.

Olsen, J., Maynes, D., Slawson, D., and Ho, K. *Comparison and equating of paper-administered, computer-administered and computerized adaptive tests of achievement.* Paper presented at the annual meeting of the American Educational Research Association, San Francisco, California, April 1986.

5

Word processing, writing, and reading

B oth reading and writing involve the manipulation of text, and both involve the sharing of meaning. Any analysis of the processes responsible for reading and writing reveal some interplay between the two language activities, despite the fact that reading is considered a receptive activity and writing a productive activity. One cannot write without reading what is written. Clearly, attitudes and achievements in writing are shaped by reading, and reading attitudes and achievements are shaped by writing. As James Squire so aptly pointed out in the Ginn Occasional Papers #1 (Ginn, P.O. Box 2649, Columbus, Ohio 43216) "How can a seventh grader be expected to write a research report if he has never read one? Can a fifth grade child write an interview, a business letter, or a diary if he is not sufficiently familiar with the particular genre to understand the particular ways in which it requires language to be used?"

The interaction of reading and writing explains why reading teachers of the eighties are devoting more of their time to teaching writing. Such instruction offers the promise of increased comprehension ability through increased attention to wording and the structure of compositions.

The role of word processing programs

Using the word processor for reading and writing instruction can result in fresh insights for both students and teachers, and fresh insights seem necessary. The American National Assessment of Educational Progress (*The Writing Report Card*) reported that students in the United States are not mastering the writing skills necessary for describing, reporting, interpreting, or analyzing facts and events. Some might even say that the writing skills of students in most countries of the world are in danger of extinction or, perhaps more optimistically, that today's students are taking advantage of more nonwriting opportunities to communicate.

It is possible that technology, in the form of telephone and television, is to blame for much of the decline in our children's writing and reading skills. Stephen J. Gould commented (*New York Review of Books,* February 27, 1986) that the telephone is the greatest single enemy of scholarship; for what our intellectual forebears used to inscribe in ink now goes once over a wire into permanent oblivion. On the other hand, it is possible that technology, in the form of word processing, videotext, and teletext communication, will also encourage and improve the reading and writing of our students.

A caveat does seem warranted. Technology alone will not improve our situation. Improved communication skills, whether in reading or writing, still require teachers with good communication skills and motivated students. Access to a word processor does not necessarily produce a good writer or reader. Educators concerned with computer applications in reading should learn how to use word processors in teaching writing and reading.

The research articles, the testimonials, the treatises, and the editorial comments listed or annotated in this chapter support the following advantages and disadvantages for the use of word processing in reading, writing, and language arts instruction.

Advantages

1. Students can quickly write their ideas on paper.
2. Students can easily edit their written ideas, moving and saving bits of information.
3. Students can see how a text would look as a finished product and easily change formats.
4. Students can increase collaborative writing efforts.
5. Students can increase their tolerance (physically and psychologically) for errors and writing problems.
6. Students can be encouraged and motivated to write more.
7. Students can keep copies of their writing activities on disk. In addition, teachers and schools can keep a permanent record on disk of a student's writing progress through the grades.
8. Students with penmanship problems can be encouraged to write, and their writing can be read by others.
9. Students can be encouraged to expand their computer literacy beyond word processing.
10. Students can be encouraged to do writing beyond what is assigned in school.
11. Publishers are putting more instructon in programs through on screen help, such as spelling checkers and outliners.

Disadvantages

1. Students must have access to many computers or many opportunities to use a few computers. Unfortunately, computers, word processing software, and printers cost more than pencils and paper.
2. Students must learn how to type using a computer keyboard (although, to some, keyboarding is relatively insignificant in terms of the overall writing process).
3. Students must learn how to use a word processor, which may be a difficult and time consuming task for some. Unfortunately, students who learn one word processor often prefer to use that one despite attempts at change.
4. Students will need to learn how to use a printer.
5. Students will probably need to learn special word processing programs that can provide help during prewriting, writing, and rewriting activities (i.e., on-line dictionaries, outline processors).
6. Students must learn that word processing programs cannot meet all their writing needs.

Teachers working with word processors and reading may find three recent journals of interest: *Research in Word Processing Newsletter* (South Dakota School of Mines and Technology, Rapid City, South Dakota 57701; *ACE Newsletter* (Jack Jobst, Humanities Department, Michigan Technological University, Houghton, Michigan 49931); and *Journal of Technical Writing and Communication* (Baywood Publishing, 120 Marine Street, Farmington, New York 11735).

Chapter five contains word processing references as well as references related to interactive fiction and literature, computer assisted composition, and the word processing-reading connection.

References

1975
Ahl, D. Computers in language arts. In O. Lecarme and R. Lewis (Eds.), *Computers in education*. Amsterdam: North-Holland Publishing, 1975.

1980
Burns, H. *A writer's tool: Computing as a mode of invention*. 1980. (ED 193 693)
Roberts, R. A computerized identikit for alien beings. *Creative Computing*, 1980, *8*, 88-89.
>   Describes and lists a program to generate descriptions of aliens—sort of a story starter for young science fiction writers.

1981
Guthrie, J. One computer literacy skill. *Journal of Reading*, 1981, *24* (5), 458-460.
>   Cites Xerox Research Center research on the use of word processors.

Liddil, B. Interactive fiction: Six micro stories. *Byte,* 1981, *6* (9), 436.

> Reviews and criticizes interactive fiction because of limited vocabulary and small choice of outcomes.

Lyons, T. Computer-assisted instruction in English composition. *Pipeline,* 1981, *6* (2), 13-14.

> Describes the College Expository Writing Program that is providing remedial basic skill instruction at the University of Colorado, Boulder.

Nelson, T. Interactive literature. *Creative Computing,* 1981, *1* (3), 42.

> Discusses interactive fiction and calls it "dialogue adventure."

1982

Ahl, D. Computer poetry: Not so new. *Creative Computing,* 1982, *8* (7), 172.

> Lists and gives sample runs of two poetry programs, POET and BARD, which date back to the 1960s and 1970s.

Alexander, J., and Swartz, F. *The dynamics of computer-assisted writing sample measurements at Ferris State College.* 1982. (ED 233 344)

Arms, V. *The computer kids and composition.* 1982. (ED 217 489)

> Describes a program of computer based technical writing instruction at Drexel University. Engineering students use the word processor for weekly assignments, research projects, proposals, and final reports. Positive attitudes toward writing, via the word processor, have been noted among students.

Bork, A. Computers and learning: Right justification and word processing. *Educational Technology,* 1982, *22* (8), 24-25.

Bradley, V. Improving students' writing with microcomputers. *Language Arts,* 1982, *59* (7), 732-743.

> Features discussions on how computers can improve students' writing through the generation of ideas, electronic mail, text analysis, and word processing. In addition, describes two exploratory studies that investigated LEAs with first graders and sentence combining with sixth graders. Concludes with a list of nine desirable features of word processors for improving writing skills.

Cronnell, B. *Computer-based practice in editing.* 1982. (ED 220 869)

> Describes procedures for CAI in text editing. After students review rules of capitalization, spelling, usage, and punctuation, they receive practice in choice (correct rule application); correction (sample sentences depict rule being studied); and dictation (oral presentation of sentence, with student entering the sentence on the computer). With feedback on each section, students can progress at their own pace or receive individual help.

Daiute, C. Word processing: Can it make even good writers better? *Electronic Learning,* 1982, *1* (4), 29-31.

> Reports on the state of word processing for classroom use in 1982 and provides historical perspective on the subject of early word processing in schools. Discussions range from issues surrounding computers and writing to the drawbacks of word processing.

De Bonis, D.M., Joseph, D., and Prezioso, J. Education's new alphabet: Alphanumeric, byte, chip. *Academic Therapy,* 1982, *18* (2), 133-140.

> Describes a computer assisted writing component for middle school students. Enumerates activities (programing, word processing, text editing) used to "stimulate vigorously the systematic language and attitudinal growth of children."

Dembart, L. Computers as writers—some bad reviews. *Los Angeles Times,* January 1, 1982, 1.

Holder, W. Software tools for writers. *Byte,* 1982, 138-163.

Humes, A. *Computer instruction on sentence combining.* 1982. (ED 239 580)

Kelly, T., and Anandam, K. *Teaching writing with the computer as helper.* 1982. (ED 214 583)

Lawler, J. *Computers in composition instruction.* 1982. (ED 226 709)
> Discusses the state of the art in CAI, CAI in prewriting activities, the composing process and CAI, and selection of courseware. Includes summaries of courseware demonstrations.

Levin, J. Microcomputers as interactive communicative media: An interactive interpreter. *The Quarterly Newsletter of the Laboratory of Comparative Human Cognition,* 1982, *4,* 34-36.

Martin, M., and Trombino, J. What a word web we can weave, when we practice..."Spider"—an idea spinning program. *Classroom Computer News,* 1982, *2* (5), 45-47.
> Describes and lists a program for simulating and then editing and printing creative writing.

McKean, K. Computers, fiction, and poetry. *Byte,* 1982, *7* (7), 50-53.
> Explores the history and current developments in computer assisted literature and provides computer generated poetry and narrative prose.

McWilliams, P. *The word processing book.* Los Angeles, CA: Prelude Press, 1982.

Nancarrow, P. *Integrating word processors into a freshman composition curriculum.* Unpublished manuscript, University of Minnesota, 1982.

Oates, W. *An evaluation of computer-assisted instruction for English grammar review.* 1982. (ED 218 930)

Schwartz, M. Computers and the teaching of writing. *Educational Technology,* 1982, *22* (11), 27-29.

Selter, C. *Wordsworth II: New wave CAI for college composition teachers.* 1982. (ED 225 151)

Shostak, R. Computer-assisted instruction: The state of the art. In J. Lawlor (Ed.), *Computers in composition instruction.* Los Alamitos, CA: SWRL Educational Research & Development, 1982.

Woodruff, E. Computers and the composing process: An examination of computer-writer interaction. In J. Lawlor (Ed.), *Computers in composition instruction.* Los Alamitos, CA: SWRL Educational Research and Development, 1982.

Wresch, W. *Prewriting, writing, and editing by computer.* 1982. (ED 213 045)
> Describes four recently developed computer programs to assist students in the writing process. The prewriting phase uses a series of questions intended to help the student think in depth about the subject. In the writing phase, CAI demonstrates how preliminary information can be structured into a composition. Text editing is facilitated by a program that searches out key facts and courseware that evaluates sentence length, word choice, and grammatical structure.

1983

Anandam, K. Computer-based feedback on writing. *Computers, Reading and Language Arts,* 1983, *1* (2), 30-34.

Arms, V. The computer and the process of composition. *Pipeline,* 1983, *8,* 16-18.

Bridwell, L., Nancarrow, P., and Ross, D. The writing process and the writing machine: Current research on word processors relevant to the teaching of composition. In R. Beach and L. Bridwell (Eds.), *New directions in composition research*. New York: Guilford Press, 1983, 381-398.

Bruce, B., and Rubin, A. What are we learning with QUILL? In M. Kamil and R. Leslie (Eds.), *Perspectives on computers and instruction for reading and writing*. Rochester, NY: National Reading Conference, 1983.

Collier, R. The word processor and revision strategies. *College Composition and Communication*, 1983, *34* (2), 149-155.

> Suggests the word processor did not significantly affect the final outcome of revision. However, the correction process seemed quicker and more comprehensive.

Collins, A. *Learning to read and write with personal computers,* Reading Education Report No. 42. Urbana, IL: University of Illinois, Center for the Study of Reading, 1983.

> Claims microcomputers and their accompanying programs can help young students learn to read and write and can improve the reading and writing skills of older students. Points out that computers can function as an information retrieval system, interactive text, automated dictionary, writing coach, text editor, editorial assistant, message system, and publication system.

Daiute, C. The computer as stylus and audience. *College Composition and Communication*, 1983, 134-145.

> Explores how computers can produce greater flexibility in the composing process by freeing writers from fundamental tasks such as information storage and retrieval, spelling corrections, recopying, and text editing.

Doyle, C. Writing and reading instruction using the microcomputer. *T.H.E. Journal*, 1983, *11* (1), 144-146.

Engberg, R. Word processors in the English classroom. *Computers, Reading and Language Arts*, 1983, *1* (1), 17-19.

> Describes how one teacher used a word processor in a junior high school English classroom.

Esbensen, B., and Esbensen, T. Word weaving: Computer-assisted creative writing. *Educational Computer Magazine*, 1983, *3* (5), 36-39.

Fluegelman, A., and Hewes, J. *Writing for the computer age.* New York: Doubleday, 1983.

Geoffrion, L. The feasibility of word processing for students with writing handicaps. *Journal of Educational Technology Systems*, 1983, *11* (3), 239-250.

> Discusses the word processor's effectiveness in assisting students with limited writing skills. In a writing project with ten hearing impaired teenagers, it was found that students were quick to learn word processing skills and were positive about the learning experience. Offers suggestions for implementation of computer assisted remedial instruction in writing.

Hennings, D. Words processed here—write with your computer. *Phi Delta Kappan*, 1983, *65* (2), 122-124.

Hertz, R. Problems of computer-assisted instruction in composition. *The Computing Teacher*, 1983, *11* (2), 62-64.

> A thoughtful critique of computer based composition instruction that maintains software that criticizes and corrects student writing (e.g., EPISTLE, Writer's Workbench) leaves much to be desired for classroom applications.

Hocking, J. *The impact of microcomputers on composition students.* 1983. (ED 229 791)

Kaake, D. Teaching elementary children touch typing as an aid to language arts instruction. *The Reading Teacher,* 1983, *36* (7), 640-644.

Kane, J. *Computers for composing.* 1983. (ED 230 978)

Kuechle, N. Reading, writing and programming. *Computers, Reading and Language Arts,* 1983, *1* (2), 7-10.

> Describes a project using BASIC, in which gifted fifth grade students composed original stories to share with classmates. Both student programers and those reading the finished products were enthusiastic about the project. Also notes improved writing skills and the stories' high interest levels.

Levin, J., and Boruta, M. Writing with computers in classrooms: You get exactly the right amount of space. *Theory into Practice,* 1983, *22,* 291-295.

Levin, J., Boruta, M., and Vasconcellos, M. Microcomputer-based environments for writing: A writer's assistant. In A. Wilkinson (Ed.), *Classroom computers and cognitive science.* New York: Academic Press, 1983.

> Discusses Writer's Assistant, a program for enhancing students' writing skills.

Levin, R., and Doyle, C. The microcomputer in the writing/reading/study lab. *T.H.E. Journal,* 1983, *10* (4), 77-79, 100.

Littlefield, P. Word processors in the classroom—two views. *Computers, Reading Language Arts,* 1983, *1* (1), 38-39.

Marcus, S., and Blau, S. Not seeing is relieving: Invisible writing with computers. *Educational Technology,* 1983, *23* (4), 12-15.

> Discusses an experiment using word processors with the text invisible as the writer composes. Results were favorable.

Piper, K. The electronic writing machine: Using word processors with students. *The Computing Teacher,* 1983-1984, *11* (5), 82-83.

> Focuses on the word processor's benefits in facilitating the mechanical process of writing. Offers suggestions for implementing CAI in the writing classroom.

Piper, K. Separating wheat from chaff: Evaluating word processing programs for language arts instruction. *Computers, Reading and Language Arts,* 1983, *1* (3), 9-14.

> Evaluation criteria for word processing programs should address compatibility with existing hardware and students' needs; ease of use, with clear easy to understand directions and documentation; quality of visual display, noting line length, spacing, letter size; and opportunity for preview by both teacher and student. Provides a three page evaluation form.

Purvis, D., Schwartz, M., and Vowell, F. *Computers, word processing, and the teaching of writing.* Cassette Recording No. 71036-012. Urbana, IL: National Council of Teachers of English, 1983.

Riel, M. Education and ecstasy: Computer chronicles of students writing together. *The Quarterly Newsletter of Laboratory of Comparative Human Cognition,* 1983, *5,* 59-67.

Schantz, L. The computer as tutor, tool, and tutee in composition. *The Computing Teacher,* 1983, *11* (3), 60-63.

> Explains that word processing for composition instruction should work in most classrooms, discusses why, and offers several references to support the optimism.

Schwartz, H. Teaching organization with word processing. *Computers, Reading and Language Arts,* 1983, *1* (3), 34-35.

> Claims that three methods of organization may help students tighten their writing via the word processor. Discusses computer capabilities of outlining, prompting (checking for coherence), and abstracting (highlighting topic or thesis sentences).

Schwartz, L. Teaching writing in the age of the word processor and personal computers. *Educational Technology,* 1983, *23* (6), 33-35.

Sharples, M. The use of computers to aid the teaching of creative writing. *AEDS Journal,* 1983, *16* (2), 79-91.

Shostak, R., and Golub, L. Problems of computer-assisted instruction in composition. *The Computing Teacher,* 1983, 62-64.

Strickland, J. *The computer as a tool for the invention stage of writing.* 1983. (ED 236 693)

Stromberg, L., and Kurth, R. *Using word processing to teach revision in written composition.* 1983. (ED 241 953)

Suttles, A. Computers and writing: Contemporary research and innovative programs. *Computers, Reading and Language Arts,* 1983, *1* (1), 33-37.

> Reviews research on computers and writing and suggests what computerized writing instruction should include: a component to ease the mechanics of revision, a means of more quickly recording thought flow, a memory to hold the writing, a mechanism for sharing writing, a means to reduce writing apprehension, an editing ability, a prewriting program to stimulate thought, and on-line aids during writing and revision.

Withley, M. The computer and writing. *English Journal,* 1983, *72* (7), 24-31.

Wresch, W. Computer essay generation. *The Computing Teacher,* 1983, (6), 63-65.

Wresch, W. Computers and composition instruction: An update. *College English,* 1983, *45,* 794-799.

1984

Borgh, K. *The effects of computer-generated spoken feedback on young children's writing with a word processor.* Unpublished doctoral dissertation, University of Wisconsin, Madison, 1984.

Boudrot, T. Word processing primer. *Teaching and Computers,* 1984, *1* (7), 31-38.

Branan, K. Moving the writing process along. *Learning,* 1984, *13* (3), 22, 24, 26.

> Points out the word processor's effectiveness in student writing assignments. Ease in making corrections plus displayed and printed text are noted as instructional features.

Bridwell, L., Nancarrow, P., and Ross, D. The writing process and the writing machine: Current research on word processors relevant to teaching composition. In R. Beach and L. Bridwell (Eds.), *New directions in composition research.* New York: Guilford Press, 1984.

Bruce, B., Michaels, S., and Watson-Gegeo, K. *Reviewing the black history show: How computers can change the writing process.* Technical Report No. 320. Urbana, IL: University of Illinois, Center for the Study of Reading, 1984.

> Discusses the effects of using a word processing program (QUILL) on classroom social organization as well as individual development of literacy skills.

Collins, A. Teaching reading and writing with personal computers. In J. Orsinau (Ed.), *A decade of reading research: Implications for practice.* Hillsdale, NJ: Erlbaum, 1984.

Daiute, C., and Kruidenier, J. *Strategies for reading one's own writing.* Unpublished manuscript, Harvard Graduate School of Education, Cambridge, 1984.

Elias, R. *Will computers liberate the comp drudge?* 1984. (ED 241 954)

Halpern, J., and Liggett, S. *Computers and composing: How the new technologies are changing writing.* Carbondale, IL: Southern Illinois University Press, 1984.

Hewes, J. The write stuff. *PC World,* January 1984, 168-172.
> Provides suggestions for using word processors, including writing, editing, formatting, and filing tips.

Hively, W. Word processing: Expressive, persuasive. *Electronic Education,* 1984, *3* (8), 34-35.
> Provides a short review of Story Tree, Story Maker, and Compupoem, programs that help students develop expressive, expository, and persuasive writing techniques.

Jarchow, E. Computers and composing: The pros and cons. *Electronic Education,* 1984, *3* (8), 38.
> Compares ten positive conclusions to ten negative conclusions for supporting the use of word processors in the classroom.

Kassnoff, D. EDITOR system: A computerized alternative to the red pen. *Electronic Education,* 1984, *4* (3), 42, 52.
> Discusses an integrated writing, grammar, and spelling program that helps students become better writers. The EDITOR program operates as a writing tutor focusing on the details of writing (phrasing, grammar, punctuation). Provides a description of EDITOR and how it operates.

Knapp, L. Word processors. *Electronic Learning,* 1984, *3* (6), 54-65.
> Provides a compendium of what to look for in a word processor for classroom use. Also includes a comparative listing of the features of thirty-five word processors.

Larsen, R. The impact of computers on composition: A polemic. *Educational Technology,* 1984, *24* (12), 22-26.

Leggett, S. "They laughed when I sat down at the piano..." or learning to write made easier by using the word processor. In S. Leggett (Ed.), *Microcomputers go to school.* Chicago: Teach'em, Inc., 1984.

Levin, J., Riel, M., Boruta, M., and Rowe, R. Muktuk meets Jaccuzi. In S. Freedman (Ed.), *The acquisition of written language.* New York: Ablex, 1984.

Madigan, C. The tools that shape vs. composing by hand vs. composing by machine. *English Education,* 1984, *16* (3), 143-150.

Mason, G. The word processor and teaching reading. *The Reading Teacher,* 1984, *37* (6), 552-553.
> Explains that word processing can help reading instruction by promoting writing and hence creative writing as well as editing. Provides brief discussions on ways the computer can help editing and creative writing as well as writing in other areas.

Mehan, H., Miller-Souviney, B., and Riel, M. Research currents: Knowledge of text editing and control of literacy skills. *Language Arts,* 1984, *61* (5), 510-515.
> Reports on using the computer to help children take control of their own literacy training through writing. Discusses fifteen references that could help teachers who want to integrate computers into their classrooms and schools for literacy training through writing.

Newman, J. Reading, writing, and computers. *Language Arts,* 1984, *61* (7), 758-763.

Reviews an innovative language arts program entitled The Puzzler. Discusses the advantages of the program, which includes as a goal the emphasis of meaning rather than decoding. According to its developers, The Puzzler is designed to support comprehension instruction on predicting, confirming, and integrating. Also discusses some of the benefits of word processing and mentions a brainstorming program called The Write Idea.

Newman, J. Some reflections on learning and computers. *Language Arts,* 1984, *61* (4), 414-417.

Claims that a great deal can be learned from watching young children's and adults' first attempts at using a word processor. Recounts experiences with both groups.

O'Brien, P. Using microcomputers in the writing class. *The Computing Teacher,* 1984, *11* (9), 20-21.

Tells how word processing can help liven up classroom writing assignments.

Oliver, L. Pitfalls in electronic writing land. *English Education,* 1984, *16* (2), 94-100.

Describes pitfalls to the use of computer assisted composition in teaching or enhancing writing skills. Discusses a few drawbacks of a computer assisted composition program called Text Analysis.

Palmer, A., Dowd, T., and James, K. Changing teacher and student attitudes through word processing. *The Computing Teacher,* 1984, *11* (9), 45-47.

Explains that student reactions to word processing are important elements in its classroom success and discusses how some sixth graders reacted to word processing.

Phenix, J., and Hannan, E. Word processing in the grade one classroom. *Language Arts,* 1984, *61* (8), 804-812.

Describes one month in a first grade classroom using Story Writer, a word processor under development for use with first graders. Includes examples of student writing.

Piazza, C., and Dawson, J. Choosing a word processor for writing instruction. *Computers, Reading and Language Arts,* 1984, *2* (1), 10-12.

Compiles ten attributes to be considered when selecting a word processor for children. Suggests strategies for introducing the word processor into the curriculum.

Piper, K. Word processing as a tool for structured writing instruction with elementary students. *AEDS Monitor,* 1984, *23,* 22-24.

Describes research in which above average and below average students were combined in pairs for word processing activities involving Apple Writer. Students participated in sentence combining lessons and exercises for 45 minutes, twice weekly for eight weeks. The research reports no gains on posttests but does suggest that word processing can be used successfully to teach sentence combining in upper elementary grades.

Pollitt, A. Warming to the wonders of the word processors: An English teacher's introduction to the computer. *The Computing Teacher,* 1984, *11* (9), 48-49.

Explains how an eighth grade language arts class produced a newspaper using a word processor.

Pufahl, J. Response to Richard M. Collier, "The word processor and revision strategies." *College Composition and Communication,* 1984, *35* (1), 91-93.

Radencich, M., and Schumm, J. To byte or not to byte. *Media & Methods,* 1984, *21* (1), 9-12.

> Provides strategies for researching and writing a term paper. Compares using the word processor and the typewriter.

Rodriques, R., and Rodriques, D. Computer-based invention: Its place and potential. *College Composition and Communication,* 1984, *35* (1), 78-87.

> Discusses the problems and potentials of computer based writing programs.

Rubin, A., and Bruce, B. *QUILL: Reading and writing with a microcomputer.* Reading Education Report No. 48. Urbana, IL: University of Illinois, Center for the Study of Reading, 1984.

> Discusses QUILL, a microcomputer word processing program designed to teach writing.

Schwartz, H. Teaching writing with computer aids. *College English,* 1984, *46* (2), 239-247.

Starshine, D., and Fortson, L. First graders use the computer: Great word processing. *The Reading Teacher,* 1984, *38* (2), 241-242.

> Describes the experiences of six and seven year olds using Bank Street Writer.

Vacc, N. Computers in adult education. *Lifelong Learning,* 1984, *7* (6), 26-28, 31.

> Describes word processing's potential for assisting individual writing skills. Discusses instructional reading activities (cloze procedures, readability evaluation, speech synthesizers, touch sensitive screens) and their effectiveness with the adult disabled reader.

Willer, A. Creative writing with computers: What do elementary students have to say? *Computers, Reading and Language Arts,* 1984, *2* (1), 39-42.

> Summarizes eight sixth grade students' opinions of word processors after a ten day period of use. Group consensus was overwhelmingly positive for computer assisted writing.

Wolff, F. Word processing is a tool for comprehension. *The Reading Teacher,* 1984, *37* (8), 799.

> Word processing can be used with upper elementary students for sharing and revising written work as well as clarifying and defending what was written.

Wresch, W. (Ed.). *The computer in composition instruction.* Urbana, IL: National Council of Teachers of English, 1984.

> Contains thirteen chapters related to computer based composition programs.

Wresch, W. Integrated computer systems to aid all stages of the writing process. *The Computing Teacher,* 1984, *12* (1), 50-51.

> Describes Writer's Helper, a word processing program to enhance the prewriting, writing, and editing process.

1985

Bruce, B., Michaels, S., and Watson-Gegeo, K. *Language Arts,* 1985, *62* (2), 143-149.

> Describes QUILL, a commercial program that serves as an information storage and retrieval system, an electronic mailbag, and a writing planner. Relates the experiences of students in Hartford using QUILL during Black History Week.

Cohen, S. Why computers in remedial language arts? *The Computing Teacher,* 1985, *12* (8), 46-47.

> Tells how word processing with remedial language arts high school students led to improved quality and quantity of written work as well as better group participation in writing assignments.

Collins, J., and Sommers, E. (Eds.). *Writing On-Line: Using Computers in the Teaching of Writing.* Upper Montclair, NJ: Boynton/Cook, 1985.

> Features sections on how and where computers fit in a writing program; how to begin using word processors; and using word processors in prewriting, writing, and editing.

Costanzo, W. Interactive text editors: A new generation of teaching tools. *Educational Technology,* 1985, *25* (12), 7-14.

> Discusses Story Tree and Adventure writer.

Daiute, C. Issues in using computers to socialize the writing process. *Educational Communication and Technology Journal,* 1985, *33,* 41-50.

Daiute, C. Writing and computers. Reading, MA: Addison-Wesley, 1985.

Degnan, S., and Hummel, J. Word processing for special education students: Worth the effort. *T.H.E. Journal,* 1985, *12* (6), 80-82.

Duin, A. Computer literacy: The impact of the information age on education. *Forum in Reading and Language Education,* 1985, *1* (2), 1-25.

> Comments on computer literacy and its impact on society and education. Discusses computers, composition instruction, and research that appears to be one of the first comprehensive reviews of both the positive and negative aspects of using word processing to teach writing.

Eiser, L. Can kids outgrow word processing programs? *Classroom Computer Learning,* 1985, *5* (6), 52-55.

> Advises that simplistic word processing programs may lack features that students use as they acquire more sophisticated skills. Evaluates Bank Street Writer, Cut and Paste, Homeword, Apple Works, Apple IIe, and Screen Writer.

Frase, L., Kiefer, K., Smith, C., and Fox, M. Theory and practice in computer aided composition. In S.W. Freedman (Ed.), *The acquisition of written language: Revision and response.* Norwood, NJ: Ablex, 1985.

Hutson, B., and Thompson, D. Moving language around on the word processor: Cognitive operations upon language. *Quarterly Newsletter of the Laboratory of Comparative Human Cognition,* 1985, *2* (7), 57-64.

> Describes a project involving groups of college students learning to write with word processors using WordStar, Grammatik, and Spellguard.

Mason, G. Why not make your own? *The Reading Teacher,* 1985, *38* (6), 598-602.

> Presents a few simple BASIC programs needed for students to write sentences without using a word processor. Includes a Texas Instruments Extended BASIC program on verbal analogies.

McNinch, G., and Hall, G. The word processor in the reading learning center. *Computers, Reading and Language Arts,* 1985, *2* (2), 32-33, 29.

> Presents two elementary level, computer based word processing activities. The first involves recognition and reorganization of sequence through time order. The second features manipulation of character traits through vocabulary.

Michaels, S. Classroom processes and the learning of text editing commands. *The Quarterly Newsletter of the Laboratory of Comparative Human Cognition,* 1985, *7* (3), 70-79.

Discusses how to use the text editor in QUILL as well as experiences using the text editor with students and teachers.

Newman, J. Cribsheets and adventure games. *Language Arts,* 1985, *62* (7), 796-802.

Discusses adventure games (i.e., interactive fiction). Provides some interesting advantages and disadvantages of using adventure games like Zork, In Search of the Most Amazing Thing, Sherwood Forest, Rendezvous with Rama, Amazon, and Fahrenheit 451.

Olds, H. A new generation of word processors. *Classroom Computer Learning,* 1985, *5* (4) 27-31.

Reports on the latest crop of word processors. Evaluates enhanced word processors, including Magic Slate, Milliken Word Processor, QUILL, and Writing Wizard; word processors with graphic capabilities, including Bank Street Storybook, Kidwriter, and Storymaker; and the idea processor, represented by ThinkTank.

Richards, M. Word processors...the new centerpiece of language arts. *Instructor and Teacher,* 1985, *2* (6), 82-86.

Recommends the word processor as a high tech tool for improving the language arts curriculum. Provides five minilessons to assist students in basic writing and editing operations: inserting or erasing words and characters; moving the cursor; moving or rearranging text; and performing the search/replace operation.

Schoenmaker, S. Language arts on the computer. *The Reading Teacher,* 1985, *38* (8), 821-822.

Describes how a microcomputer, Bank Street Writer, and a printer can help remedial readers expand their vocabulary, comprehension, and story sense skills.

Schwartz, H. *Interactive writing.* New York: Holt, Rinehart and Winston, 1985.

Solomon, G. The reading-writing connection: Four word processing activities. *Electronic Learning,* 1985, *5* (1), 46-47.

Presents four types of word processing activities: cloze, rearranging sentences, finding character attributes, and writing sequels. Also includes four teacher recommended programs: Missing Links, Plato's Cave, Story Tree, and Microzine.

Solomon, G. Writing with computers. *Electronic Learning,* 1985, *5* (3), 39-43.

Discusses use of word processors as aids for prewriting, writing, and postwriting activities. Also includes five activities that can be used with word processors to teach and enhance writing instruction.

Wagner, W., O'Toole, W., and Kazelskis, R. Learning word processing skills with limited instruction: An exploratory study with college students. *Educational Technology,* 1985, *25* (2), 26-28.

Finds that students learn word processing best from demonstrations and hands on experiences.

1986

Anderson-Inman, Lynne. The reading-writing connection: Classroom applications for the computer. *Computing Teacher,* 1986, *14* (3), 23-26.

    Explores the relationship between reading and writing with specific reference to word processing. Includes discussions on using the language experience approach as well as text and graphics with word processing.

Balajthy, E., McKeveny, R., and Lacitignola, L. Microcomputers and the improvement of revision skills. *Computing Teacher,* 1986, *14* (4), 28-31.

    Suggests some important instructional techniques (i.e., modeling and monitoring) for teaching revision skills.

Costanzo, W. Reading interactive fiction: Implications of a new literary genre. *Educational Technology,* 1986, *26* (6), 31-35.

    Describes many of the best interactive fiction and literature programs available as of June 1986. Also discusses the difference between interactive fiction (e.g., *Where in the World Is Carmen San Diego?*) and interactive literature (e.g., *Treasure Island*).

Daiute, C. Physical and cognitive factors in revising: Insights from studies with computers. *Research in the Teaching of English,* 1986, *20,* 141-159.

Haas, C., and Hayes, J. What did I just say? Reading problems with the machine. *Research in the Teaching of English,* 1986, *20,* 22-37.

Heffron, K. Literacy with the computer. *The Reading Teacher,* 1986, *40* (2), 152-155.

    Suggests that word processing can be integrated into all subject areas and tells how one school did it.

McCloskey, M. Word processors find homes in both classroom and office. *T.H.E. Journal,* 1986, *14* (4), 12-14.

    Describes word processing applications in the classroom and home.

Newman, J. Online: Electronic mail and newspapers. *Language Arts,* 1986, *63* (7), 736-741.

    Discusses electronic mail using QUILL and classroom newspapers using *The Newsroom* and *Newspaper Maker.*

Opack, M., and Perushek, B. Effective instruction in word processing: Maximizing minimal competence. *Educational Technology,* 1986, *26* (12), 33-36.

    Describes a college level class in word processing.

Pearson, H., and Wilkinson, A. The use of the word processor in assisting children's writing development. *Educational Review,* 1986, *38,* 169-187.

Rodrigues, D., and Rodriques, R. *Teaching writing with a word processor, grades 7-13.* Urbana, IL: National Council of Teachers of English, 1986.

    Contains a theory and research section; however, most of the content is devoted to computer writing suggestions.

Selter, C. *Computer-assisted instruction in composition.* Urbana, IL: National Council Teachers of English, 1986.

    Discusses how individuals can create their own computer assisted instruction programs for composition.

1987

Barker, T. Studies in word processing and writing. *Computers in the Schools,* 1987, *4* (1), 78-87.

> Reviews research on word processing and writing. Section titles are Surveys of Research on Word Processing and Writing, Studies of Attitudes toward Word Processing, Studies of Composing Behavior, Studies of Collaboration, Studies of Revising, Studies of Reading and Writing, and Implications for Instruction.

Newman, J. Improving with a word processor. *Language Arts,* 1987, *64* (1), 110-115.

> Presents three uses of word processors with reading and writing activities: One activity involves inserting "forgery text" in a passage and inviting students to detect the forgery, a second involves students entering comments while they study a text or poem (through the insertion of text in a file containing the text or poem), and the third involves synonym substitution.

Newman, J. Learning about language. *Language Arts,* 1987, *64* (3), 319-326.

> Highlights the texts *Teaching Humanties in the Microelectronic Age* and *Language in Use.* Discusses Fr Ed Writer, a public domain word processor for the Apple Computer.

O'Donnell, H. Computerized spelling checkers and text editors: Their potential in the classroom. *Journal of Reading,* 1987, *30* (4), 362-365.

> Reviews research studies on spelling checkers and text editors available from ERIC / RCS.

6
Readability

R eadability formulas have been used in reading instruction and research for many decades. They are designed to help teachers, writers, and publishers evaluate reading materials to meet the instructional needs of students. Many of the commonly used readability formulas have been computerized. To use a computer version of a readability formula, the teacher must type in a passage. The computer program then counts any number of reading variables, including letters, words, lines, sentences, and punctuation marks, before computing the estimates of readability.

For example, the Fry readability formula calls for counting words and estimating syllables. The Raygor formula calls for counting words with more than five letters. The Dale-Chall and Spache formulas require counting letters, checking against a word list in memory, and computer addition of a mathematical constant. Virtually any readability formula or graph can be computerized, but there are some problems.

First, computerized versions of readability formulas are no better than their noncomputerized versions. A readability formula, whether computerized or not, is still unable to quantify the special, interactive relationships between reader and text. Readability formulas do not measure the content of text as much as the text itself, counting only surface features and ignoring other variables.

Second, while computerized versions of readability formulas can give rapid estimates, teachers cannot easily enter text for analysis. Each readability program has specific text entry directions. These change from program to program and are associated with the features (good and bad) of the word processor on which the readability formula is being run. The text entry directions must deal with such features of written text as hyphenating, apposition, ellipses, dashes, ending sentences, underlining, capitalizing, and signalling proper nouns—features of the written language that are not quantified in readability formulas but that do affect comprehensibility.

Unfortunately, many computer based readability formulas do not provide adequate directions, and users are left to solve text entry problems on their own. Therefore, word processors are often inadequate for dealing with many features of written text.

Third, the more complex the readability formula, the less accurate the results. For example, anyone using computer based versions of the Dale-Chall or Spache formulas must necessarily make visual checks to determine if roots of some words are on the appropriate word list. This is not easy. The user must understand special rules for determining whether a word can be considered to be included on a particular word list. Furthermore, some situations cannot be predicted until a user analyzes a text. No computer based formulas are broad enough to yield results exactly the same as those derived by a reading specialist. At present, manual procedures are more accurate than computerized versions of readability formulas.

Chapter six reviews the available research on computer based readability and text analysis. The following references present both the advantages and the disadvantages of using computers in readability assessment.

References

1963

Danielson, W., and Bryan, S. Computer automation of two readability formulas. *Journalism Quarterly,* 1963, *40,* 201-206.

1968

Fang, I. By computer Flesch's Reading Ease Score and a syllable counter. *Behavioral Science,* 1968, *13,* 249-251.

1969

Carroll, M., and Roeloffs, R. Computer selection of key words using word frequency analysis. *American Documentation,* 1969, *20* (3), 227-233.

Gillman, D., and Moreau, N. Effects of reducing verbal content in CAI. *AV Communication Review,* 1969, *17,* 291-298.

Klare, G., Rowe, P., St. John, M., and Stolurow, L. Automation of the Flesch Reading Ease Readability Formula with various options. *Reading Research Quarterly,* 1969, *4* (4), 550-559.

1970

Coke, E., and Rothkopf, E. Note on a simple algorithm for a computer produced reading ease score. *Journal of Applied Psychology,* 1970, *54,* 209-210.

> Compares Flesch Reading Ease scores based on syllable counts by humans with computerized scores based on vowels per word, consonants per word, and letters per word (in place of syllables). A correlation of .92 was found between scores based on syllable counts and scores based on vowels per word.

Jacobson, M., and MacDougall, M. Computer management of information and structure in computer supported instructional materials. *Educational Technol-*

ogy, 1970, *10,* 39-42.

Uses readability measures to evaluate texts and make changes in text content.

1973

Kinkaid, J. *Use of the automated readability index for evaluating peer-prepared materials for use in adult reading education.* 1973. (ED 068 814)

Tells how the automated readability index (ARI) was used to create three versions of a story at different reading levels. The ARI appears to have resulted in story versions appropriate for the intended audiences.

1974

Strong, S. An algorithm for generating structural surrogates of English text. *Journal of the American Society for Information Science,* 1974, *25* (1), 10-24.

1975

Barry, J., and Stevenson, T. Using the computer to calculate the Dale-Chall formula. *Journal of Reading,* 1975, *19* (3), 218-222.

Explains the ease of use and accuracy of calculating textbook readability levels by computer.

Coleman, M., and Liau, T. A computer readability formula designed for machine scoring. *Journal of Applied Psychology,* 1975, *60* (2), 283-284.

Points out that there is no need to count syllables, since word length in letters is a better predictor than word length in syllables. The formula described uses both letters and sentences per 100 words.

Moe, A., and Arnold, R. Computer assisted readability levels of twenty-five Newbery books. *Reading Improvement,* 1975, *12,* 59-64.

Uses the computerized versions of the Lorge formula and the Fry graph to estimate the readability of Newbery books.

Seigel, A., and Wolf, J. Computer analysis of textual comprehensibility. In O. Lecarme and R. Lewis (Eds.), *Computers in Education.* Amsterdam: North-Holland Publishing Company, 1975.

Describes computer text analysis to determine comprehensibility. Discusses research groups involved in text analysis research. As of 1975, the authors felt eleven measures of comprehensibility were possible, including Guilford's semantic units, evaluation of symbolic implications, and cognition of figural units.

Shamo, G. Predicting syllable count by computer. *Journalism Quarterly,* 1975, *52,* 344-346.

Thomas, G., Hartley, R., and Kincaid, J. Test-retest and interanalyst reliability of the Automated Readability Index, Flesch Reading Ease Score, and the FOG count. *Journal of Reading Behavior,* 1975, *7* (2), 149-154.

Considers all formulas reliable estimates of readability.

1976

Harris, A., and Jacobson, M. Predicting twelfth graders' comprehension scores. *Journal of Reading,* 1976, *20* (1), 43-46.

Uses the Harris-Jacobsen readability formula to estimate comprehension scores of twelfth graders.

Herndon, M. An approach toward computer control of redundancy in textual materials. *Journal of Reading Behavior,* 1976, *8* (3), 259-271.

Describes an attempt to develop a program for detecting and editing redundancy in text.

1979

Barry, J. Computerized readability levels—their need and use. *Journal of Educational Data Processing,* 1979, *16,* 10-22.

Walker, N., and Boillot, M. A computerized reading level analysis. *Educational Technology,* 1979, *19* (1), 47-49.

Describes a computer based readability analysis scheme that uses the Fry graph and Flesch formula.

1980

Goodman, D., and Schwab, S. Computerized testing for readability. *Creative Computing,* 1980, *6* (4), 46, 48, 50-51.

Moe, A. Analyzing text with computers. *Educational Technology,* 1980, *20* (7), 29-31.

1981

Angier, N. Bell's letters. *Discover.* 1981, *2* (7), 78-79.

Describes Writer's Workbench system of text analysis developed by Bell Laboratories. The Gettysburg Address and a section from *A Tale of Two Cities* are analyzed with the system.

Blanchard, J. Readability of the MMPI. *Perceptual and Motor Skills,* 1981, *52,* 985-986.

Describes a study in which the MMPI was analyzed by computer for word and syllable counts in as many nonrecurring samples as possible. Readability estimates equal ninth to tenth grade.

Braby, R., and Kincaid, J. Computer aided authoring and editing. *Journal of Educational Technology Systems,* 1981-1982, *10* (2), 109-124.

Describes TAEG (Navy's Training Analysis and Evaluation Group) efforts to develop programs helping authors to write simply. Authoring routines automatically format and compose text and merge stored graphics with it. Editing routines include flagging uncommon words, suggesting substitutes for awkward or difficult words and phrases, and indicating the readability.

Carlson, R. Reading level difficulty. *Creative Computing,* 1981, *6* (4), 60-61.

Judd, D. Avoid readability formula drudgery: Use your school's microcomputer. *The Reading Teacher,* 1981, *35* (1), 7-8.

Noonan, L. Reading level determination. *Creative Computing,* 1981, *7* (3), 166-168, 170, 172-173.

Nottingham, R. FOG index. *Creative Computing,* 1981, *7* (4), 152-154.

1982

Cherry, L. Writing tools. *IEEE Transactions on Communication,* 1982, *30* (1), 100-104.

Discusses Writer's Workbench and its attempts to evaluate documents and produce better written prose.

Keller, P. Maryland micro: A prototype readability formula for small computers. *The Reading Teacher,* 1982, *35* (7), 778-782.

Klass, P. Software augments manual readability. *Aviation Week & Space Technology,* January 11, 1982, 106.

Describes the Navy's Flesch-Kincaid readability formula and the need for improved technical writing. Also refers to Bell Laboratories' use of the Writer's Workbench.

Macdonald, N., Frase, L., Gingrich, P., and Keenan, S. The writer's workbench: Computer aids for text analysis. *IEEE Transactions on Communication*, 1982, *20*, 1-14.

Schuyler, M. A readability formula program for use on microcomputers. *Journal of Reading*, 1982, *35* (6), 572-589.

>Presents the source code for a readability formula that uses several different formulas.

1983

Kiefer, K., and Smith, C. Textual analysis with computers: Tests of Bell Laboratories' computer software. *Research in the Teaching of English*, 1983, *17*, 201-214.

1984

Brown, R., and Byrd, C. *Reading expectancy and regression formulas.* 1984. (ED 240 538)

>Explains that microcomputer programs can be used to "develop a regression equation that will more accurately predict class performance than rule of thumb formulas."

Glynn, S., and Britton, B. Supporting readers' comprehension through effective text design. *Educational Technology*, 1984, *24* (10), 40-43.

>Serves as required reading for anyone interested in designing text for better comprehension. Especially of interest to reading educators who may want to design or evaluate comprehension software.

Kretschmer, J. Computerizing and comparing the Rix readability index. *Journal of Reading*, 1984, *27* (6), 490-499.

>Presents the RIXRATE computer based readability formula along with its source code so it can be copied. The RIXRATE formula uses word and sentence length data as variables for determining readability. A comparison with a few other short formulas indicates there is some degree of uniformity among the formulas.

Noe, K., and Standal, T. Readability: Old cautions for the new technology. *The Reading Teacher*, 1984, *37* (7), 673-674.

>Computer based readability software packages are now commercially available and offer reading analyses, including many formulas. Authors caution the user to remember that readability data, whether computer derived or not, should be considered as ballpark indicators of readability levels.

1985

Duffelmeyer, F. Estimating readability with a computer: Beware the aura of precision. *The Reading Teacher*, 1985, *38* (4), 392-394.

>Presents advantages and disadvantages of using a computer based readability formula called the RIXRATE. While RIXRATE is faster and less tedious than most noncomputer efforts at readability, Duffelmeyer suggests that teachers not abandon good judgment as they review computer based readability results.

Dunsmore, G. Readability assessments of elementary level microcomputer courseware. *AEDS Journal*, 1985, *18* (4), 267-276.

>Reports research that sought to investigate the accuracy of the Minnesota Educational Computing Consortium (MECC) readability program, which is a

part of the set of programs call School Utilities Volume 2. The program includes the Spache and Dale-Chall readability formulas.

Frase, L., MacDonald, N., and Keenan, S. Intuitions, algorithms, and a science of text design. In T. Duffy and R. Waller (Eds.), *Designing usable text.* New York: Academic Press, 1985.

Gross, P., and Sadowski, K. FOGINDEX – A readability formula for microcomputers. *Journal of Reading,* 1985, *28* (7), 614-618.

A computer based version of the FOG (by Gunning) readability formula is presented with source code so the program can be copied. The FOG formula measures percentage of three and more syllable words in determining readability. (No comparisons are made to other computer based readability formulas in the discussion.)

Noe, K., and Standal, T. Computer applications of readability formulas: Some cautions. *Computers, Reading and Language Arts,* 1985, *2* (2), 16-17, 43.

Otts, D. The reading estimate program: A computerized method for calculating the Raygor readability estimate. *Computers, Reading and Language Arts,* 1985, *2* (2), 30-1.

1986

Hague, S., and Mason, G. Using the computer's readability measure to teach students to revise their writing. *Journal of Reading,* 1986, *30* (1), 14-17.

Reveals that computer based readability formulas and word processing can be used in tandem to support classroom rewriting activities.

1987

Standal, T. Computer-measured readability. *Computers in the Schools,* 1987, *4* (1), 88-94.

Discusses many of the problems facing computer based readability estimates and reviews some readability programs.

7
Reading readiness and beginning reading

Increasing numbers of preschools and kindergartens are using curricula in which microcomputers play significant roles. Many of these preschool programs are intended to allow children to discover how to control computers rather than to use the computers to teach or provide reading readiness for the children. At the University of Maryland's Center for Young Children, where a computer was used in 1981-1982, some young children quickly took control of Tasman Turtle, a computer controlled robot, while others seemed less well equipped to deal with it. The Maryland Center program allowed children to experiment with on screen LOGO and DELTA DRAWING. Parents were involved in all phases of the computer project. The impact on reading interests, attitudes, and acquisition was not evaluated.

Programs at other centers often have gone beyond exploring LOGO. At the University of Pittsburgh, young children use LOGO, but they also use drill and practice programs in counting and in number and letter recognition. Still other centers use computers for checking children's mathematics and for teaching children to control the computer using BASIC (Ross & Campbell, 1983). Some centers even involve young children in controlling robots with computer programs (Shanahan, 1983).

As one might anticipate, there has been a lack of agreement on how to introduce children to computers; indeed, there is even a lack of agreement on whether to introduce young children to computers at all. Some experts maintain that age six is too late, while others maintain that six is too early. Despite these disagreements, emerging research conducted at the University of Wisconsin's Laboratory Preschool suggests that the social interaction outcomes resulting from introducing computers into classrooms are very positive. Experiences suggest that girls may be more likely to take control of computers when the opportunity is presented to them at early ages. And, since children discover the world through play, experts in many preschool settings recommend that their first experiences with computers be with games.

A number of experts have suggested that computers be used in the language experience approach to beginning reading (Casey, 1984). Recommendations to this end appear in journal articles and in books detailing the multiple uses of word processing programs in teaching. Some of these publications recommend that the teacher should type in the children's stories, while others suggest the children do so, learning keyboarding (typing) as they go along. Many fear children will practice errors in typing as little hands attempt to master the adult sized keyboard with or without typing instruction (Dacus & Dacus, 1983).

Very few comprehensive microcomputer programs for introducing beginners to reading have been developed because of the intensely individual nature of learning to read and the heavy speech requirements for beginning reading instruction. The relatively few computers that can be found in first grade classrooms is another compelling reason; the chance for profit seems small at present. Nevertheless, one massive effort has led to the development of Writing to Read, an instructional program combining computer taught letter phonics tutorials and games (with speech) with a language experience approach in which children type their own stories on electric typewriters (often employing invented spellings), make letters and words in clay, and read quantities of children's books (Hawkins, 1982).

In spite of the few comprehensive beginning reading programs, the availability of speech producing peripherals is beginning to foster the development of many new reading programs for young children. The increasing accessibility of speech for microcomputer programs in beginning programs has great promise for the future. Already prototype programs can pronounce words the beginning reader indicates are unknown (Clements, 1985). Others can provide audiovisual demonstrations of phonic blending and the additions of affixes and inflectional endings. These current developments suggest that teachers of reading readiness and beginning reading someday may have roles different from their present roles.

Chapter seven contains references that describe computer based reading readiness and beginning reading efforts in many diverse locations.

References

1981

Brandt, R. (Ed.) On reading, writing, and computers: A conversation with John Henry Martin. *Educational Leadership*, 1981, *39*, 60-64.

Dusewicz, R. Technology in the education of young children. *Journal of Children in Contemporary Society*, 1981, *14* (1), 3-14.

Kimmel, S. Programs for preschoolers: Starting out young. *Creative Computing,* 1981, *7* (10), 44-53.

Describes some preschool programs (circa, 1981).

Lally, M. Computer-assisted teaching of sight-word recognition for mentally retarded school children. *American Journal of Mental Deficiency,* 1981, *85* (4), 383-388.

Piestrup, A. *Preschool children use Apple II to test reading skills programs.* 1981. (ED 202 476)

Tells how fifty-five three and four year old children learned terms (above, below, left, right) needed to operate a computer and care for the diskettes during a three week tryout at a nursery school at Stanford University. Used as an activity center, the computer was accepted by all children and teachers.

Smith, P. The impact of computerization on children's toys and games. *Journal of Children in Contemporary Society,* 1981, *14* (1), 73-82.

Spring, C., and Perry, L. Computer-assisted instruction in word-decoding for educationally-handicapped children. *Journal of Educational Technology Systems,* 1981, *10* (2), 149-163.

Swigger, K., and Campbell, J. *Computers and the nursery school.* 1981. (ED 202 476)

Describes how children three to four years old used microcomputers to learn visual discrimination skills.

1982

Clements, D. *Microcomputers in early education: Rationale and outline for teacher training.* 1982. (ED 223 328)

Outlines Teaching with Microcomputers—the Early Years, a college course designed for early childhood educators.

Hawkins, P. Retired educator + IBM + 300 talking personal computers + 600 selectric typewriters + 10,000 kindergarten and first grade students = a test of the theory that children could learn to read by first learning to write. *IPD News,* 1982, *1* (3), 1-7.

Describes IBM's Writing to Read program and a sequel involving cassette tapes and comic strips for teaching reading to functionally illiterate young adults.

Hungate, H. Computers in the kindergarten. *The Computing Teacher,* 1982, *9* (5), 15-18.

Kohl, H. Should I buy my child a computer? *Harvard Magazine,* September-October 1982, 14-21.

Preschoolers learn using microcomputers. *Classroom Computer News,* 1982, *2* (5), 13-14.

Describes a pilot study at Stanford University that found preschoolers can use microcomputers to develop reading readiness skills. The study showed preschoolers are not afraid of the microcomputer and gains in achievement can be expected.

Smith-Willis, D., Riley, M., and Smith, D. Visual discrimination and preschoolers. *Educational Computer,* 1982, *2* (6), 19-20.

Vonstein, J. *An evaluation of the microcomputer as a facilitator of indirect learning for the kindergarten child.* Unpublished doctoral dissertation, Florida Atlantic University, 1982.

Watt, D. LOGO in the schools. *Byte,* 1982, *7* (8), 116-139.

1983

Barnes, B., and Hill, S. Should young children use microcomputers: LOGO before Lego? *The Computing Teacher,* 1983, *10* (9), 11-14.

Carlson, E. Teach your child programming. *Creative Computing,* 1983, *9* (4), 168-176.

> Suggests programing activities appropriate to the developmental ages of children, based on Papert's work. Recommends single finger turtle graphics commands for the very young.

Clements, D. The ABCs and beyond: Computers, language arts, and the young child. *Computers, Reading and Language Arts,* 1983, *1* (3), 15-18.

> Describes fifteen teacher controlled programs covering prereading and reading skills and five language arts oriented exploratory programs that are child controlled.

Dacus, J., and Dacus, D. Time bomb in educational computing. *Educational Computer,* 1983, *3* (6), 50-51.

> Describes how New Mexico State University personnel encountered opposition to teaching keyboarding to young children and eventually set a minimum of fourth grade for the children they taught.

D'Angelo, K. Computer books for young students: Diverse and difficult. *The Reading Teacher,* 1983, *36* (7), 626-633.

> Presents (with short annotations) a list of computer information books for young readers. The author seems to feel that many of the computer books available for children are difficult for children to read and understand.

Dickson, W. Little programs for little kids. *Family Computing,* 1983, *1* (2), 64-68.

> Suggests software, lists simple little programs (two for the Commodore 64 and two for the Apple), and tells how to use them with young children.

Dickson, W., and Borgh, K. Software for preschoolers. *Family Computing,* 1983, *1* (3), 66-67.

Embry, D. Preschoolers + computers = ABC: Music CAI. *Educational Computer,* 1983, *3* (2), 30-31.

Favaro, P. My five year old knows BASIC. *Creative Computing,* 1983, *9* (4), 158-166.

> Suggests programs parents might buy for preschoolers and states cautions.

Frank, M. (Ed.). *Young children in a computerized environment.* New York: Haworth Press, 1983.

> Contains sections on the impact of computers on teaching methodologies, on children's toys and games, and on the ethical development of children.

Hines, S. Computer programming abilities of five year old children. *Educational Computer,* 1983, *39* (40), 10-12.

Karoff, P. Computerized Head Start. *Teaching, Learning, Computing,* 1983, *1* (1), 44-50.

> Details the disagreements between experts over using computers with young children.

Muller, A. Preschoolers at the computer. *The Commodore Microcomputer Magazine,* 1983, *4* (4), 86-89.

Murphy, B. Educational programs for the very young. *Creative Computing,* 1983, *9* (10), 107-118.

> Recommends a number of programs.

PC Perspectives in Computing. Writing to Read is tested in schools. *PC Perspectives in Computing,* 1983, *3* (2), 49.

Porter, M. Juggles, bumbles and junior. *PCjr Magazine,* 1983, *1* (2), 9-14.
Describes development of a company specializing in software for young children.

Ross, S., and Campbell, L. Computer-based education in the Montessori classroom: A compatible mixture. *T.H.E. Journal,* 1983, *10* (6), 105-109.
Describes a tryout of computers and software in a Montessori first grade. Children loved checking math solutions and learning BASIC commands.

Reed, S. Preschool computing: What's too young? *Family Computing,* 1983, *1* (3), 55-59.
Describes how two young children learn to use the computer in their home.

Reed, S. Practicing what you teach. *Family Computing,* 1983, *1* (3), 60-63.
Reports an interview with a researcher employed by the University of Wisconsin's Laboratory Preschool.

Shanahan, D. Robots in the kindergarten. *Post Time,* 1983, *1* (11), 4.
Describes programing Big Trak robot with kindergartners.

Swigger, K., Brennan, C., and Swigger, B. Behavioral characteristics and their influence on preschool children's selection of programs. *Journal of Computer Based Instruction,* 1983, *9* (Special Issue), 137-143.

Vaidya, S. Using LOGO to stimulate children's fantasy. *Educational Technology,* 1983, *23* (12), 25-26.
Discusses using student generated LOGO graphics, as sources for story narratives with preschoolers.

Watt, M. Electronic thinker toys: Six programs from The Learning Company help children to think. *Popular Computing,* June 1983, 161-172.

Weyer, S. Computers for communication. *Childhood Education,* 1983, *59* (3), 227-231.

Ziajka, A. Microcomputers in early childhood education. *Young Children,* 1983, *38* (5), 61-67.

1984

Association for Supervision and Curriculum Development. Early results of computer-based reading and writing program impressive. *ASCD Update,* 1984, *26* (2), 2.
Describes a speech in which John Henry Martin elaborates on the field testing of Writing to Read by IBM.

Brady, E., and Hill, S. Research in review: Young children and microcomputers. *Young Children,* 1984, *39* (3), 49-61.
Reports work in progress to answer questions about roles of microcomputers in the preschool curriculum, their effects on children's learning styles, their uses in play, and the equity in their use.

Casey, J. *Beginning reading instruction: Using the LEA approach with and without micro-computer intervention.* 1984. (ED 245 192)
Describes a program in which kindergarten children received a reading lesson using the language experience approach in two different contexts. In the first, children's stories were transcribed on paper. Computer display, plus voice synthesis, were used in the second context. The resulting discussion was "more enthusiastic, involving and produced longer and richer language contributions from all participants."

Chandler, D. *Young learners and the microcomputer.* Milton Keynes, England: Open University Press. 1984.

> Provides information about using computers with elementary school age children. The publisher suggests both parents and teachers use the book as a commentary on educational issues surrounding computers and young children. All chapters would be of interest to reading professionals, especially Words Which Dance in Light, about word processing, writing, and children. Appendixes include Choosing software: A checklist; Relevant books; Relevant journals; Major software sources; and Useful addresses.

Chatman, S., Love-Clark, P., and Ash, M. *Microcomputers in early childhood psychological research.* Paper presented at the annual meeting of the American Educational Research Association, New Orleans, 1984.

Cuffaro, H. Microcomputers in education: Why is earlier better? *Teachers College Record,* 1984, *85* (4), 559-568.

> Discusses some disadvantages of using computers with three to seven year olds. Further speculates that the computer may not have much to offer children who are under eight years of age.

Davy, J. Mindstorms in the lamplight. *Teachers College Record,* 1984, *85* (4), 549-558.

> Discusses some aspects of using LOGO with young children.

D'Ignazio, F. Computing to read. *Compute,* February 1984, 124, 128, 129.

> Discusses how the computer helped a four year old learn to read and write without formal instruction.

Murphy, R., and Appel, R. *Evaluation of the Writing to Read instructional system 1982-1984: Second year report.* Princeton, NJ: Educational Testing Service, 1984.

> Provides a complete report of the evaluation of the Writing to Read educational system with kindergartners and first graders. Results indicate the system had a significant impact on writing achievement of young children. The impact on their reading achievement was apparent in kindergarten classes, but less so in first grade classes, especially among low scoring children.

Ohanion, S. IBM's Writing to Read: Hot new item or same old stew? *Classroom Computer Learning,* 1984, *4* (8), 30, 33.

Powell, B. Five-year-old authors. *Family Computing,* 1984, *2* (6), 58-60.

Rotenberg, L. Booting up for reading: Two nationwide programs that use computers to teach reading. *Teaching and Computers,* 1984, *1* (8), 16-19.

> Describes IBM's Writing to Read as implemented in Cary, North Carolina, and the Individual Reading Instruction System (IRIS) of the World Institute for Computer Assisted Teaching (WICAT).

Sheingold, K. The microcomputer as a medium for young children. In P.F. Campbell and G.G. Fein (Eds.), *Microcomputers in early education: Conceptualizing the issues.* Reston, VA: Reston Publishing, 1984.

> Explores concerns about microcomputers for young children and suggests uses and teachers' roles.

Strasma, J. Commodore clinic. *RUN Magazine,* 1984, *1* (1), 14.

> Names preschool programs for the Commodore 64 computer.

Swigger, K., and Swigger, B. Social patterns and computer use among preschool children. *AEDS Journal,* 1984, *17* (3), 35-41.

Describes a North Texas State University study indicating that most children prefer to approach the computer with friends and that introducing the computer did not change existing social patterns in the preschool classroom.

Taylor, M., Howe, M., and Dootson, D. *Microcomputers in the early childhood classroom* (videotape). Lynnwood, WA: Edmunds Community College Bookstore, 1984.

Shows three, four, and five year old children reacting to a computer in their classroom.

Turkle, S. The intimate machine. *Science,* 1984, *5* (3), 40-46.

Suggests that LOGO can be observed as a sort of Rorschach test revealing how children structure their tasks in order to accomplish them. States that girls deal with formal systems differently but just as competently as boys when allowed to discover how to manipulate the computer.

Vaidya, S. Making LOGO accessible to preschool children. *Educational Technology,* 1984, *24* (7), 30-31.

Warash, B. *Computer language experience approach.* 1984 (ED 244 264)

Discusses a computer based language experience program at West Virginia University Child Development Lab. Preschoolers use LOGO graphics to construct computer drawings, then dictate their accompanying stories to the teacher for transcription. Observation indicates children are more involved and verbalize significantly more with the computer drawings as compared to the hand drawn works.

Worden, P., and Kee, D. *Parent-child interaction and computer learning: An alphabet game for preschoolers.* 1984. (ED 243 601)

Describes a research project involving ten three year olds and their mothers. It was found that significantly more verbal interchange between parent and child occurred when reading a traditional alphabet book, as compared to playing a computer alphabet game. Suggests that software for preschoolers be designed with a stimulus for rich verbal interchange.

Zajonc, A. computer pedagogy? Questions concerning the new educational technology. *Teachers College Record,* 1984, *85* (4), 569-577.

Questions the need to use computers with young children because computers are unable to nurture those "capacities and structures" upon which childhood development depends. Also mentions that computers are perhaps best left to older students (twelve years) during concrete operational stages.

1985

Borgh, K., and Dickson, W. Two preschoolers sharing one microcomputer: Creating prosocial behavior with hardware and software. In P. Campbell and G. Fein (Eds.), *Young children and microcomputers: Conceptualizing the issues.* Reston, VA: Reston, 1985.

Clements, D. *Computers in early and primary education,* Englewood Cliffs, NJ: Prentice-Hall, 1985.

Contains many chapters of interest to reading professionals, especially The ABCs and Beyond, which contains sections on supporting young children's writing, writing computer programs that write English, books that talk to you, readiness skills, sight vocabulary and spelling, reading for comprehension, examining language arts and reading software critically, and what research tells us about teaching language arts with computers.

Johnson, J. Characteristics of preschoolers interested in microcomputers. *Journal of Educational Research,* 1985, *78* (5), 299-305.

Reports a three month study that investigated the relationships that might exist between preschool children's interests in microcomputers and cognitive as well as behavioral characteristics. Results indicate that preschoolers need some representational knowledge (as opposed to concrete) competency. In addition, those young students who exhibit single minded, sequential, abstract play attributes may enjoy greater success using computers than those who do not possess such attributes.

1986

Beaty, J., and Tucker, W. *The computer as a paintbrush: Creative uses for the personal computer in the preschool classroom.* Columbus, OH: Merrill, 1986.

Contains chapters on the computer as a playmate, alphabet block, abacus, building block, crayon, paintbrush, chatterbox, the computer in the preschool classroom, and choosing software for the preliterate child.

Glover, S. A field study of the use of cognitive-developmental principles in microcomputer design for young children. *Journal of Educational Research,* 1986, *79* (6), 325-332.

Compares software featuring cognitive-developmental principles to traditional software. The software was designed to teach letter recognition and number judgment. "It appears that the software designed in accord with cognitive-developmental principles significantly enhanced learning compared to software not so designed."

Goodwin, L., Goodwin, W., Nansel, A., and Helm, C. Cognitive and affective effects of various types of microcomputer use by preschoolers. *American Educational Research Journal,* 1986, *23* (3), 348-356.

Investigates the effects of microcomputer use on preschoolers' knowledge of basic reading readiness concepts and on their attitudes toward the microcomputer. The results indicate no effect on prereading skills by microcomputers and relatively low levels of interest in microcomputers.

1987

Goodwin, L., Goodwin, W., and Garel, M. Use of microcomputers with preschoolers. *Early Childhood Research Quarterly,* 1987.

Irwin, M. Connections: Young children, reading, writing, and computers. *Computers in the Schools,* 1987, *4* (1), 27-37.

Includes introducing children to books and computers, finding software for beginning readers, and using text programs and word processors with young readers.

8
Computer managed reading instruction

While most of the excitement about computer use in helping children read is generated by the new instructional software, there is some excitement about our increased ability to keep track of children's progress and to provide approprite materials by use of the computer. Databases are the filing, storage, and retrieval programs that may improve our instructional capabilities and gauge the success of our endeavors. One very promising database is The Nebraska Reading Retrieval System, a state sponsored computer program designed to share expert opinions and materials knowledge with Nebraska's teachers. Another is the Educational Products Information Exchange (EPIE) database of educational software. This database, when printed out as The Educational Software Selector (TESS), is probably the most complete listing of evaluations of educational software to be found.

The databases most used by school reading educators are computerized reading management systems. These systems provide a variety of tests and computer programs that both score the tests and create files for school districts, buildings, or classes in such a way that reports are quickly available to provide summaries of student reading performance at all three of these levels or for each student for whom scores have been entered.

Computerized reading management systems are of five general types: commercial mail in or networked mainframe programs, commercially developed microcomputer programs supporting no particular set of teaching materials, microcomputer programs supporting a basal reading series, mainframe and minicomputer instructional programs including a management system, and microcomputer programs developed as part of school district projects.

Commercial mail in or networked mainframe programs

Among the mail in or networked programs are the Croft Computerized Management System, Learning Unlimited Systems, and Individual Criterion Referenced Tests (ICRT from Educational Development Corporation). Teachers using such systems send completed test response cards or answer sheets to collection points and receive printout class lists, prescriptions, and groups needing particular skills by mail in ten days to two weeks. Usually both pretests and posttests are provided. Prescriptions are usually stated both in materials prepared by the authors of the system and materials customized at the request of the school district using the system.

Commercially developed microcomputer management systems

Among the commercial computerized reading management systems are AIDS (Assisted Instructional Development System); GESI (Instructional Management System by Gulf Educational Systems); CRMS (Computer Based Reading Management System by Educational Activities); K Thru College (Soft-Mark); CAMP (Computerized Assisted Management System); Fountain Valley Teacher Support System – Computerized Management System; M MICRO (Microcomputer Managed Information for Your Criterion Referenced Objectives); MIMS (Microcomputer Instructional Management System); the Talley Special Education Management System; Skillcorp's CMS Reading; and The System (James Rennix), a Commodore computer based program for managing records of Chapter I students. Most of these use card readers to input test information from criterion referenced reading skill tests provided as part of the management system. These programs write prescriptions that include numerous supplementary reading materials as well as the materials input by the users.

Mainframe and minicomputer programs including a management system

Three companies offer reading programs that operate with computers much larger than micros. Used in schools, these programs are made available to students at terminals connected to a central (host) computer. The Dolphin Reading Program (Timeshare Division, Houghton-Mifflin) offers remediation in reading skills arranged to match those presented in the Houghton Mifflin Reading Series. The many programs available from the Computer Curriculum Corporation (CCC) not only make use of computer delivered diagnostic tests to determine level of student entry into the various skill strands, but also monitor student responses so placement levels are automatically changed to correspond to student success or lack of it. A third company marketing reading programs, CDC (Control Data Corporation), has several versions of their Basic Skills Reading Curriculum for remedial or literacy work at reading levels three to eight. These are available at terminals connected to PLATO networks, most of which are based on university campuses. Like the CCC programs, those from CDC also offer online pretesting, constant monitoring, upward or downward reassignment based on performance, and posttesting. Programs from both CDC and CCC are being redesigned and reprogramed to run on microcomputers.

Microcomputer programs developed as part of school district projects

An increasing number of schools are using local and federal funds to create reading management systems to fit their own needs. Two programs have met the standards of the National Diffusion Network (NDN), a federally funded agency created to disseminate information about outstanding educational efforts nationwide. The first of these, Mastery Management, was developed by the CAM Demonstration Evaluation Center of Hopkins, Minnesota, Public Schools. Originally created for tracking student progress in reading and mathematics, this system is easily modifable for storage and retrieval of a variety of school data. It resembles a list of blanks for 900 students, with 40 tidbits of information written after each name.

The second, Computer Assisted Diagnostic and Prescriptive Program (CADPP), was developed by the Buckingham County Schools to help teachers create prescriptions in math and reading. The prescriptions call for use of materials available in the classroom to which the child is assigned and entered into the computer's memory by the teacher. It is designed to run on the Apple II computer and to generate prescriptions and progress reports for children in grades three to nine.

Several other Lighthouse projects selected for diffusion by NDM include a CMI component. Among these are I CARE, which manages CAI and audiovisual remedial reading instruction vocational students (grades 9-12) in Blue Mountain High School, Schuylkill Haven, Pennsylvania. Another is the Computer Assisted Instructor Program of the Merrimack Education Center in Chelmsford, Massachusetts. At the Merrimack Center, the self-managing instructional packages of the Computer Curriculum Corporation are supplemented with more traditional instruction managed by a locally developed CMI program. A third is the Demonstration Reading Program at Sierra Junior High School in Bakersfield, California. It bases comprehension instruction on the PRI, McGraw-Hill's program for writing prescriptions based on computer scored tests. A fourth is Project Clover, which involves the use of MSRTS (Migrant Student Record Transfer System) for maintaining records on migrant school children in 49 states, Puerto Rico, and the District of Columbia. Teachers input information on their present students and request information about newly arrived students. The information may be about health, standardized test scores, interests, book levels, and state mandated performance test scores.

A fifth, HOSTS (Help One Student to Succeed), started as a remedial reading program in Vancouver, Washington. It is now used in more than 150 schools in at least twelve states. The major role of the computer in HOSTS is in scoring tests and prescribing instruction from its six disk database. The instruction is carried on by volunteer tutors.

A large number of school districts are using computers to aid in the management of their reading programs. Often these efforts lead to combinations of locally produced computer programs with commercially available programs. For example, the Spencerport, New York, School System is using ICRT (Educational Development Corporation) to generate pupil prescriptions and at the same time is creating (with a local software company) a computer program for generating compensatory Individual Educational Plans (IEPs) capitalizing on the information made available by the ICRT program.

The references in chapter eight provide an overview of the major attempts to development computer managed reading instruction across the past two decades. Much more research is needed, particularly in the area of computer managed instruction for microcomputers that use inexpensive, teacher adaptive software.

References

1970

Kooi, B., and Geddes, C. The teacher's role in computer assisted instructional management. *Educational Technology,* 1970, *10* (2), 42-45.

1974

Aaron, R., and Muench, S. The effects of a computer managed individualized treatment program on the achievement of behaviorally disordered, delinquent adolescents. *Reading Research Quarterly,* 1974, *10* (2), 228-243.

Describes a program in which delinquents in a Georgia Youth Development Center were randomly assigned to experimental or control groups. The experimental groups earned significantly greater reading scores. The experimental group was taught with PLAN, *a computer managed reading and mathematics program developed for Westinghouse Learning Corporation.*

Fey, T. *A comparison of computer and teacher prepared individualized reading prescriptions.* Unpublished doctoral dissertation, University of Florida, 1974.

Describes a program in which the Gilmore Oral Reading Inventory (McGraw-Hill) and an interest inventory were administered to fifth graders. A group of classroom teachers and a group of reading teachers then picked books and remedial materials for each pupil tested. A computer program prescribed from these same data. The computer generated prescriptions closely matched the reading teachers' prescriptions.

1976

Hendon, C. *A comparison of reading and vocabulary achievement of elementary students taught with two reading methods.* Unpublished doctoral dissertation, University of Kansas, 1976.

Compares basal reading instruction with and without computer managed instruction in forty classrooms. Results favored the non-CMI classrooms.

1978

Baker, F. *Computer-managed instruction: Theory and practice.* Englewood Cliffs, NJ: Educational Technology Publications, 1978.

Describes the history and development of computer managed instruction prior to 1978; one of the most substantive works on CMI.

Blachowicz, C., and Fairweather, P. A computer assisted preservice program in reading. *Reading Horizons,* 1978, *19,* 71-74.

Describes an experimental project at Northwestern University involving the application of computers to the operation of a preservice program for teacher preparation in reading. Using a competency based model, the computer managed the students' entry into and progress through a series of on-line, interactive tutorials by assessing their initial behaviors, assigning lesson plans, guiding use of bibliographical database, and monitoring progress.

1979

Bozeman, W. Computer managed instruction: State of the art. *AEDS Journal,* 1979, *12* (3), 116-137.

Contains an excellent analysis of the literature. Answers two questions: What CMI programs are available? What evidence exists concerning the effectiveness of CMI? Discusses five major CMI projects (circa 1979).

1980

Hazen, M. An argument in favor of multimethod research and evaluation in CAI and CMI instruction. *AEDS Journal,* 1980, *13* (4), 275-284.

Describes a metaanalysis on the literature concerning the effectiveness of CAI and CMI.

1981

Haugo, J. Management applications of the microcomputer: Promises and pitfalls. *AEDS Journal,* 1981, *14* (4), 182-187.

Examines the advantages and disadvantages of using microcomputers for CMI.

Hedges, W. Lightening the load with computer managed instruction. *Classroom Computer News,* 1981, *1* (6), 34.

Discusses CMI, including some CMI programs commercially available in 1981.

McIsaac, D., and Baker, F. Computer managed instruction system implementation on a microcomputer. *Educational Technology,* 1981, *21* (10), 40-46.

Describes the evolution of the Wisconsin WIS-SIM CMI project to microcomputers.

1982

Ingebo, G., Yagi, K., Leitner, D., Miller, S., and Miller, P. *Evaluation report on three new instruction programs: Help One Student to Succeed, prescription learning, computer assisted instruction.* Portland, OR: Portland Public Schools, 1982.

Finds the HOSTS (Help One Student to Succeed) program leads to more favorable results than supplementary CAI in reading and mathematics for Chapter I students. HOSTS uses computer databases to generate prescriptions implemented by volunteer tutors.

Roberts, S. The effects of split-day scheduling and computer-managed instruction on the reading achievement of intermediate students. *Dissertation Abstracts International,* 1982, *43,* 1482A.

Describes a study in which intermediate students were divided into three groups: control, split day scheduling, and computer managed. No statistically significant differences in reading achievement were found among the groups, each using the same basal reading program with the varied methods of instructional support.

1983

Meyer, L. *Evaluation research in basic skills with incarcerated adults.* 1983. (ED 237 954)

Provides findings of a study to determine effectiveness of traditional vs. computer managed instruction in basic skills programs for incarcerated adults in Illinois. Significant gains for both control groups were reported after three months of instruction, with language scores increasing most dramatically, followed by math gains. Reading comprehension showed lowest gains.

1984

Bilyeu, L. Computer tracks second graders' book preferences and accomplishments. *The Reading Teacher,* 1984, *38* (3), 358-359.

Explains how computers were used to record and tabulate data on several aspects of children's literature.

1985

Holmes, J.N. *1984-85 evaluation report: HOSTS pilot project at Cleveland High School.* Portland, OR: Portland Public Schools, 1985.

Describes HOSTS materials as providing testing and prescriptions in six major skill areas at six grade levels. These are implemented through a computerized database of teaching materials.

Payton, W. Our schools: The good news. *California School Boards,* 1985, *44* (2), 26-27.

Describes tutoring program at Loma Prieta, California, where computers use test results to generate prescriptions for tutors. The computers search for materials to prescribe from a database stored on six Apple disks.

1986

Reinhold, F. Buying a hardware/software system. *Electronic Learning,* 1986, *5* (5), 42-47.

  Discusses different integrated learning systems (ILS) and focuses on several companies that sell them.

Smith, J. Managing reading. *Electronic Learning,* 1986, *5* (7), 24-28.

  Describes how publishers have incorporated computer based management and instructional systems into their basal reading series and provides examples.

9

Speech technology and reading

Some of the most exciting advances in computer technology have been in the area of speech production and recognition. Several inexpensive microcomputer peripherals, which have become available in the past five years, finally make practical the application of speech technology to computers. These devices are particularly significant for the field of reading since they make it possible for even nonreaders to communicate and learn from a computer. As a consequence, the computer's capability for providing direct instruction in reading has been vastly improved.

Speech production

The most successful speech peripherals for microcomputers are in the area of speech production rather than speech recognition. Many hardware peripherals are available for producing speech. These devices differ greatly in terms of speech quality, voice types, and overall utility. There are two general approaches to providing speech output with computers: speech digitization and text to speech synthesis.

Text to speech synthesizers use mathematical and grammatical models that have been developed for all of the phonemes in English. The computer reads individual letters in a word to form the phonemes. The phonemes are then strung together, or synthesized, to form words. The advantage of this type of approach is that anything that can be spelled phonetically can be spoken.

Phoneme based synthesizers have widespread applications. For instance, visually handicapped persons can type individual letters into the computer and the letters can be fed into a synthesizer and spoken back as whole words. This makes it possible for the visually handicapped to write fluently using a word processor, correcting normal typographical errors as they occur based on the audio feedback. It has allowed many visually handicapped people to move into computer related occupations.

Another exciting application of speech synthesis can be seen in a recent program entitled Talking Textwriter (Scholastic). This program uses text to speech synthesis in the context of a simple word processor. Young students use the word processor, then with a simple command whatever they have written will be spoken by the computer. Not only does this reinforce students, but it provides them the opportunity of reviewing their spelling. Words that are misspelled when read back by the computer will be mispronounced. This helps students identify where a spelling error has been made. They can adjust the spelling until it sounds and looks correct.

There are some distinct disadvantages, however, to text to speech synthesizers. The audio quality of synthesized speech is often poor, particularly when more than one word at a time must be spoken. Most synthesizers use only one model for a particular phoneme. This means the voice is always the same, usually that of a male adult. Female voices, children's voices, or unfamiliar patterns of male voices are not possible. Also, because the algorithms focus on the phonemes, the subtle tonality and stress patterns of words and sentences cannot be taken into account. Consequently, speech quality is reduced.

Speech digitizers are another type of speech peripheral. Digitizers do not base their output on models of the human voice, but on human speech that has been recorded and converted to a digital signal. Consequently, with digitizers it is possible to distinguish many voices. Also, because the speech is recorded rather than modeled, it will reflect more accurately the inflections and intonations of the original speaker.

Not all digital voice systems are created alike or sound alike. Currently, there are only a few microcomputer peripherals that will play back digitized voice. Voice quality and quantity vary greatly depending on the frequency with which the voice is sampled during the recording process, chip type, and the encoding/decoding algorithms employed. Some types of voice digitizers use a lot of the computer's memory but provide good audio quality, while others use less computer memory and have poorer audio quality. The differences in the memory requirements of these devices are not insignificant. Many sample speech at a rate of 4,000 bytes per second, which means that the average floppy disk can hold about 25 seconds of speech. Since much of the disk must be used for the program itself, often only 10-15 seconds of speech are available. One of the first major reading series to use this type of speech digitizer was the IBM Writing to Read program. While this program uses audio to help teach phonics, the application of audio is highly limited because of the high sampling rate of the digitizer.

More recent digital speech devices use a sophisticated electronic technique, linear predictive coding (LPC), to compress the audio data so it can be stored at a rate of 200 bytes per second. Consequently, LPC digitizers can store up to 6 minutes of continuous audio on a floppy disk. The trade-off is that the audio quality is slightly reduced. Several publishers have developed software using this type of device. The smaller memory requirements make it much easier to fit the audio into a variety of educational applications. The Houston Independent School District Department of Technology has developed two major software series in language arts that make use of LPC speech. One series, Harmony English as a Second Language, uses audio for modeling English. The other is the Language Literacy System, a large K-2 software package for teaching reading and writing.

Regardless of type, speech digitizers have clear drawbacks for some applications. First, the speech must be prerecorded. Therefore, if a student types a word into the computer, it will not be pronounced unless it was previously recorded. This limits spontaneous interaction with the computer. Second, it is often more costly to develop software using digital speech because of the time and effort involved in recording and editing the soundtracks. Consequently, many software manufacturers have been reluctant to develop software for this peripheral.

Since each approach to speech production has limitations, an obvious way of improving speech peripherals is to combine the two types of approaches into a single peripheral. Not surprisingly, microcomputer speech boards have been developed that contain both digital and synthesized speech chips. Programs are just beginning to take advantage of their combined capability. Given the greater flexibility such composite speech devices provide, it appears likely that many educational publishers will begin to use them.

Speech recognition

The concept of freely conversing with a machine is one of the most intriguing in all of science fiction. Unfortunately, for the most part, this concept remains fiction. Nonetheless, there have been significant advances in this area.

Speech recognition devices attempt to sample auditory data and match the data with models for specific vocabulary items or, in some cases, specific phonemes. In order to do this the computer must first learn the distinguishing characteristics of a particular speaker's voice. The speaker is asked to say certain words several times while the computer analyzes the person's voice qualities. These qualities are then incorporated into the model used to analyze all subsequent utterances. Even with this modeling, most microcomputers can handle vocabularies of only 100 to 300 words with accuracy.

The primary barrier to the successful development of accurate speech recognition devices is the complexity of human language. There is tremendous variance in the acoustical features of human voices both within and between speakers. A single word, even when spoken by the same person, can lead to literally thousands of different wave forms across different frequencies, depending on the pitch, stress, and volume of the speaker. Correctly interpreting data is still a problem for even the most sophisticated computers. Most devices presume certain things about the speaker in order to limit the complexity of the data. They often presume the speaker to be an adult English speaker. The more a voice deviates from the audio pattern of an English speaking adult, the more difficult recognition becomes. Consequently, most speech recognition devices tend to be much less accurate at recognizing young children or speakers with strong accents.

Another major drawback to voice recognition devices is that most are highly susceptible to interference from other noises in the environment. The susceptibility of voice recognition devices to errors caused by external noise has been one of the biggest reasons why school applications of this technology have been so scarce. School classrooms are inherently noisy.

More than hardware

Even though speech hardware has become increasingly sophisticated, software applications are still in their infancy. This should not be surprising. When sound capability was added to movies, it was still many years before producers consistently used sound to its full effect. Much needs to be learned about how and when to use audio with software.

An early study (Mock, 1976) on the use of audio combined with text in educational television suggests that the effects of audio vary with reading ability. In addition, Mock suggests that the timing of the audio relative to the presentation of text is crucial to the reader's visual attention. Research is needed on the use of audio with computers to see if the findings from educational television transfer.

The future of speech technology for reading instruction

Taken as a whole, the future of computer assisted speech technology for the field of reading is excellent. The promise of the technology for reading instruction has been demonstrated by a steadily increasing volume of application software. This software has been used to address the obvious elements of phonics and all phases of reading instruction. Speech peripherals may soon play a major role in beginning reading instruction. Until now it has been difficult to create instructionally effective software for primary and preschool children. Students have been caught in a dilemma. If they cannot read the directions, they cannot operate the computer. If they cannot operate the computer, they cannot use it to learn to read. Speech technology offers a way out. The computer can literally talk the student through the use of a program. This means that even totally illiterate users can make full use of computer assisted instruction. Consequently, computers equipped with speech devices could have a tremendous impact on all forms of instruction at the primary level and with adult illiterates.

Chapter nine reviews the available research on computer applications in reading using speech.

References

1976

Mock, K. *Children's attention to television: The effects of audio-visual attention factors on children's television viewing habits.* Paper presented at the American Educational Research Association annual meeting, San Francisco, California, 1976.

> Explains that eye movement recordings were used in a study of eight to ten year old children to determine the nature of visual attention while viewing selected segments from an educational television program. Findings suggest that voice overs should be delayed until the student has had the opportunity to orient to the text.

1981

Levinson, S., and Liberman, M. Speech recognition by computer. *Scientific American,* 1981, *244* (4), 64-76.

> States that after forty years of research, the automatic recognition of speech by computers remains a Utopian goal. Current devices have small vocabularies and little ability to deal with fluent sequences of words. Explains Bell Laboratories' prototype system involving word decoding and decision making about which word (within sentence syntax context) and which sentence within a semantic context called "word concept." Predicts continued progress.

Lin, K., Frantz, G., and Goudie, K. Computer-generated speech: The voice of the future. *Personal Computing,* March 1981, 84-89.

1983

Cater, J. *Electronically speaking: Computer speech generation.* Indianapolis, IN: H.W. Sams, 1983.

Ciarcia, S. Use ADPCM for highly intelligible speech synthesis. *Byte,* 1983, *8* (6), 35-48.

> Describes all of the major approaches to speech synthesis, then provides a do it yourself model for making your own speech synthesizer. This article is for the more technically oriented.

Elliot, L. Performance of children aged nine to seventeen years on a test of speech intelligibility in noise using sentence material with controlled word predictability. *Journal of the Acoustical Society of America,* 1983, *66* (3), 643-651.

Gould, J., Conti, J., and Hovanyecz, R. Composing letters with a simulated listening typewriter. *Communications of the ACM,* 1983, *26* (4), 295-308.

Harvey, W. Voice synthesis: A new technology comes to school. *Electronic Learning,* 1983, *3* (2), 68-73

> Explains clearly how voice synthesis works. One of the few articles that discusses voice technology specifically in relationship to schools. Includes a section of ten questions to ask when selecting a voice synthesizer and a source list of available speech peripherals.

Luce, P.A., Feustel, T.C., and Pisoni, D.B. Capacity demands in short-term memory for synthetic and natural speech. *Human Factors,* 1983, *25* (1), 17-32.

> Reports three experiments indicating that synthetic speech is more difficult to understand than natural speech because it places increased processing demands on short term memory.

1984

Bergheim, K. Micros prick up their ears. *InfoWorld,* 1984, *6* (32).

> Explains how the recent availability of new speech chips has led to a resurgence in the use of speech peripherals with computers.

Bristow, G. *Electronic Speech Synthesis.* New York: McGraw-Hill, 1984.

> Serves as an excellent resource for those with or without a technical orientation. The readers guide directs readers to the most appropriate chapters.

Bruckert, E. A new text-to-speech product produces dynamic human-quality voice. *Speech Technology,* 1984, *2* (2), 114-119.

Hagan, D. *Microcomputer resource book for special education.* Reston, VA: Reston Publishing, 1984.

> Contains much useful information on applications of speech technology for the handicapped. Designs specific applications of the technology for different types of handicaps and lists resources.

Hillinger, M. Issues in the design of speech-based phonics software. Unpublished manuscript (available from Houghton Mifflin, TSC Division, P.O. Box 683, Hanover, New Hampshire 03755), 1984.

> Describes the development of the Sound Ideas reading software that used the ECHO Plus Speech Synthesizer.

Mella, M. More than a whisper of hope for computers you can talk to. *Business Week,* December 17, 1984, 92-93.

> Describes recent development by IBM of a speech to text device. This type of speech peripheral makes it possible to dictate directly into a computer and have the speech converted to text. Notes that many manufacturers of speech peripherals have been operating at a loss, but are continuing to obtain funding because of the increasing promise of the technology.

Nelson, M. *Talking chips.* New York: McGraw-Hill, 1984.

Rangel, D., Mercado, L., and Daniel, D. *Aspects of developing CAI for English as a second language.* Paper presented at the National Educational Computing Conference, Dayton, Ohio, 1984.

> Describes the Harmony English as a Second Language courseware developed by the Houston Independent School District. This is one of the largest

bodies of courseware to use digital speech technology with microcomputer software. Discusses the methodology used in the courseware and the advantages of using digital speech technology for this type of application.

Schulman, R., Wojno, J., and Catterson, C. Making computers talk and listen. *Newsweek,* October 15, 1984, 3.

Describes recent advances in the application of voice input devices. Worth noting are references to the use of voice input devices for automated phone systems.

Smith, G. Five voice synthsizers. *Byte,* September 1984, 337-339.

Provides a brief theoretical overview of speech synthesis and then compares five different types of commonly used speech chips.

Wagers, W., and Scott, B. Will fifth-generation computers converse with humans? *Electronic Products,* 1984, *9* (9), 53-55.

Argues that current speech technology methods are insufficient to handle the demands of fifth generation computers. Describes a new type of signal processing approach called CORETECHS.

1985

Casey, J. Making micros talk. *Electronic Learning,* 1985, *5* (2), 16, 21-22, 62.

Describes three forms of computer based speech: digital, text to speech synthesis, and the software speech. Discusses advantages and disadvantages of each type of system for educational applications. Includes names and addresses of suppliers of educational speech software and hardware.

Greene, B., and Pisoni, D. Perception of synthetic speech by adults and children: Research on processing voice output from text-to-speech systems. In L.E. Bernstein (Ed.), *The vocally impaired,* Volume 2. New York: Academic Press, 1985.

Explains the state of the art in text to speech systems, with summations of recent research and suggestions for future directions in voice input/output research. An interesting note is that comprehension of synthesized speech is found to improve dramatically with a small amount of practice, although it seldom equals comprehension of normal speech.

Holcomb, R. Use a speech synthesizer to teach basic vocabulary. *Tech Trends,* 1985, *30* (4), 18-19.

Explains that the speech synthesizer can provide immediate feedback, repetition designed for individual needs, opportunity to integrate new information at learner's pace, assistance in record keeping, and individualized instruction.

Linggard, R. *Electronic synthesis of speech.* New York: Cambridge University Press, 1985.

Nelson, M. Voice system: Perfect teacher's aid. *Electronic Education,* 1985, *4* (5), 23, 28.

Discusses a voice based learning system, the Scott Instruments Voice Entry Terminal (VET).

Nusbaum, H., and Pisoni, D. Constraints on the perception of synthetic speech generated by rule. *Behavior Research Methods, Instruments, and Computers,* 1985, *17,* 235-242.

1986

Friedland, L. The sounds aren't silent. *Sky,* 1986, *15* (1), 11-19.

Describes computer based research into the voice apparatus with which we create speech and some of the implications and applications of this research into computer produced speech.

Mason, G. The new speaking programs. *The Reading Teacher,* 1986, *39* (6), 618-620.

Discusses speech peripherals in reading instruction and the IBM Writing to Read program, which uses speech.

Olson, R., Foltz, G., and Wise, B. Reading instruction and remediation with the aid of computer speech. *Behavior Research Methods, Instruments, and Computers,* 1986, *18,* 93-99.

1987

Barbour, A. Computerized speech: Talking its way into the classroom. *Electronic Learning,* 1987, *6* (4), 15-16.

Discusses the speech capabilities of the Talking Text Writer (Scholastic) and Writing to Read (IBM).

In press

Greene, B., Logan, J., and Pisoni, D. Perception of synthetic speech produced automatically by rule: Intelligibility of eight text-to-speech systems. *Behavioral Research Methods, Instruments, and Computers,* in press.

Compares the intelligibility of eight computerized synthetic speech systems with natural speech. Systems include both mainframe and microcomputer devices or programs. The best system equalled natural speech only with initial consonant phonemes, producing an overall error rate of only 3 to 4 percent for isolated monosyllabic words.

10

Legibility, reading, and computers

I t is estimated that by the year 2000 there will be more than 20 million users of video display terminals (VDTs) or cathode ray tubes (CRTs) in the United States alone. This should not startle anyone in the reading community. Visual display terminals in many forms have been with us for a quarter of a century. However, few reading researchers have addressed the question of whether reading text printed on an electronic display is different from reading text printed on paper.

An essential element of this question is legibility. During the early part of the century questions about how print could be made most readable were of widespread interest. How big should type be? How can eye fatigue be reduced? How should children's books be printed? Excellent summaries from this era of legibility research can be found in Tinker (1963) and Watts and Nisbet (1974). Today, technical and societal changes are once again pushing questions of legibility to the forefront.

Radiation and fatigue effects

Many frequent users of video display terminals are concerned about radiation and fatigue effects. Studies by the National Institute of Occupational Safety and Health (NIOSH) and by individual researchers (e.g., Terrana, 1980) show that users of video display terminals are not exposed to excessive radiation. However, studies by Gunnarsson and Soderberg (1983), Jelden (1981), Oestberg (1974), and Sauter et al. (1983) show that concerns about visual fatigue may be legitimate. All of these studies report that reading from VDTs causes more visual fatigue then reading from print.

Computer based comprehension

The question of whether VDTs negatively affect reading comprehension has not been fully addressed. Chapman and Tipton (1985), in looking at VDT reading with television, found a significant reduction in comprehension as compared to paper print. Muter et al. (1982), however, found no significant difference in comprehension. In a related issue, researchers consistently find that reading rate is significantly slower for text presented electronically (Hoover, 1977; Muter et al., 1982). This finding may simply reflect subjects' lack of familiarity with the medium or it may be related to the fact that most electronic displays contain about one third the amount of text of book pages. Line length also may be a factor, since 40 character lines were used in these studies. Kolers, Duchnicky, and Ferguson (1981) found that reading speed on a CRT was 17 percent faster with 80 characters per line than with 40 larger characters per line.

The type of visual contrast on an electronic display may be significant. Print is usually displayed with negative contrast, dark text on a white background, while VDTs usually have positive contrast, illuminated text on a dark background. Bauer and Cavonius (1980) and Radl (1980) reported improved performance with negative contrast displays. One should be careful, however, in generalizing from these or any other results involving VDTs. As luminosity increases, other aspects of the display, such as flicker sensitivity, change. Most VDTs flicker at approximately 50 cycles per second, and this flickering may be disruptive and may trigger seizures in epileptics.

One of the critical distinctions between electronic display and conventional print is that electronic displays are dynamic. The displays exist in four dimensions — height, width, depth, and time. The designer of electronic displays must be concerned not only with how text is printed, but when. The human visual system is extremely sensitive to temporal factors. Sudden changes in the visual display, such as flashing letters or words, immediately attract attention (Smith & Goodwin, 1971). These changes have the potential to either improve or reduce legibility depending on how they are used. Smith and Goodwin found that search time was improved by the use of dynamic cues such as flashing letters. However, anything that can attract attention can also distract if it is used inappropriately. In a series of eye movement studies, O'Bryan and Silverman (1974) found that the visual attention of poor readers was frequently misdirected by the animation of graphics adjacent to the text being taught. In some cases the distraction was so powerful that young beginning readers never fixated on the text.

In conclusion, the legibility of electronic displays is of increasing concern. Use of VDTs is increasing and the physical construction of display terminals is changing rapidly. Efforts are underway to develop small, portable, "flat screen" displays for use with small computers. New approaches to creating electronic displays, such as liquid crystal displays (LCDs) and electroluminescent screens, are challenging cathode ray tubes. Each of these devices creates an image that differs markedly from those of cathode ray tubes. Consequently, much of the previous research on VDT/CRT legibility may not transfer. However, the economic importance of these devices has already started new research in the area of legibility.

Chapter ten presents references that should help to clarify some of the issues surrounding legibility, reading, and computers.

References

1963

Tinker, M. *The legibility of print.* Ames, IA: Iowa State University Press, 1963.
Contains a detailed discussion of studies of legibility going back to the turn of the century, as well as Tinker's own exhaustive research in this area. The classic reference in the field of legibility.

1968

Gould, J. Visual factors in the design of computer-controlled CRT displays. *Human Factors,* 1968, *10* (4), 359-375.

1971

Smith, S., and Goodwin, N. Blink coding for information display. *Human Factors,* 1971, *13* (3), 283-290.
Studies time required to search a display of random digits for a target item. Subjects were able to identify a target item 50 percent faster when it blinked.

1974

O'Bryan, K., and Silverman, H. *Experimental program eye movement study: Research report.* 1974. (ED 126 870)
Reports a study in which several segments of videotape from an educational television show were shown to 30 children aged nine to eleven, divided into two groups — poor readers and nonreaders. Film recordings of eye movements were made. Qualitative analysis was performed by overlaying a 1/16 second fixation onto drawings of segment scenes. The purpose of the lessons was to teach basic sight vocabulary. Most screens contained cartoon or live characters who depicted a word or sentence shown at the bottom of the screen. The study showed that the children's eye movements were consistently drawn away from the text and to the animated characters whenever they moved. Silhouettes without faces proved substantially less distracting than silhouettes with faces. It was also noted that the character speaking drew all of the eye movements.

Oestberg, O. *Fatigue in clerical work with CRT computer terminals.* Paper presented at Manniskor och Datoren, Stockholm, Sweden, 1974.

> Discusses effects of room illumination on visual fatigue. Finds that for people wearing eyeglasses, a viewing distance of about 13 inches tended to reduce visual fatigue from eye convergence and accomodation, while 20 inches was recommended as a viewing distance for those with normal vision.

Watts, L., and Nisbet, J. *Legibility in children's books: A review of research.* London: NFER Publishers, 1974.

> Discusses legibility research and legibility factors as they relate to children's reading.

1975

McConkie, G., and Rayner, K. The span of the effective stimulus during a fixation in reading. *Perception & Psychophysics,* 1975, *17* (6), 578-586.

> Reports a study that found that subjects acquire word length information on a CRT display of text at least 12 to 15 character positions to the right of the fixation point. This seemed to influence saccade length. Specific letter and word perception was accurate no more than ten spaces to the right of the fixation point.

Rayner, K. Visual attention in reading: Eye movements reflect cognitive processes. *Memory and Cognition,* 1975, *5* (4), 443-448.

> Reports a study using computer controlled displays and computer data gathering that found main verbs to be fixated longer than other words in sentences.

1976

Just, M., and Carpenter, P. Eye fixations and cognitive processes. *Cognitive Psychology,* 1976, *8,* 441-480.

> Finds that when subjects are shown computer controlled pictures and print, print that conflicts with pictures on the same screen takes longer to read.

1977

Hoover, T. *Empirical study of reading and comprehension as a function of CRT display.* 1977. (ED 161 002)

> Reports research in which college students read and answered questions about four passages displayed on CRT. Two passages were presented with text on every line and two were presented with text on every other line. No differences in rate or comprehension were found, although rates were not high and comprehension scores were very low.

1978

Krebs, M. Design principles for the use of color in displays. *SID international symposium digest of technical papers.* Los Angeles, CA: Society for Information Display, 1978.

> Presents a detailed, technical discussion of the effects of color in electronic displays.

Rayner, K. Eye movements in reading and information processing. *Psychological Bulletin,* 1978, *85,* 618-660.

> Summarizes research Rayner and his colleagues conducted on eye movement. In most of the studies, readers read from computer controlled CRT displays, so findings are relevant to that medium.

1979

Merrill, P., and Bunderson, V. *Guidelines for employing graphics in a videodisc training delivery system.* 1979. (ED 196 413)

Gives guidelines for use of color, line, motion, and pictures (as opposed to text) and presents questions for research.

Moore, M., Nawrocki, L., and Simutis, Z. *The instructional effectiveness of three levels of graphics displays for computer assisted instruction.* 1979. (ED 178 057)

Reports research with CRT reading of text supplemented with one of three levels of graphics. Low level graphics (such as line drawings or boxes around text) as helpful as medium or high level graphics were.

1980

Bauer, D., and Cavonius, C. Improving the legibility of visual display units through contrast reversal. In E. Grandjean and E. Vigliani (Eds.), *Ergonomic aspects of visual display terminals.* London: Taylor & Francis, 1980.

Describes research in which subjects were asked to read nonsense words and then type them into a terminal or to detect discrepancies between what was presented on the terminal and what was printed on paper. The text was presented either in positive or negative contrast. Subjects preferred the negative contrast (dark text on an illuminated light background).

Cakier, A., Hart, D., and Stewart, T. *Visual display terminals.* New York: John Wiley & Sons, 1980.

Discusses display devices exhaustively. Contains an excellent chapter on the ergonomics of using video display terminals, as well as a checklist for determining the effectiveness of displays.

Galitz, W. *Human factors in office automation.* Atlanta, GA: Life Office Management Association, 1980.

Contains a good (but somewhat dated) collection of research on human factors in office design. The role of room illumination in relation to visual display terminals is discusssed in detail. Includes a number of specific recommendations teachers could use to determine the optimal location of microcomputers within a classroom or lab. In general, recommends setting the computer on the higher lumination or brightness setting so the lumination of the screen is slightly higher than that of the room in general.

Radl, G. Experimental investigations for optimal presentation-mode and colours of symbol on the CRT screen. In E. Grandjean and E. Vigliani (Eds.), *Ergonomic aspects of visual display terminals.* London: Taylor & Francis, 1980.

Reports research in which adults transcribed letters from CRT displays for five minutes using two different types of contrast—illuminated letters on a dark background (positive contrast) and dark letters on an illuminated background (negative contrast). Subjects preferred negative contrast displays.

Terrana, T., Merluzzi, F., and Gindici, E. Electromagnetic radiation emitted by visual display units. In E. Grandjean and E. Vigliani (Eds.), *Ergonomic aspects of visual display terminals.* London: Taylor & Francis, 1980.

Analyzes radiation emissions from CRTs used as computer terminals, showing that X-ray and radio frequency emissions are no higher than natural background levels.

1981

Darnell, M.J., and Neal, A.S. Effect of the amount and format of displayed text on text editing performance. *Human Factors,* 1981, *23,* 220.

Compares the proofreading performance of 28 typists with two types of display. One display used a conventional format of 20 lines of 80 characters each. The second used a format consisting of a single line of only 32 characters. After a moderate amount of practice, no difference was found in text editing performance.

Jelden, D. The microcomputer as a multiuser interactive instructional system. *AEDS Journal,* 1981, *14* (4), 208-217.

Reports a study of 201 college students using CAI. Reading fatigue was reported by 21 percent of the students after 30 minutes of instruction.

Kolers, P., Dachnichy, R., and Ferguson, D. Eye-movement measurement of readability of CRT displays. *Human Factors,* 1981, *23,* 517-527.

Reports research in which eye movement was recorded as college students read texts presented on a CRT in two different spacings, two different character densities, and at five different scrolling rates. Reading speed was 17 percent slower with 40 characters per line than with 80. Pages scrolled at rates 10 or 20 percent faster than the preferred scrolling rate appeared to lead to more efficient scanning with no significant reduction in comprehension.

Matula, R. Effects of visual display units on the eyes: A bibliography (1972-1980). *Human Factors,* 1981, *23* (5), 581.

Provides a complete bibliography on this topic.

Mourant, R., Lakshmanan, R., and Chantadisai, R. Visual fatigue and cathode ray tube display terminals. *Human Factors,* 1981, *23,* 529-540.

Reports two studies of the physical effect of eye fatigue on a CRT and on hard copy. In the first study, two subjects spent four three hour sessions reading. Eye fatigue was measured by indicated durations to move from a near point and focus on a far point (and vice versa). Fatigue was not visible in the hard copy group. In the second study, subjects were measured for two four hour sessions. Measurable eye fatigue was present for the CRT group after two hours.

1982

Bruce, M., and Foster, J. Visibility of colored characters on colored background in viewdata displays. *Visible Language,* 1982, *16* (4), 382-390.

Measures the ability of adult subjects to recognize six combinations of colored letters on colored background. The luminance of each color was found to be a major factor affecting legibility. Concludes that a light color should not be mixed with another light color (white and yellow); that the dark colors (red and blue) should be paired with a light color; and that the medium colors (green and magenta) should be paired with colors from one of the other groups.

Grandjean, E., and Vigilani, E. *Ergonomic aspects of visual display terminals.* London: Taylor & Francis, 1982.

Contains one of the most comprehensive collections of research on VDTs.

Mason, G., Edwards, J., and Shetler, C. *Reading from the cathode-ray tube: A comparison with book-page reading.* Unpublished manuscript, University of Georgia, 1982.

Muter, P., Latremouille, S., Treurniet, W., and Beam, P. Extended reading of continuous text on television screens. *Human Factors,* 1982, *24,* 501-508.

> Reports on thirty-two subjects who read short stories for two hours. Half of the subjects read from a CRT display and half from a book. Both groups were seated comfortably on a couch for the viewing period. Comprehension was found to be the same for both reading groups, but subjects reading from the CRT displays read 28.5 percent slower than those reading from books.

1983

Gould, J., and Grischkowsky, N. Doing the same work with paper and cathode ray tube displays (CRT). *Human Factors,* 1983, *24,* 329-338.

> Reports on twenty-four subjects who proofread from a CRT on one day and from hard copy on another. Physical measures of participants' vision were made, as well as a subjective survey of visual comfort. Proofreading times and accuracy also were measured. There were no significant differences in vision or in ratings of visual fatigue. Proofreading accuracy was no different for the two conditions, but subjects did proofread the paper copy 20 to 30 percent faster.

Gunnarsson, E., and Soderberg, I. Eye strain resulting from VDT work at the Swedish Telecommunications Administration. *Applied Ergonomics,* 1983, *14,* 61-69.

> Studies employees at the Swedish Telecommunciations Administration. The amount of time spent at CRTS was varied between two levels, normal and intensified. Both subjective and physiological measures of visual fatigue were made. Near point accommodation and conversion, indicators of visual fatigue, were greater on days when CRT use was heavy. Verbal reports of fatigue on those days increased.

National Research Council. *Video displays, work and vision.* Washington, DC: National Academy Press, 1983.

> Includes findings from NIOSH studies as well as analyses by many top researchers in the field. Appendix A reviews the research methodology employed in most of the major studies to date and concludes that the findings of most studies are questionable due to poor research techniques. One of the most current and thorough books on the topic of VDTS.

Sauter, S., Gottlieb, M., Jones, K., Dodson, V., and Rohrer, R. Job and health implications of VDT use: Initial results of the Wisconsin-NIOSH study. *Communications of the ACM,* 1983, *26* (4), 284-294.

> Studies the relationship between video terminals and health. The National Institute for Occupational Safety and Health compared 248 office workers using display terminals with 85 office workers doing similar work with printed material. Both physical and subjective measures of stress were recorded. There was little evidence of higher stress among those workers using the CRTS. Most subjective reports of eyestrain were related to inadequate lighting.

Veigh, R. *Television's teletext.* New York: North-Holland, 1983.

> Discusses videotext systems. The videotext industry has attempted to establish display guidelines to improve legibility. The chapter on display standards describes these display guidelines in great detail.

Watson, A., and Ahumada, A. *A look at motion in the frequencey domain.* NASA Technical Memorandum 84352. Moffett Field, CA: Ames Research Center, 1983.

Describes the visual field in terms of spatial and temporal frequency. One of the first attempts to integrate, in detail, the role of temporal conditions to create a unified description of perception. Shows that in order to process motion in displays only a limited amount of information need be processed. Defines a region called the "window of visibility" that defines the limits of visual sensitivity.

1984

Gould, J., and Grischkowsky, N. Doing the same work with hard copy and with CRT terminals. *Human Factors,* 1984, *26,* 323-337.

Potter, M. Rapid serial visual presentation (RSVP); A method for studying language processing. In D. Kieras and M. Just (Eds.), *New methods in reading comprehension research.* Hillsdale, NJ: Erlbaum, 1984.

Salomon, G. Television is "easy" and print is "tough": The differential investment of mental effort in learning as a function of perceptions and attributions. *Journal of Educational Psychology,* 1984, *76,* 647-658.

1985

Chapman, A., and Tipton, J. *The presentation of written passages on television: A comparison of three methods.* Lexington: The Kentucky Network, 1985.

Compares three methods of displaying text on a television screen: scrolling, page by page, and slow reveal (letters print one at a time as if being typed). Display time was held constant for all three methods. No significant differences in comprehension were found. A posthoc study showed that comprehension improved by a third for students reading the same passages on paper.

Daniel, D. *Construct of legibility in the reading environment of a microcomputer.* 1985. (ED 225 908)

Contains an extensive review of previous legibility research in an attempt to determine the relevancy of legibility research to reading from a visual display terminal. A new model for defining legibility in the context of a computer is introduced. Argues that in order to adequately define legibility in the dynamic medium of a computer, a four dimensional construct must be used. Factors of height, width, depth, and time interact to form new parameters of legibility.

Haas, C., and Hayes, J. *Effects of text display variables on reading tasks: Computer screen vs. hard copy.* CDC Technical Report No. 3. Pittsburgh, PA: Carnegie-Mellon University, Communication Design Center, 1985.

Haas, C., and Hayes, J. *Reading on the computer: A comparison of standard and advanced computer display and hard copy.* CDC Technical Report No. 7. Pittsburgh, PA: Carnegie-Mellon University, Communication Design Center, 1985.

Monk, A. (Ed.). *Fundamentals of human-computer interaction.* New York: Academic Press, 1985.

Consists of an outstanding collection of research on communication between humans and computers. Includes much of the groundbreaking research being performed at the University of York in the United Kingdom. Chapter 2 contains one of the most current treatises on reading electronically presented text. The chapter on how to use speech communication is one of the few papers in the field of artificial speech that looks at when and how to apply speech.

Webb, S. *A discussion about the problems of displaying text on televison for maximum reading comprehension.* Lexington, KY: The Kentucky Network, 1985.

Discusses changes in methods used for displaying text on television and possible effects on legibility.

11

The optical era and reading

C omputer technology develops in leaps and bounds. The development of the transistor was one leap, the advent of the microcomputer another. Now, the field is poised on the verge of another leap into the optical era. That move could have profound impact on reading education.

Laserdisks

Optical storage has been with us since the late seventies. Optical disks were first introduced as a medium for storing video information. They were 12 inch diameter plastic disks into which millions of pieces of information had been embedded using a tiny laser. More than 50,000 video frames could be stored on a single disk. This meant that 30 to 60 minutes of video could be stored on the disk, one frame at a time, and then played back just like movie film. Laserdisk players were introduced in 1978 as a consumer item for playing movies.

Interactive videodisks

An offshoot of the analog optical format is the videodisk. With a videodisk, digital data are added to a disk that can be read by a computer. This information contains instructions controlling the playback of video and audio data, allowing segments to be branched based on student input. Videodisks have found a strong niche in industrial training. However, the cost of videodisk production remains high, particularly when film footage must be created. In some types of training, flight simulation for example, the industry can afford to underwrite the cost of developing the material. Public schools, however, require low cost materials. Although a few excellent instructional videodisks have been developed for schools, major educational publishers generally do not produce videodisks. The volume of available videodisk courseware and players in schools is far below that needed to have a major instructional impact on public education. Moreover, new optical disk formats, particularly CDI (compact disk interactive), are now providing alternative optical formats for instruction.

Compact disks

In 1983 a slightly scaled down optical disk, called a CD ROM (Compact Disk Read Only Memory) was introduced in Europe and the United States. Like its cousin the laserdisk, CD ROM is an optical storage medium designed to hold a vast amount of information. The development of compact disks represented an important breakthrough in storage technology because they were designed to store digital rather than analog data. Computers are digital devices. Consequently, compact disks can be used to store text rather than just video.

The first type of digital data to be encoded on compact disks was audio information in the form of music. Digital audio made it possible to achieve very high levels of musical fidelity. In addition, optical disks are touched only by a light beam during the read process, and therefore do not wear as do traditional records. Consequently, when commercially produced audio compact disks were introduced in 1983, they received rapid acceptance. Compact disks are expected to outdistance records and cassettes as the primary medium for storing music.

CD ROM

Though capable of storing vast amounts of data, early versions of the compact disk suffered from some basic limitations. The digital information was occasionally misread by the player. An error might occur only once in every 10,000 bytes of information. While such a tiny error would be completely inaudible in an audio signal, it would wreak havoc in a computer program. Consequently, few computer storage applications were attempted. This problem was quickly overcome, and, in 1985, both Sony and Phillips introduced compact optical disks specifically for use in the computer industry. This format of the optical disk was called CD ROM. CD ROMS contained digital information like CD audiodisks, but used a complex system of error correction to ensure incredible accuracy.

Each CD ROM disk has the capacity to store over 600 million bytes of information, or approximately 250,000 pages of text. This incredible volume of storage constitutes a dramatic leap in storage capacity for small computers. Optical disks will enable microcomputers to access huge databases of information, as large as those of most mainframe computers. Moreover, the information can be searched and retrieved in a matter of seconds.

In late 1985, Grolier introduced one of the first commercial CD ROM disks. Grolier had put its entire encyclopedia on one compact disk, with room to spare. Any item, anywhere in the encyclopedia, could be searched and accessed in less than two seconds. All that was required were a standard microcomputer and a CD ROM player. The price for the compact disk itself was less than $200.

In 1987, Microsoft introduced Bookshelf, a CD ROM library of ten reference works (dictionary, almanac, etc.) for IBM or compatible personal computers. The Bookshelf sells for less than $300.

Compact disk interactive

In March 1986, the first major technical conference on CD ROM technology was held in Seattle. This conference was to be a critical benchmark for CD ROM technology because Sony and Phillips made a startling announcement. They announced a new format for an entirely new type of machine. They called this format CDI (compact disk interactive). CDI was intended to be a truly interactive format, combining all the capabilities of CD ROM and CD audio. In addition, CDI would have the capability for both still and running video. The most exciting aspect of this technology was that a CDI player was not a computer peripheral. It might best be described as a Trojan Computer. The device would look like a CD audio player and would play CD audio disks. However, a fully equipped microcomputer was housed inside. By running a cable to the TV set, whole libraries of information as well as video could be viewed. The information could be accessed and manipulated using a simple hand controller, already found on current audio players.

CDI machines are not expected to be completed and available to the public until sometime in late 1987 or early 1988. As of this writing, they are only a set of technical specifications. However, given the record of the companies involved and the existing success of optical technology, there is little reason to doubt that this technology will arrive.

A new publishing medium

In looking at the cost of compact disks as a publishing medium, it is important to look at the cost of the medium as opposed to the cost of the information. In 1986, several major factories for premastering and mastering compact disks were created in the United States. These facilities can stamp out one compact disk in less than five seconds at a reproduction cost of less than $5. That is equivalent to publishing 250,000 pages of information flawlessly at a printing cost of less than one cent for every 5,000 pages.

Though optical reproduction is highly cost efficient, one should not conclude that books, encyclopedias, databases, and other forms of information will suddenly become dramatically cheaper. The information itself must be paid for first. For example, a medical textbook might still cost as much in optical form because of the value of the information. However, in situations where a copyright can be obtained inexpensively, or where reproduction rights need not be purchased—as in the case of public documents—the cost of publication is dramatically reduced.

The promise

In the second edition of *Computer Applications in Reading,* we hinted that computers may take the place of books in the distant future. With the advent of optical technology, the future looks considerably closer. We have taken a dramatic leap beyond the electronic book, to the electronic encyclopedia, perhaps the electronic library. Major reference works such as ERIC, the Library of Congress Card Catalog, and the Readers Guide to Periodicals have already been put on CD ROM disks. If these and other references are put in CD ROM or CDI format, the impact upon schools could be dramatic. Given the reproduction costs previously described, it is reasonable to assume that an entire reference library could be put in a single classroom (if not at every student's desk) for a low cost. Students would have access to enormous volumes of information that could be instantly searched and retrieved. This could potentially change the entire nature of student research in schools.

Textbook use in public schools may be affected as well. It is debatable whether putting textbooks on-line would make them more affordable. The information still must be paid for. However, because optical textbooks would be interactive, they would be significantly more powerful as learning tools. One company has already created (not yet released for sale) a segment of a textbook that uses interactive optical technology to teach the history of the J.F. Kennedy presidential administration. Key terms, when pointed to in the text, are defined using text and audio. A picture, when pointed to, suddenly comes to life showing an actual film clip of President Kennedy. By pointing at a reference in the text to Kennedy's famous Berlin speech, the student can suddenly hear and see the actual speech.

Limitations

There are still a number of factors that inhibit the use of CD ROM and CDI technology. First, for optical technology to affect large numbers of students, low cost CD players must become available. The development of CD players for noneducational purposes could make this a reality. Second, low cost, portable, high resolution monitors will need to become available. Finally, a sufficient body of low cost educational optical courseware will need to be created to justify the cost of schools purchasing CD devices.

Getting information on optical technology

The CD optical technology industry is new, and detailed information is difficult to find. Only vague references have been made to optical technology in educational journals. The best single source of information on CD ROM technology at this time is *CD ROM: The New Papyrus* (Lambert & Ropiequet, 1986). This hefty textbook was published in association with the first international conference on CD ROM technology sponsored by Microsoft. The text contains both general and technical papers presented at the conference. Another good source of information about optical technology is an industry newsletter entitled *CD Data Report* (Langley Publications, 1350 Beverly Road, Suite 115-124, McLean, Virginia 22101).

As optical technology emerges, several computer magazines are beginning to devote space to this topic. The entire April 1986 issue of *Byte* magazine was devoted to optical technology. More consumer oriented magazines such as *Video Review* and *High Technology* are beginning to carry reports on optical technology.

Because optical technology is so new, no formal research studies can be cited as to its educational effectiveness. But optical technology creates the potential for putting enormous quantities of reference information in a student's hands. Yet many students currently do not know how to use reference materials in conventional text formats. How should we teach them to deal with electronic versions of these reference materials? How should these electronic reference materials be designed so that students can easily use them? Recent research in the areas of artificial intelligence, ergonomics, and information science may be helpful in answering these questions.

Chapter eleven contains references about optical technology and its possible applications to education and reading.

References

1985

Blair, D., and Maron, M. An evaluation of retrieval effectiveness for a full-text document-retrieval system. *Communication of the ACM,* March 1985, 289-299.

> Presents a fairly technical analysis of problems of retrieving large text documents from large electronic data bases.

Lee, E., and MacGregor, J. Minimizing user search time in menu retrieval systems. *Human Factors,* 1985, *27* (2), 157-162.

Roth, J. *Essential guide to CD ROM.* Westport, CT: Meckler Publishing, 1985.

Schuford, R. CD ROMs and their kin. *Byte,* November 1985, 137-150.

1986

Bairstow, J. CD-ROM: Mass storage for the mass market. *High Technology,* October 1986, 44-49.

> Explains clearly and concisely CD ROM and CDI technology. Discusses the potential effects of cheap mass optical storage on the business and consumer markets.

Browning, E. Sony's perseverance helped it win market for mini-CD players. *Wall Street Journal,* February 27, 1986, 1, 10.

> Provides a brief history of the development of the compact disk.

Chen, P. The compact disk ROM: How it works. *IEEE Spectrum,* April 1986, 44-49.

Lambert, S., and Ropiequet, S. (Eds.). *CD ROM: The new papyrus.* Redmond, WA: Microsoft Press, 1986.

> Provides a definitive source on CD ROMs. Contains information about CD ROM, videodisk, CDI, theoretical issues about the design of electronic media, and electronic text as instructional text.

McGinty, T. Text crunching. *Electronic Learning,* 1986, *5* (6), 22-26.

> Discusses the possible uses of CD ROM disks for educational applications.

Oren, T., and Kildall, G. The compact disk ROM. *Applications Software,* April 1986, 49-54.

Raleigh, L. Interactive compact discs: The next step in CD technology. *Classroom Computer Learning,* September 1986, 46-51.

> Provides a brief overview of CDI technology and plans to develop CDI products.

Waurzyniak, P. Optical discs. *Info World,* December 1986, 51-55.

> Reviews CD ROM technology, including WORM (write once, read many).

Zoelick, B. CD ROM software development. *Byte,* May 1986, 177-192.

> Discusses file structure as it relates to CD ROM development. Given the enormous number of files a CD can hold, the design of the index to those files is critical.

1987

Brewer, B. Read when you are, CD-I. *PC World,* 1987, *5* (4), 252-255.

Presents the many features of CD-I, including audio, video, and interactive with a personal computer.

Byers, T. Built by association. *PC World,* 1987, *5* (4), 244-250.

Discusses the concept of hypertext as a means to access the large amounts of data found in CD ROM devices. Hypertext is "a text storage system in which the documents and their context...[are] indexed not alphabetically or numberically but by association—the way we think."

Helgerson, L. Optical discs: New storage media for education. *T.H.E. Journal,* 1987, *14* (7), 50-51.

Reviews the latest development in the fields of interactive video, CD-ROM, and CD-I in education.

McManus, R. The reference ROM. *PC World,* 1987, *5* (4), 236-239.

Discusses Microsoft Corporation's Bookshelf, a CD ROM database that uses a personal computer and word processor to access information from such sources as *The American Heritage Dictionary. The World Almanac,* and *Chicago Manual of Style.*

12

The future: Some predictions

P ast editions of this book included predictions about the future of computers in reading. Our initial predictions were from the vantage point of 1978 (first edition). In 1982 (second edition) we tried again. Nearly everything we predicted came to pass sooner than we had predicted.

However, a few of our predictions were wrong because we did not anticipate the problems the schools would face in using computers for reading education. First, teachers and administrators are struggling to stay abreast of computer based education developments and ahead of student and parent inquiries. Many teachers and administrators are unaware of available reading programs. Second, software developments have not kept pace with hardware developments. Hardware developments follow the rules of science and the mandates of business economics; software developments follow the educational economics of school boards and the preferences of buyers who may or may not be knowledgeable about computers and software. Finally, we are seldom able to match the capabilities of the computer to the diverse needs of learners. Our computer based reading programs have been slow to address what we know about the learning and teaching processes in reading. Even though these problems will not disappear soon, we are enough encouraged by our many successful predictions to venture a few more.

A prediction: More simulations

A simulation is a model of a physical system that operates with clearly defined rules. Using a computer based model of the physical system, students can conduct experiments that help them understand the behaviors of the system. When students become able to optimize the operation of the system, it is assumed learning has occurred.

Today's simulations, with respect to reading education, can be grouped into three categories: simulations that *cannot* readily support the reading curriculum, simulations that *can* support the reading curriculum, and simulations that *do* support the reading curriculum.

The first type of simulation might possibly support the classroom curriculum if it contained more accompanying texts or other noncomputer instructional support materials. This simulation does not directly relate to anything found in the curriculum; it is often gamelike. To make such simulations usable, teachers must help students meet reading demands, develop suitable instructional strategies, create supportive materials, and figure out how and where the simulation might support some part of the curriculum.

Although the second type of simulation can support the reading curriculum, it is not so designed. This type provides text based materials such as student manuals, teacher's guides, handouts, and worksheets to support the simulation content. However, the teacher must determine how and when to use it in the curriculum.

The third type of simulation is designed to support the reading curriculum or any other curriculum of the school. Text based materials and the computer simulations they accompany are carefully coordinated parts of the curriculum. Students use such a simulation as they would any other curriculum based activity. Unfortunately, few simulations are available that have text based coordination with the curriculum because simulations that are an integral part of classroom texts have not been produced.

Simulations often increase the work of content area teachers and reading educators. Not only must teachers help students meet the reading demands of their classroom text, but also the reading demands of the additional text for the simulation presented on the screen, its documentation, and any instructional support materials. In spite of this, most experts predict that there will be an increase in the use of simulations as reading tasks to be accomplished in school.

A prediction: More artificial intelligence in reading

Artificial intelligence (AI) researchers attempt to engineer thinking and learning and to simulate or model intelligent functions of humans. One function they are trying to simulate is reading. There are at least two reasons why this is a most difficult task.

First, we are still struggling to understand how humans read. Since reading professionals and cognitive scientists do not understand many of the reading processes, they cannot create a program to emulate those processes. One day computers may "read," but not until we discover more about how humans read.

Second, computers store and manipulate information electromagnetically with basically unitary processing; humans store and manipulate information electrochemically, completing many processing functions at once. Although new multiple processing computers have been developed, they are still very limited in capability when compared to the human brain.

As mentioned earlier in this text, many educational publishers claim to have AI components in their programs. Clearly, today's computers are not genuinely able to think and learn. The computer merely reconstructs the programer's algorithms when a problem is presented.

We predict that claims about the use of artificial intelligence will increase. Reading educators should use their critical reading and reasoning skills in interpreting these claims.

A prediction: Programing and authoring

If teachers wish to create or modify programs to meet the instructional needs of their own students, they have four choices: hire a programer, learn a programing language, learn an authoring language, or purchase a program that contains an authoring option.

The first option is unlikely; seldom is creating or modifying a program an easy task, and good programers are expensive. Furthermore, quality instructional computer programs with text and graphics take a lot of time and effort to produce – not to mention the time required to learn a programing language such as LOGO, BASIC, or Pascal. Of course, teachers may choose to use an authoring language such as SUPERPILOT. While authoring languages are easier to use than programing languages, learning how to use them to develop a program requires a great deal of time. However, schools can purchase software programs that offer authoring options in the programs. Authoring options permit a teacher to delete, add, or modify the content of a program, and they are relatively easy to learn. For example, an elementary teacher can use an authoring system to enter the weekly spelling or basal reader lesson words into a drill and practice vocabulary program. Since most teachers seem to want to add, delete, or modify the contents of their program to meet the instructional needs of their students, we predict that more educational software publishers will include authoring options in their programs.

A prediction: More telecommunications and satellite communications

As computer use increases in the schools, computer based telecommunications and satellite communications will become more readily available.

Telecommunications

To use the most common form of telecommunications, microcomputer users can plug a modem (*mo*dulate/*dem*odulate device) into the computer and a nearby telephone jack, dial and connect with a host computer, and then exchange information with the host computer and other computers connected with the host computer. Teachers and students using modems and microcomputers can receive and exchange information on virtually any topic.

One type of telecommunication, the on-line database or teletext, can be reached through subscription to a database or teletext service. This type of telecommunication service can provide students access to general, all purpose information (e.g., political, business, sports) and bibliographic information (e.g., magazines, newspapers, journals). Since information is generally delivered in text format, students who have trouble reading their texts may have more trouble reading information from telecommunication sources. The largest telecommunication source accessible from the classroom is CompuServe, which provides access to many educational forums and databases: learning and physical disabilities, educational research, EPIE, foreign language, LOGO, Academic American Encyclopedia, and educational travel, to name but a few.

In the future, reading and content area teachers can expect their duties to include helping students learn to read and use on-line databases and forums.

Satellites

Satellite communication is just beginning. One example of satellite communication is software distribution via satellite to schools. Television stations will broadcast the software to a satellite, and schools or school districts will access the software with satellite receivers (dishes). (For more information see *Electronic Learning,* 1978, *6* (6), 6.)

A prediction: Robots in reading

It seems appropriate that the third edition of *Computer Applications in Reading* should end with robots (from the Czech word *robota,* which means forced labor or slave). In the earlier editions we speculated on the future, but we made no mention of robots. However, since reading teachers have always used every means imaginable to teach reading, it should surprise few readers that robots may someday be used to teach reading.

If you have doubts about robots in reading, consider these recent events: an orchestra in Japan featured a robot guest organist, two robots played Ping Pong in San Francisco, a robot sheared 200 sheep in Australia, and a robot in California listened to music being played and then printed out the score.

We predict much greater use of robots in reading programs of the future as they approach "human equivalence" (a term coined by the robotist Hans Moravec at Carnegie Mellon University). It takes only a little imagination to see students programing robots to compete in classroom treasure hunts. Of course, students will have to program the robots to read clues, predict solutions, and relate the proper sequences of instructions. We think students will love it and improve their own reading in the process.

Simulation references

1979

Boysen, V., and Thomas, R. Interactive computer simulation of reading skill weaknesses. *Journal of Computer-Based Instruction,* 1979, *5* (3), 45-49.

Describes the development of simulations for use in reading assessment using the PLATO IV terminal and Tutor authoring language.

1982

Gross, E. *Computer simulations stimulate inductive thinking.* A presentation at the twentieth annual conference of the Association for Educational Data Systems, Orlando, Florida, May 1982.

1983

Anderson, R. Innovative microcomputer games and simulations: An introduction. *Simulations & Games,* 1983, *14* (1), 3-10.

Edwards, L. Teaching higher level thinking skills through computer courseware. *AEDS Monitor,* 1983, *21,* 28-30.

States that computer based simulations and problem solving software can help students develop higher level thinking skills when teachers learn how, when, and with whom they should be used.

Jones, K. Simulations for language skills. *Reading-Canada-Lecture,* 1983, *2* (1), 63-68.

Snyder, T., and Dockerman, D. Getting to "Aha!" *Electronic Learning,* 1984, *3* (8), 26, 28.

Claims that computer based simulations, most of which require students to read text that accompanies the simulation, can be successful for many reasons. Discusses some aspects of a simulation's effectiveness in the classroom.

Willis, J., and Kuchinskas, G. Simulations = fun + language learning. *Computers, Reading and Language Arts*, 1983, *1* (3), 24-26.

>Discusses the history of educational simulations, their theoretical foundations, and instructional advantages. Describes The Oregon Trail, Change Agent, Tribbles, and The Human Adventure.

1984

Balajthy, E. Computer simulations and reading. *The Reading Teacher*, 1984, *37* (7), 590-593.

>Explains that simulations offer much for reading, language arts, and English teachers. While most simulations are for science and social studies, they still involve language activities. Reading teachers can help students better use simulations by assuring that students can read and understand the text.

Bronson, R. Computer simulation: "What is it and how is it done?" *Byte*, March 1984, 95-101.

1985

Hallgren, R. Systematic development of a computer simulation program. *Electronic Learning*, 1985, *5* (2), 17-20.

1986

Brady, P. Computer simulations and reading instruction. *The Computing Teacher*, 1986, *14* (2), 34-36.

>Introduces the reader to the simulation "Where in the world is Carmen San Diego." This simulation provides practice on the reference skill of locating information and the reading comprehension skills of attending to detail, recognizing cause and effect, and drawing inferences.

Price, R., and Sassi, A. Sailing in search of whales. *Electronic Learning*, 1986, *5* (5), 62.

>Reviews The Voyage of the Mini (Holt, Rinehart and Winston). This interactive videodisk program contains some of the first simulations present with video (film). Reading teachers will find the videodisk presentations of interest, as well as the student guides and workbooks.

Artificial intelligence references

1979

Shank, R. Philosophical perspectives in artificial intelligence. In M. Ringle (Ed.), *Philosophical perspectives in artificial intelligence*. Atlantic Highlands, NJ: Humanities Press, 1979.

1981

Wilson, K., and Bates, M. Artificial intelligence in computer-based language instruction. *The Volta Review*, 1981, *83*, 336-349.

1982

Moursund, D. Artificial mind (editor's message). *The Computing Teacher*, 1982, *9* (9), 3-4.

Shank, R. *Dynamic memory: A theory of reminding and learning in computers and people*. Cambridge, MA: Cambridge University Press, 1982.

Schank, R. *Reading and understanding: Teaching from the perspective of artificial intelligence*. Hillsdale, NJ: Erlbaum, 1982.

>Discusses the links between artificial intelligence and practical as well as theoretical issues surrounding teaching children to read.

Waltz, D. Artificial intelligence. *Scientific American*, 1982, *247* (4), 118-135.

Winston, P., and Brown, R. (Eds.). *Artificial intelligence: An MIT perspective*, volumes 1 and 2. Cambridge, MA: MIT Press, 1982.

1984

Dehn, N. An AI perspective on reading comprehension. In J. Flood (Ed.), *Understanding reading comprehension*. Newark, DE: International Reading Association, 1984.

McGrath, D. Artificial intelligence: A tutorial for educators. *Electronic Learning*, 1984, *4* (1), 39-43.

> Offers educators an easy to read explanation of AI concepts and presents some examples of AI programs.

1985

Balajthy, E. Artificial intelligence and the teaching of reading and writing by computers. *Journal of Reading*, 1985, *29* (1), 23-32.

> Discusses AI and its potential impact on reading as well as what teachers can do to help foster future development of AI principles in reading software.

Brady, H. Artificial intelligence: What's in it for educators? *Classroom Computer Learning*, 1985, *6* (4), 26-29.

> Covers expert systems as well as language and image processing as they relate to education.

Brady, H. Hang on to the power to imagine: An interview with Joseph Weizenbaum. *Classroom Computer Learning*, 1985, *6* (3), 24-27.

> Presents an evocative interview with a seminal figure in artificial intelligence and a critic of some computer applications in the schools.

1987

Burns, D. REMark: Beyond expert systems. *PC World*, 1987, *5* (4), 63, 66, 68, 72-73.

> Questions the ability of AI programs to totally emulate intelligence if they cannot imitate human intuition.

Programing and authoring references

1979

Spitler, C., and Corgan, V. Rules for authoring computer assisted instruction programs. *Educational Technology*, 1979, *19* (11), 12-20.

1981

Jelden, D. A CAI "coursewriter" system for the microcomputer. *AEDS Journal*, 1981, *44* (3), 17-26.

Scandura, J. Microcomputer systems for authoring diagnosis and instruction in rule based subject mater. *Educational Technology*, 1981, *21* (1), 13-19.

> Describes a system of task analysis called structural learning theory, then relates this theory to attempts to develop microcomputer based authoring systems.

Wagner, W. Author languages: Instruction without programming. *Classroom Computer News*, 1981, *1* (6), 42-43.

> Defines what an authoring language is and describes briefly eight authoring languages currently available (circa 1981).

Wise, W. Improving user/machine interaction. *AEDS Journal,* 1981, *15* (1), 23-30.
Discusses educational concepts bearing on the ease of interaction between users and their computer programs. Concepts reviewed are typographical cuing, advanced organizers, paced output, contextual clues, and conceptual hierarchies.

1982

Merrill, D. Doing it with authoring systems. *Educational Technology,* 1982, *22* (5), 36-38.
Discusses the hierarchy of computer languages from machine code to the authoring language PILOT, then compares this to a hierarchy of educational and psychological theory. Concludes that both authoring languages and specific instructional templates are required for the development of true authoring systems.

1983

Chan, J. What micros do for reading comprehension. *The Reading Teacher,* 1983, *36* (7), 692-693.
Explains how computer programing may help students develop comprehension skills such as details, sequence and organization, perceiving relationships, comparison and contrast, and predicting outcomes.

Mason, G. Computer use doesn't require sophistication in programming. *The Reading Teacher,* 1983, *37* (3), 329-330.
Suggests several books teachers can use to learn more about writing computer programs.

Wepner, Shirley. Computer flowcharts: Road maps to reading skills. *Computers, Reading and Language Arts,* 1983, *1* (2), 14-17.
Illustrates the use of flowcharts to help students learn sequential organization of ideas, recognize main idea, identify supporting details, understand flowcharting arrangement, and recognize critical words.

1984

Clements, D., and Gulla, D. Effects of computer programming on young children's cognition. *Journal of Educational Psychology,* 1984, *76* (6), 1051-1058.

Dickinson, J. Write your own adventure stories. *Teaching and Computers,* January 1984, 25-29.
Presents a step by step plan for writing and programing an interactive adventure story with upper elementary students. Includes ideas on teaching plot, setting, scenario, and developing characters.

1985

Bork, A., Pomicter, N., Peck, M., and Veloso, S. Toward coherence in learning to program. *AEDS Monitor,* 1985, *24,* 16-19.
Explains that learning to program can lead to learning beyond programing if programing is part of a coherent, integrated curriculum.

Linn, M. The cognitive consequences of programming instruction in classrooms. *Educational Researcher,* 1985, *14* (5), 14-29.

Newkirk, T. Writing and programming: Two modes of composing. *Computers, Reading and Language Arts,* 1985, *2* (2), 40-43.
Discusses the parallels between LOGO activities and writing prose.

Richgels, D. Five easy steps in microcomputer programming. *Computers, Reading and Language Arts,* 1985, *2* (2), 40-43.

> Presents an instructional approach on how to teach BASIC for purposes of programing reading software.

Schubert, N. Reading teachers as programmers: Writing computer assisted instruction. *The Reading Teacher,* 1985, *39* (9), 930-932.

> Explains that teachers can write CAI programs in many reading instruction areas. Demonstrates a compound word program.

Telecommunication references

1982

Tydeman, J., Lipinski, H., Adler, R., Nylan, M., and Zwimpfy, L. *Teletex and videotex in the United States.* New York: McGraw-Hill, 1982.

1983

Nerby, C., and Paradis, E. Micros compensate for varied reading levels. *Journal of Reading,* 1983, *27* (3), 272.

> Presents databases for storing information about stories for students to use in story selection as ways to enhance reading interest.

Paisley, W. Computerizing information: Lessons of a videotex trial. *Journal of Communication,* 1983, *33,* 153-161.

Quinn, C., Mehan, H., Levin, J., and Black, S. Real education in non-real time: The use of electronic message systems for instruction. *Instructional Science,* 1983, *11,* 313-327.

> Discusses the use of E-mail (electronic message systems) for instruction.

Robinson, B. *Reading and the video screen.* 1983. (ED 257 429)

> Discusses the potential of teletext and interactive cable television to help educators. Includes forty references.

1984

Akers, J., and Vanis, B. The Nebraska reading retrieval system (NRRS): A microcomputer assisted system for writing individual reading programs. *Computers, Reading and Language Arts,* 1984, *1* (4), 23-26.

> Explains how a statewide database allows teachers and schools to exchange reading information and activities for corrective and remedial purposes.

Butcher, D. Online searching: How to get instant information. *Electronic Learning,* 1984, *4* (3), 39-40, 90.

> Provides information about on-line databases for school use.

Casteel, C. Computer skill banks for classroom and clinic. *The Reading Teacher,* 1984, *38* (3), 294-297.

> Describes the use of computer based skill banks, material banks, assessment banks, and banks for prescriptive suggestions.

Neuman, S. Teletext/videotex: The future of the print media. *Journal of Reading,* 1984, *27* (4), 340-344.

> Reviews the state of teletext and videotex. Teletext refers to noninteractive information sent to television viewers (subscribers). Teletex refers to interactive on-line systems.

Pollard, J., and Holznagel, D. *Electronic mail.* 1984. (ED 248 880)

Shea, G. Information services: The new frontier of communication. *Electronic Learning,* 1984, *4* (3), 33-34, 88-89.
> Provides an overview of telecommunication opportunities available to schools that have computers.

1985

Alber, A. *Videotex/teletext: Principles and practices.* New York: McGraw-Hill, 1985.
> Provides a general overview of today's electronic information services.

Blurton, C. Enhance your students' thinking, problem solving, and research skills. *AEDS Monitor,* 1985, *23,* 8-9.
> Discusses how databases can be used to encourage thinking skills.

Crook, C. Electronic messaging and the social organization of information. *Quarterly Newsletter of the Laboratory of Comparative Human Cognition,* 1985, *7* (3), 65-69.
> Discusses how information is transmitted in an electronic message environment.

Slatta, R. The banquet's set. *Electronic Education,* 1985, *4* (4), 12-13.
> Presents the major electronically accessible resource databases, including CompuServe, Delphi, Dialog, EduNet, MDC, System Development Corporation, and In-Search.

1986

Duranti, A. Framing discourse in a new medium: Openings in electronic mail. *Quarterly Newsletter of the Laboratory of Comparative Human Cognition,* 1986, *8* (2), 64-71.
> Analyzes E-mail traffic between an instructor and students. Suggests some implications for E-mail in schools. Includes many E-mail references.

Scott, B. Mind meetings. *On-Line Today,* 1986, *5* (8), 12-16.
> Describes many educational forums and databases available from CompuServe.

Robot references

1983

Keller, J., and Shannahan, D. Robots in the kindergarten. *The Computing Teacher,* 1983, *10* (9), 66-67.

1984

Barnett, H., and Better, J. The language of robots. *Computers, Reading and Language Arts,* 1984, *1* (4), 35-37, 58.
> Describes using a programable robot (TOPO) to help teach and reinforce language skills, including reading and writing.

Appendix A

Sources of reading and language arts software

Academic Hallmarks
    P.O. Box 998
    Durango, CO 81301
Acorn Software Products, Inc.
    634 N. Carolina Avenue, SE
    Washington, DC 20003
Active Learning Systems
    P.O. Box 1984
    Midland, MI 48640
Activision Home Computer Products, Inc.
    2350 Bayshore Frontage Road
    Mountain View, CA 94043
Addison-Wesley Publishing Company
    2725 Sand Hill Road
    Menlo Park, CA 94025
Advanced Ideas, Inc.
    2902 San Pablo Avenue
    Berkeley, CA 94702
Advanced Technology Applications
    3019 Governor Drive
    San Diego, CA 92122
Adventure International
    P.O. Box 17329
    Longwood, CA 32750
Agency for Instructional Technology
    P.O. Box A
    Bloomington, IN 47402
Agriculture Computer Services
    P.O. Box 5034
    Oregon City, OR 97045
Ahead Designs
    699 N. Vulcan
    Encinitas, CA 92024

Alphanetics Software
    P.O. Box 339
    Forestville, CA 95436
American Educational Computer
    2450 Embarcadero Way
    Palo Alto, CA 94303
American Micro-Media
    P.O. Box 306
    Red Hook, NY 12571
American Peripherals
    122 Bangor Street
    Lindenhurst, NY 11757
American Software Design Company
    7450 Ivyston Avenue, S
    Cottage Grove, MN 55016
Amidon Publications
    1966 Benson Avenue
    St. Paul, MN 55116
Andent
    1000 North Avenue
    Waukegan, IL 60085
Anthistle Systems/Programming
    563 Patricia Drive
    Oakville, Ontario
    Canada L6K 1M4
Apple Computer, Inc.
    10260 Bandley Drive
    Cupertino, CA 95014
Aquarius People Materials
    P.O. Box 128
    Indian Rocks Beach, FL 33535
Artworx Software Company, Inc.
    150 N. Main Street
    Fairport, NY 14450

Ashton-Tate
    3600 Wilshire Boulevard
    Los Angeles, CA 90010
AT&T Bell Laboratories
    6 Corporate Plaza
    Piscataway, NJ 08854
Atari, Inc.
    1265 Borregas Avenue
    Sunnyvale, CA 94086
Athena Software
    727 Swarthmore Drive
    Newark, DE 19711
Automated Simulations
    1988 Leghorn Street
    Mountainview, CA 94043
Avalon Hill/Microcomputer games
    4517 Hartford Road.
    Baltimore, MD 21214
Avante-Garde Publishing Corporation
    37B Commercial Boulevard
    Novato, CA 94947
A/V Concepts Corporation
    30 Montauk Boulevard
    Aokdale, NY 11769
A.V. Systems
    P.O. Box 49210
    Los Angeles, CA 90049
Bainum Dunbar, Inc.
    6427 Hillcroft, Suite 133
    Houston, TX 77081
Bantam Software
    666 Fifth Avenue
    New York, NY 10103
Barron Enterprises
    714 Willow Glen Road
    Santa Barbara, CA 93105
Basics & Beyond, Inc.
    P.O. Box 10
    Amawalk, NY 10501
B.E.A.R., Inc.
    479 Fulton Avenue
    Hempstead, NY 11550
Bede Software, Inc.
    P.O. Box 2053
    Princeton, NJ 08540
Behavioral Engineering
    230 Mount Hermon, Suite 207
    Scotts Valley, CA 95066

Bell Laboratories
    (see AT&T)
Bertamax, Inc.
    101 Nickerson Street, Suite 500
    Seattle, WA 98109
B5 Software
    1024 Bainbridge Plaza
    Columbus, OH 43228
BLS
    2503 Fairlee Road
    Wilmington, DE 19810
Bluebird's Computer Software
    P.O. Box 339
    Wyandotte, MI 48192
Blue Lakes Computing
    3240 University Avenue
    Madison, WI 53705
Blythe Valley Software
    P.O. Box 333
    Oakhurst, CA 93664
Bob Baker Software
    5845 Topp Court
    Carmichael, CA 95608
Bolt, Beranek and Newman, Inc.
    10 Moulton Street
    Cambridge, MA 02238
Book Lures, Inc.
    P.O. Box 9450
    O'Fallon, MO 63366
Borg-Warner Educational Systems
    600 W. University Drive
    Arlington Heights, IL 60004
BrainBank, Inc.
    220 Fifth Avenue
    New York, NY 10001
Brittanica
    (see Encyclopedia Brittanica)
Broderbund Software
    17 Paul Drive
    San Rafael, CA 94903
Buckingham County Schools
    c/o Debra Glowinski
    Dillwyn, VA 23936
Bureau Of Business Practice
    24 Rope Ferry Road
    Waterford, CT 06386
Byte By Byte
    1183 West 1380
    North Provo, UT 84604

Bytes of Learning
        150 Consumers Road
        Toronto, Ontario
        Canada M2J 1P9
C & C Software
        5713 Kentford Circle
        Wichita, KS 67220
Captain Software
        P.O. Box 575
        San Francisco, CA 94107
Cardinal Software
        13646 Jefferson Davis Highway
        Woodbridge, VA 22191
CASA Software
        2103 34 Street
        Lubbock, TX 79411
CBS College Publishing
        383 Madison Avenue
        New York, NY 10017
CBS Software
        One Fawcett Place
        Greenwich, CT 06836
CCC
        (see Computer Curriculum
        Corporation)
Center for Educational
Exper/Dev/Evaluation
        218 Lindquist Center
        University of Iowa
        Iowa City, IA 52242
Chalk Board, Inc.
        3772 Pleasantdale Road
        Atlanta, GA 30340
Chariot Software Group
        3101 Fourth Avenue
        San Diego, CA 92103
Charles Mann & Associates
        55722 Santa Fe Trail
        Yucca Valley, CA 92284
Chicago Systems, Inc.
        P.O. Box 429
        Western Springs, IL 60558
Classifies Software
        8986 S. Overhill
        DeSoto, KS 66018
Class 1 Systems
        17909 Maple
        Lansing, IL 60438

Classroom Consortia Media
        57 Bay Street
        Staten Island, NY 10301
Coeur d'Alene Schools
        311 N. Tenth Street
        Coeur d'Alene, ID 83814
Cognitronics Corporation
        25 Crescent Street
        Stamford, CT 06906
Columbia Computing Services
        8611 S. 212 Street
        Kent, WA 98031
Combase, Inc.
        333 Sibley Street, Suite 890
        St. Paul, MN 55101
Command Data Computer House
        320 Summit
        Milford, MI 48042
Commodore Computer Systems
        1200 Wilson Drive
        West Chester, PA 19380
Comp Ed
        P.O. Box 35461
        Phoenix, AZ 85069
COMPress
        P.O. Box 102
        Wentworth, NH 03282
ComputAbility Corporation
        101 Route 46 E
        Pine Brook, NJ 07058
Compu-Tations
        P.O. Box 502
        Troy, MI 48099
Computer Applications Tomorrow
        P.O. Box 605
        Birmingham, MI 48012
Computer Assisted Instruction, Inc.
        6115 28 Street, SE
        Grand Rapids, MI 49506
Computer Curriculum Corporation
        P.O. Box 10080
        Palo Alto, CA 94303
Computer-Ed
        1 Everett Road
        Carmel, NY 10512
Computer Island
        227 Hampton Green
        Staten Island, NY 10312

Computer applications in reading

Computer Using Educators (CUE)
333 Main Street
Redwood City, CA 94063
Computing Adventures, Ltd.
P.O. Box 15565
Phoenix, AZ 85060
Compuware
15 Center Road
Randolph, NJ 07869
Concept Educational Software
P.O. Box 6184
Allentown, PA 18001
Conduit
The University of Iowa
Oak Dale Campus
Iowa City, IA 52242
Control Data Publishing Company,
Inc.
3601 W. 77 Street
Bloomington, MN 55420
Coronado Courseware
P.O. Box 85271, Suite 171
San Diego, CA 92128
Cove View Press
P.O. Box 810
Arcata, CA 95521
Creative Curriculum, Inc.
15632 Producer Lane
Huntington Beach, CA 92649
Creative Publications
Warehouse
5005 W. 100 Street
Oak Lawn, IL 60453
Cross Educational Software
P.O. Box 1536
Ruston, LA 71270
CSR Computer Systems Research
P.O. Box 45
Avon, CT 06001
CTW Software
1 Lincoln Plaza
New York, NY 10023
Cuenjay
P.O. Box 791
Livermore, CA 94550
Curriculum Applications
P.O. Box 264
Arlington, MA 12174

Cybernetic Information Systems
P.O. Box 9032
Schenectady, NY 12309
Data Command
329 E. Court Street
Kankakee, IL 60901
Datamost
20660 Nordhoff Street
Chatsworth, CA 91311
Datatech Software Systems
19312 E. Eldorado Drive
Aurora, CO 80013
Davidson & Associates
6069 Groveoak Plaza, 12
Rancho Palos Verdes, CA 90274
DCH Educational Software
125 Spring Street
Lexington, MA 02173
DCM Products
(through Radio Shack)
DEC Computing
5307 Lynnwood Drive
West Lafayette, IN 47906
DesignWare
185 Berry Street
San Francisco, CA 94107
Digital Marketing Corporation
2363 Boulevard Circle 8
Walnut Creek, CA 94595
Disney Electronics
6153 Fairmount Avenue
San Diego, CA 92120
Diversified Educational Enterprises
725 Main Street
Lafayette, IN 47901
DLM Teaching Resources
One DLM Park
Allen, TX 75002
Dynacomp, Inc.
1427 Monroe Avenue
Rochester, NY 14618
Dynatek Information Systems
586 Concord Avenue
Williston Park, NY 11596
EAS, Inc.
108 Morgate Circle
Royal Palm Beach, FL 33411
E. David & Associates
22 Russett Lane
Storrs, CT 06268

Educational Activities
 P.O. Box 392
 Freeport, NY 11520
Educational Computing Systems
 106 Fairbanks Road
 Oak Ridge, TN 37830
Educational Media Associates
 342 W. Robert E. Lee
 New Orleans, LA 70124
Educational Software & Marketing
Company
 1045 Outer Park, Suite 110
 Springfield, IL 62704
Educational Teaching Aids
 199 Carpenter Avenue
 Wheeling, IL 60090
Edupro
 445 E. Charleston Road
 Palo Alto, CA 94306
EduSoft
 P.O. Box 2560
 Berkeley, CA 94702
EduTech, Inc.
 303 Lamartine Street
 Jamaica Plain, MA 02130
Edutek Corp.
 P.O. Box 60354
 Palo Alto, CA 94306
EduWare Services
 185 Berry Street
 San Francisco, CA 94107
Electronic Arts
 2755 Campus Drive
 San Mateo, CA 94403
EliteSoftware
 (through Radio Shack)
EMC Publishing
 300 York Avenue
 St. Paul, MN 55101
Encyclopedia Brittanica Educational
Corporation
 425 N. Michigan Avenue
 Chicago, IL 60611
Floppy Enterprises
 716 E. Fillmore
 Eau Claire, WI 54701
Fortier, G.
 6815 Pie IX
 Montreal, Quebec
 Canada H1X 2C7

Friendlee Software
 6041 West View Drive, S
 Orange, CA 92669
M.D. Fullmer & Associates
 1132 San Jose
 San Jose, CA 95120
Funk Vocab-Ware
 4825 Province Line Road
 Princeton, NJ 18540
Gamco Industries
 P.O. Box 1911
 Big Spring, TX 79721
George Earl Software
 1302 S. General McMullen
 San Antonio, TX 78237
Gessler Educational Software
 900 Broadway
 New York, NY 10003
Ginn and Company
 191 Spring Street
 Lexington, MA 02173
Grolier Educational Software
 Sherman Turnpike
 Danbury, CT 06816
Grolier Electronic Publishing
 95 Madison Avenue
 New York, NY 10016
H & H Enterprises
 946 Tennessee
 Lawrence, KS 66044
Harcourt Brace Jovanovich, Publishers
 1250 Sixth Avenue
 San Diego, CA 92101
Hartley Courseware
 P.O. Box 431
 Dimondale, MI 48821
Harvard Associates
 P.O. Box 2579
 Springfield, OH 45501
Hayden Software, Inc.
 600 Suffolk Street
 Lowell, MA 01854
D.C. Heath
 (see DCH Educational Software)
High Technology, Inc.
 P.O. Box B-14665
 Oklahoma City, OK 73106
Hoffman Educational Systems
 1720 Flower Avenue
 Duarte, CA 91010

Holt, Rinehart and Winston
383 Madison Avenue
New York, NY 10017

Hopkins Public Schools, Evaluation
Center
1001 Highway 7
Hopkins, MN 55343

HOSTS Corporation
1800 D Street, Suite 2
Vancouver, WA 98663-3332

Houghton Mifflin Company
One Beacon Street
Boston, MA 02108

Houston Independent School District
Center for Educational
Technology
5300 San Felipe
Houston, TX 77056

HRM Software
175 Tompkins Avenue
Pleasantville, NY 10570

IBM (Systems Products Division)
P.O. Box 1328
Boca Raton, FL 33432

ICT/Taylor
(see
Instructional/Communications
Technology)

Ideatech Company
P.O. Box 62451
Sunnyvale, CA 94088

Imagic
981 University Avenue
Los Gatos, CA 95030

INET Corporation
8450 Central Avenue
Newark, CA 94560

Infocom, Inc.
P.O. Box 478
Cresskill, NJ 07626

Information Unlimited Software, Inc.
2401 Marinship Way
Sausalito, CA 94965

Instructional/Communications
Technology, Inc.
10 Stepar Plaza
Huntington Station, NY 11746

Intellectual Software
798 North Avenue
Bridgeport, CT 06606

InterLearn
P.O. Box 342
Cardiff by the Sea, CA 92007

International Software Marketing
120 E. Washington Street, Suite
121
Syracuse, NY 13202

Island Software
P.O. Box 300
Lake Grove, NY 11755

Jagdstaffel Software
645 Brenda Lee Drive
San Jose, CA 95123

Jamestown Publishers
P.O. Box 6743
Providence, RI 02940

J & S Software
14 Vanderventer Avenue
Port Washington, NY 11050

J/C Enterprises
P.O. Box 441186
Miami, FL 33144

JL Educational & Computer Services
P.O. Box 35142
Dallas TX 75235

Jostens Learning Systems, Inc.
600 W. University Drive
Arlington Heights, IL
60004-1889

Kapstrom Educational Software
5952 Royal Lane, Suite 124
Dallas, TX 75230

Kendall/Hunt Publishing Company
P.O. Box 539
2460 Kerper Boulevard
Dubuque, IA 52004-0539

Koala Technologies Corporation
2065 Junction Avenue
San Jose, CA 95131

Krell Software Corporation
1320 Stony Brook Road
Stony Brook, NY 11790

K-12 Micromedia
172 Broadway
Woodcliff Lake, NJ 07675

Lane Robbins Computer Programs
P.O. Box 365
Somerset, NJ 08873

Laureate Learning Systems
1 Mill Street
Burlington, VT 05401

The Learning Company
545 Middlefield Road, Suite 170
Menlo Park, CA 94025

The Learning Seed Company
21250 N. Andover Road
Kildeer, IL 60047

Learning Unlimited
P.O. Box 12586
Research Triangle Park
Durham, NC 27709

Learning Well
200 S. Service Road
Roslyn Heights, NY 11577

Lewis & Lewis
P.O. Box 84287
San Diego, CA 92138

Lightning Software
P.O. Box 11725
Palo Alto, CA 94306

Like-to-Learn Company
P.O. Box 1904
Sherman, TX 75090

Little Bee Educational Programs
P.O. Box 262
Massillon, OH 44648

Little Shaver Software
267 Bel Forest Drive
Belleair Bluffs, FL 33540

Living Videotext
2432 Charleston Road
Mountain View, CA 94043

Logical Systems, Inc.
P.O. Box 23956
Milwaukee, WI 53223

Logidisque
c.p. 485, succ. Place d'Armas
Montreal, Quebec
Canada H2Y 3H3

Logo Computer Systems
555 W. 57 Street, Suite 1236
New York, NY 10019

Macrotronics, Inc.
1125 N. Golden State Boulevard
Turlock, CA 95380

MCE, Inc.
157 S. Kalamazoo Mall, 250
Kalamazoo, MI 49007

McGraw-Hill
1221 Avenue of the Americas
New York, NY 10020

Michael C. McKenna
Reading Center, Box 142
The Wichita State University
Wichita, KS 67208

MECC
(see Minnesota Educational
Computing Consortium)

Media Basics, Inc.
Larchmont Plaza
Larchmont, NY 10538

Media Materials
2936 Remington Avenue
Baltimore, MD 21211

Megahaus
5703 Oberlin Drive
San Diego, CA 92112

Melcher Software
412 Hollybrook Drive
Midland, MI 48640

Merit Audio Visual
P.O. Box 392
New York, NY 10024

Merry Bee Communications
815 Crest Drive
Omaha, NE 68046

Microcomputer Games
(see Avalon Hill)

Microcomputer Workshops
Courseware
225 Westchester Avenue
Port Chester, NY 10573

Micro-Ed, Inc.
P.O. Box 24156
Minneapolis, MN 55424

MicroLab, Inc.
2699 Skokie Valley Road
Highland Park, IL 60035

Micro Learningware
P.O. Box 307
Mankato, MN 56001

Micromedia Software
276 Oakland Street
Wellesley, MA 02181

Microphys Programs, Inc.
1737 W. Second Street
Brooklyn, NY 11223

Micro Power & Light
12820 Hillcrest Road, #224
Dallas, TX 75230

Computer applications in reading

MicroPro International Corporation
33 San Pablo Avenue
San Rafael, CA 94903
Microrim
3925 159 Avenue, NE
Redmond, WA 98052
Microsoft Consumer Products
10800 N.E. Eighth, Suite 819
Bellevue, WA 98004
Midwest Educational Software
P.O. Box 214
Farmington, MI 48024
Millenium Software
24 E. 22 Street
New York, NY 10010
Milliken Publishing Company
1100 Research Boulevard
St. Louis, MO 63132
Milton Bradley Company
443 Shaker Road
E. Longmeadow, MA 01028
Mindscape, Inc.
3444 Dundee Road
Northbrook, IL 60062
Minnesota Educational Computing
Consortium
3490 Lexington Avenue, N
St. Paul, MN 55112
M-R Information Systems
59 Seminole Avenue
Wayne, NJ 07470
Muse Software
347 N. Charles Street
Baltimore, MD 21201
Joseph Nichols Publisher
P.O. Box 2394
Tulsa, OK 74101
NTS Software
680 N. Arrowhead Drive
Rialto, CA 92367
On-Line Systems
36575 Mudge Ranch Road
Coarsegold, CA 93614
Orange Cherry Media
52 Griffin Avenue
Bedford Hills, NY 10507
Palantir Software
(through Radio Shack)
Peachtree Software
3445 Peachtree Road, NE
Atlanta, GA 30326

Permabound/Hertzber—New Method
Vandalia Road
Jacksonville, FL 62650
Persimmon Software
502C Savannah Street
Greensboro, NC 27406
Personal Bibliographic Software, Inc.
P.O. Box 4250
Ann Arbor, MI 48106
Personal Business Systems
4306 Upton Avenue, S
Minneapolis, MN 55410
Personal Software, Inc.
592 Weddell Drive
Sunnyvale, CA 95086
P.I.E.
1714 Illinois
Lawrence, KS 66044
PLATO/WICAT Systems, Inc.
8800 Queen Avenue, S
Minneapolis, MN 55431
The Porter Company
P.O. Box 415
Pittsford, NY 14534
Potomac Micro Resources, Inc.
P.O. Box 277
Riverdale, MD 20737
Powerbase
(through Radio Shack)
Precision Software
3452 North Ride Circle
Jacksonville, FL 32217
The Professor
959 N.W. 53 Street
Fort Lauderdale, FL 33309
Program Design, Inc.
P.O. Box 4779
Greenwich, CT 06830
The Psychological Corporation
7500 Old Oak Boulevard
Cleveland, OH 44130
Radio Shack Education Division
1400 One Tandy Center
Ft. Worth, TX 76102
RAF Software (Rank and File)
(through Radio Shack)
Random House School Division
201 E. 50 Street
New York, NY 10022
Raptor Systems, Inc.
324 S. Main Street
Stillwater, MN 55082

Ravagraph Co.
3635 E. 3800, S
Salt Lake City, UT 84109
RDA Systems, Inc.
3355 Lenox Road.
Atlanta, GA 30326
Reader's Disgest Microcomputer
Division
Pleasantville, NY 10570
Regents/ALA Company
2 Park Avenue
New York, NY 10016
Research Design Associates
P.O. Box 848
Stony Brook, NY 11790
Resource Software International
330 New Brunswick Avenue
Fords, NJ 08863
Reston Publishing
11480 Sunset Hills Road
Reston, VA 22090
Retail Sciences, Inc.
Corporate Square, Suite 700
Atlanta, GA 30329
Right on Programs (Division of
Computeam)
140 E. Main Street
Huntington, NY 11743
Ritam Corporation
209 N. 16 Street
Fairfield, IA 52556
Samna Corporation
2700 N.E. Expressway Access
Road, NE
Atlanta, GA 30345
Sandpiper Software
P.O. Box 336
Maynard, MA 07154
Scandura Training Systems, Inc.
1249 Greentree Lane
Narberth, PA 19072
Scarborough Systems
25 N. Broadway
Tarrytown, NY 10003
Scholastic, Inc.
Warehouse
1290 Wall Street
West Syndhurst, NJ 07071

School & Home Courseware
301 W. Mesa
Fresno, CA 93704
Schoolhouse Computing, Ltd.
P.O. Box 588
Oak Ridge, Ontario
Canada L0G 1P0
Schoolhouse Software
290 Brighton
Elk Grove, IL 60007
Helen J. Schwartz
P.O. Box 911
Rochester, MI 48063
Science Research Associates
155 N. Wacker Drive
Chicago, IL 60606
Scott, Foresman & Company
1900 E. Lake Avenue
Glenview, IL 60025
Sensible Software
210 S. Woodward, Suite 229
Birmingham, MI 48011
Serendipity Systems, Inc.
419 W. Seneca Street
Ithaca, NY 14850
Seven Hills Software
2310 Oxford Road
Tallahassee, FL 32304
Shenandoah Software
1111 Mt. Clinton Pike
Harrisonburg, VA 22801
Sierra
Sierra On-Line Building
Coarsegold, CA 93614
Simon & Schuster
Sylvan Avenue
Englewood Cliffs, NJ 07632
Simpac Educational Systems
1105 N. Main Street, Suite 11-C
Gainesville, FL 32601
Skillcorp Software, Inc.
1711 McGaw Avenue
Irvine, CA 92714
Sliwa Enterprises, Inc.
2360-J George Washington
Highway
Yorktown, VA 23692
The Small Computer Company
(through Radio Shack)

Computer applications in reading

The Smallsystem Center
P.O. Box 268
New Hartford, CT 06057

Society for Visual Education
1345 Diversey Parkway
Chicago, IL 60614

SoftEd
511 Sycamore Circle
Ridgeland, MS 39157

Softape
10756 Van Owen
North Hollywood, CA 91605

Soft Shoppe
P.O. Box 5223
Mesa, AZ 85201

SOFTSWAP
San Mateo County Office of
Education
333 Main Street
Redwood City, CA 94063

Software Productions
1287 W. King Avenue
Columbus, OH 43212

Software Research Corporation
3939 Quadra Street
Victoria, British Columbia
Canada V8X 1J5

Software Technology for Computers
153 California Street
Newton, MA 02178

South Coast Writing Improvement
Project
University of California
Santa Barbara, CA 93106

Southwest EdPsych Services
P.O. Box 1870
Phoenix, AZ 85001

Spin-a-Test Publishing Company
3177 Hogarth Drive
Sacramento, CA 95827

Spinnaker Software Corporation
1 Kendall Square
Cambridge, MA 02139

Springboard Software, Inc.
7807 Creekridge Circle
Minneapolis, MN 55435

SRA
(see Science Research
Associates)

Sterling Swift Publishing Company
7901 South IH-35
Austin, TX 78744

Stockard Microcomputer Software
1744 Willow Point Drive
Shreveport, LA 71119

Stoneware
1930 Fourth Street
San Rafael, CA 94901

Sunburst Communications, Inc.
39 Washington Street
Pleasantville, NY 10570

SVE
(see Society for Visual
Education)

Synergistic Software
5221 120 Avenue, SE
Bellevue, WA 98006

Sysdata
7671 Old Central Avenue, NE
Minneapolis, MN 55432

Systems Design Lab
2612 Artesia Boulevard
Redondo Beach, CA 90278

Tamarack Software, Inc.
P.O. Box 247
Darby, MT 59829

Tara, Ltd.
P.O. Box 118
Selden, NY 11784

Teacher's Pet Software
P.O. Box 50065
Palo Alto, CA 94303

Teacher Support Software
P.O. Box 7125
Gainesville, FL 32605-7125

The Teaching Assistant
22 Seward Drive
Huntington Station, NY 11746

Teach Yourself by Computer Software
2128 W. Jefferson Road
Pittsford, NY 14534

Teck Associates
P.O. Box 8732
White Bear Lake, MN 55110

Telephone Software Connection
P.O. Box 6548
Torrance, CA 90504

T.H.E.S.I.S.
  P.O. Box 147
  Garden City, MI 48135
Think Network, Inc.
  P.O. Box 6124
  New York, NY 10128
Thorobred Software
  10 Olympic Plaza
  Murray, KY 42071
T.I.E.S.
  1925 County Road B2
  Roseville, MN 55113
Touch Technologies
  609 S. Escondido Boulevard,
  Suite 101
  Escondido, CA 92025
Triton Products Company
  P.O. Box 8123
  San Francisco, CA 94128
The 22nd Ave. Workshop
  P.O. Box 3425
  Eugene, OR 97403
2-Bit Software
  P.O. Box 2036, Department
  EC1
  Del Mar, CA 92014
Tycom Associates
  68 Velma Avenue
  Pittsfield, MA 01201
TYC Software
  40 Stuyvesant Manor
  Geneseo, NY 14454
Tyson Educational Systems
  P.O. Box 2478
  Miami, FL 33055
Unicom
  297 Elmwood Avenue
  Providence, RI 02907
Unicorn Software
  1775 E. Tropicana Avenue,
  Suite 3
  Las Vegas, NV 89109
Unify
  (through Radio Shack)
University of California
  Mathematics/Computer
  Education Project
  Lawrence Hall of Science
  Berkeley, CA 94720

Ventura Educational Systems
  3440 Brokenhill Street
  Newbury Park, CA 91320
Versa Computing, Inc.
  3541 Old Conejo Road,
  Suite 104
  Newbury Park, CA 91320
VIP Technologies
  (through Radio Shack)
Walt Disney Personal Computer
Software
  (see Disney)
Weekly Reader Family Software
  (see Xerox Education
  Publications)
Whalley Computer Associates
  38 Foster Road
  Southwick, MA 10077
Wichita Public Schools
  Wichita, KS 67201
Windham Classics
  (see Spinnaker Software
  Corporation)
Woodbury Software
  127 White Oak Lane
  Old Bridge, NJ 08857
Word Associates
  55 Sutter Street, Suite 361
  San Francisco, CA 94104
World Book Discovery, Inc.
  5700 Lombardo Centre, Suite
  120
  Seven Hills, OH 44131
Xerox Education Publications
  245 Long Hill Road
  Middletown, CT 06457
Yale University
  Department of Anthropology
  New Haven, CT 06520
Zephyr Services
  306 S. Homewood Avenue
  Pittsburgh, PA 15208
Zweig Associates
  1711 McGaw Avenue
  Irvine, CA 92714

Appendix B

Integrated learning systems

An educator and a businessperson are largely responsible for the early developments of large scale integrated learning systems in computer based reading: Patrick Suppes of Computer Curriculum Corporation—CCC—and William Norris of Control Data Corporation—PLATO. Together, these men have spent hundreds of millions of public and private dollars developing computer based activities across the educational spectrum. This appendix is about the companies and projects they represent.

References about the efforts of CDC, PLATO-WICAT, and CCC in computer based reading can be found throughout the previous editions of *Computer Applications in Reading* and in other chapters of this text. In the past few years, four other companies have developed integrated learning systems for reading: Houghton Mifflin/TSC-Dolphin (Box 683, Hanover, NJ 03755), Wasatch (1214 Wilmington Avenue, Salt Lake City, UT 84106), Cemcorp (1300 Bay Street, Toronto, Ontario, Canada M5R3K8), and Ideal Learning (327 South Marshall Road, Shakopee, MN 55379).

Computer Curriculum Corporation

In the area of integrated learning systems, the Computer Curriculum Corporation has been a perennial leader. Suppes is the company's cofounder (with Richard Atkinson) and president. CCC, like PLATO, is devoted to research, development, evaluation, and delivery of computer based instruction.

CCC programs are delivered by the MICROHOST (minicomputer) Instructional System, which has its own student terminals. However, the system can use as student terminals any Apple IIe, IBM PC, Sony SMC-70, or Atari ST microcomputer.

The MICROHOST system individualizes instruction by monitoring each student's progress and providing exercises at a difficulty level matching the student's success level. Teacher handbooks provide information about the structure and content of the course, directions for using the course, suggestions for monitoring student progress, sample exercises, bibliographies, and skill objectives.

CCC courses cover many grade levels and contain thousands of exercises of two basic types: strand and lesson. In strand structured courses, each strand consists of a series of exercises in a specific skills area. The student's daily work contains exercises progressing from simple to difficult strands. In lesson structured courses, daily work focuses on one particular topic.

Individualized instruction is achieved by analyzing student progress, by diagnosing concept knowledge, and by selecting and generating appropriate exercises. All exercises use computer delivered reinforcement and help prompts.

CCC courses in reading

Audio Reading, Grades 1 and 2 (strand structured)

Presents exercises in beginning reading skills covering letter identification; patterns; sight words; and word, sentence, and passage comprehension. Uses digital speech for audio instruction and motivational messages.

Basic Reading, Grade 2 (strand structured)

Provides reading exercises on single and multiple sentences as well as sentence combining to form stories. Introduces basic sentence patterns and gradually increases sentence complexity.

Reading, Grades 3-6 (strand structured)

Focuses on reading skills at the sentence level. Provides exercises in vocabulary, comprehension, and study skills activities.

Reading for Comprehension, Grades 3-6 (strand structured)

Provides reading exercises on vocabulary, comprehension, study skills, and paragraphs. The paragraphs strand integrates skills developed in other strands and uses reading selections from content area topics and different types of prose.

Reader's Workshop, Grades 3-6 (lesson structured)

Develops reading skills using selections from various content areas and different types of prose. Activities feature a number of on-line resources during a lesson. For example, a student can use an on-line illustrated glossary or ask for tutorial help.

Practical Reading Skills, Grades 5-Adult (lesson structured)

Focuses on functional reading skills with practical, everyday materials such as charts, maps, schedules, menus, labels, and advertisements. Some subject areas include entertainment, health, transportation, and consumer sources.

Critical Reading Skills, Grades 7-Adult (strand structured)

Provides exercises on vocabulary and comprehension skills featuring an offline textbook with 150 selections from various content areas. Extensive tutorial messages guide students in analysis and interpretation of the text content.

Adult Reading Skills, Adult (strand structured)

Develops vocabulary, comprehension, and study skills in content of interest to adults. Features elementary reading skills for adult.

CCC courses in language arts

Language Arts, Grades 3-6 (strand structured)

Provides exercises about verb use, subject-verb agreement, pronoun use, and other elements of grammar for elementary students.

Fundamentals of English, Grades 7-Adult (lesson structured)

Presents exercises about language at the sentence unit. Activities include run on sentences and sentence fragments.

Adult Language Skills, Adult (strand structured)

Provides exercises about language use for adults.

English as a second language, Grade 4-Adult (strand structured)

Provides instruction in English vocabulary and grammar through listening, reading, and writing activities. Digital speech system allows students to hear exercises and explanations in English.

Writing: Process and Skills, Grades 6-Adult (module structured)

Consists of two modules, Writing Process and Writing Instruction. Writing Process develops writing competency by guiding students as they generate ideas, organize, write, evaluate, and rewrite their own compositions with CCC's word processor Wordshop. (Wordshop is a trademark of CCC.)

CCC courses with Dial-A-Drill

Dial-A-Drill courses provide instructional activities with a digital speech system by telephone. Students respond by using a touchtone phone keypad.

Dial-A-Drill Reading, Grades 1-4 (lesson structured)

Gives students practice in four reading skills areas: word patterns, vocabulary, comprehension, and study skills. Students are guided through lessons in eight workbooks by telephone directions.

Dial-A-Drill Practical Reading, Grades 5-Adult (lesson structured)

Develops functional reading skills with practical, everyday materials, including schedules, menus, labels, advertisements, directions, and applications. Some subject areas include entertainment, health, transportation, consumer, and study skills. A student workbook contains all the graphics, most of the exercises, and a glossary.

Dial-A-Drill Spelling, Grades 2-8 (strand structured)

Gives students practice in spelling words frequently taught in grades 2-8.

PLATO / WICAT

PLATO/WICAT Systems was a joint venture of WICAT and United School Services of America, a subsidiary of Control Data Corporation. As such, PLATO/WICAT Systems offered computer based products and services for grades K-12 that were not available from either WICAT or PLATO (CDC). The PLATO/WICAT partnership began in February 1985 and ended October 1986 (See *Electronic Learning*, 1987, *6*, 9-10). Both companies intend to continue services to the approximately 150,000 students using the 325 PLATO/WICAT integrated learning systems. Many of the programs described may not be abandoned, but will be available from WICAT and CDC separately or, perhaps, cast in other formats for use elsewhere.

PLATO/WICAT used a System 300 minicomputer to run its own software and support thirty student workstations. The System can provide computer assisted instruction, testing, computer managed instruction, administrative applications, and an authoring language entitled WISE. In addition, it can provide audio, graphics, and animation to support instructional activities. As mentioned, the System 300 comes with its own student workstations. However, schools can obtain adapters to use IBM PC, IBM PCjr, or Apple IIe/c computers as student workstations.

In September 1985, PLATO/WICAT announced the Local PLATO Delivery System (LPDS). If features an IBM PC/AT compatible computer (with hard disk) that can support up to thirty IBM PC compatible computers as student workstations or workstations that come with LPDS. All PLATO/WICAT System 300 and LPDS programs allow up to thirty students to work at various activities or lessons within a curriculum such as Primary Reading or Reading Comprehension.

PLATO / WICAT System 300 software

Primary Reading, Grades K-3

The primary reading curriculum features 285 lessons covering over a thousand skill activities. Each activity lasts a few minutes and features both teaching and practice. The lessons use audio, graphics, and printed presentations of material. Skill activities include letter discrimination, picture sequencing, letter identification, letter sounds, sight words and sentences, and sentence and paragraph comprehension. Help prompts are available in audio and printed formats. Student performance summaries are also available.

Reading Comprehension, Grades 4-8

The reading comprehension curriculum features 565 lessons presented in the context of newspaper articles and stories. Skill activities include drawing inferences and conclusions, providing justification for conclusions and inferences, judging the validity of an argument, determining the relationship of parts of a story to the whole, interpretating data in nontext formats, and identifying appropriate summaries of a text. Help prompts and student performance summaries are available.

Language Arts, Grades 3-6

The language arts curriculum features over 300 activities in three components: language arts skills, sentence combining, and spelling.

There are two parts to language arts skills: Choose It and Proof It. In Choose It, students use irregular verbs and frequently confused words. In Proof It, students practice proofreading punctuation and generalized capitalization. Sentence combining has students combine two or more sentences into one. Spelling programs help make the repetitive task of spelling more inspiring by using audio and graphics. Student performance summaries are available.

Writing, Grades K-6

The writing curriculum features two components: Writing 1 and Writing 2. Writing 1 has three activities: Calendar, Listen and Do, and Make a Story. Writing 2 also has two activities: Creative Writing and Informative Writing.

The writing curriculum helps students learn to organize information, formulate ideas, and communicate ideas in writing. Word processing, combined with audio and graphic prompts, helps students learn to write for various purposes.

In addition to the curricula described, PLATO/WICAT System 300 offers an English as a second language curriculum.

PLATO / WICAT lpds software
Basic Skills/Basic Reading Skills, Grades 3-8

Two hundred fifty-four lessons cover 112 skills with activities on word structure, vocabulary, and comprehension development. The curriculum is organized into nine courses: Making New Words (Parts 1 and 2), Understanding New Words (Parts 1 and 2), Understanding What You Read (Parts 1 and 2), Thinking About What You Read (Parts 1 and 2), and Judging What You Read. Student performance summaries are available.

High School Skills/High School Reading Skills

Seventy lessons are organized into five courses; Practical Reading, General Reading, Prose Literature, Poetry, and Drama. Thirty-nine skills are presented in a variety of activities covering vocabulary, identifying main ideas and supporting ideas, and making inferences. Student performance summaries are available.

PLATO/Control Data Corporation

In 1959 and 1960, researchers at the University of Illinois developed a computerized teaching system named Programmed Logic for Automated Teaching Operation (PLATO). PLATO first used the ILLIAC I computer and then, with the support of Control Data Corporation, switched to a CDC mainframe computer. Thus, the PLATO/CDC link was forged. PLATO computer based activities in reading and mathematics flourished throughout the 1970s and early 1980s. No other company has devoted as much of its resources to research, development, evaluation, and delivery of computer based instruction, both in reading and other curricular areas. Some estimates place the money spent by CDC on computer based instruction at the one billion dollar mark.

Commercial introduction of PLATO software was through a Control Data Corporation Education Company for main frame and minicomputers in 1976-1977. It was not until the early 1980s that PLATO software became available for many popular microcomputers. (For those interested in the history of PLATO reading software, see Volumes 1 and 2 of *Computer Applications in Reading.*)

Today, most PLATO software is available in the following formats: (1) main frame, online, time sharing; (2) a minicomputer system entitled CDC Education Workstation; and (3) microcomputers.

PLATO courses in reading

Reading Readiness, Grades K-3

Provides activities on memory skills, visual discrimination, word detail, and letter naming.

Basic Skills Reading Instructional Series, Grades 2-9

Covers twenty-eight curricular areas: Basic Word Building, More Basic Word Building, Complex Word Building, Prefixes, Suffixes and Compound Words, More Prefixes and Suffixes, and Prefixes and Suffixes in Content, Selecting the Proper Words, Choosing the Proper Words, Dealing with Confusing Words, Word Meanings, Applying New Words, Understanding and Using New Words, Locating Basic Facts, More Basic Facts about Reading, Understanding What You Read, Remembering What You Read, Interpreting What You Read, Understanding Basic Facts, Understanding More of What You Read, Describers and Conclusions, Different Types of Describers and Conclusions, Understanding the Whole Story, Fact and Nonfact, Author's Purpose, Evaluating What You Read, Author's Purpose and Your Conclusion, and Separating Fact from Opinion.

High School Skills/Reading Instructional Series, Grades 6-11

This PLATO series covers nine curricula areas. The multiple disk series features groups of activities including: Practical Reading 1 and 2; General Reading 1 and 2; Prose Literature 1, 2, and 3; Poetry; and Drama.

Other PLATO programs of possible interest to reading educators include Basic Grammar Skills and High School Writing Skills.

INDEX

A

Aaron, R.　132
Aaronson, D.　90
Abegglen, S.　41
Abram, S.　81, 88
Adair, J.　6
Adams, A.　12
Adler, R.　168
Aggen, W.　93
Ahl, D.　102, 103
Ahumada, A.　151
Akers, J.　168
Alber, A.　169
Alessi, S.　17, 64, 75, 77
Alexander, C.　31
Alexander, J.　103
Alfano, J.　86
Allred, R.　16, 95
Alne, D.　76
Alpert, D.　7
Anandam, K.　104
Anchorage Borough School District
　14
Anderson, B　28
Anderson, J.　99
Anderson, R.　54, 75, 91, 164
Anderson, T.　75
Anderson-Inman, Lynne　113
Andolina, M.　98
Anelli, C.　75
Angier, N.　118
Angle, H.　71, 72, 96, 97
Aoki, P.　45
Appel, R.　126
Argento, B.J.　76
Arms, V.　103, 104
Armstrong, J.　12
Arnold, R.　117
Ascher, C.　15
Ash, M.　126
Ashmore, T.　82
Askwall, S.　70, 93, 98
Association for Supervision and
　Curriculum Development　125
Atkinson, R.　6, 7, 9, 23, 24, 25
Attala, E.　9
Auten, A.　15, 30, 55

B

Bairstow, J.　158
Baker, F.　7, 8, 9, 133, 134
Balajthy, E.　33, 34, 35, 44, 55, 61,
　113, 165, 166
Ballard, R.　8
Ballas, M.　78

Barber, B.　38
Barbour, A.　143
Barker, T.　114
Barnes, B.　124
Barnes, D.　7
Barnes, H.　77
Barnett, H.　169
Barr, A.　24
Barrett, B.　10
Barrett, S.　17
Barro, S.　7
Barry, J.　117, 118
Barry, P.　39
Bass, G.　58, 82
Bass, R.　7
Bates, M.　165
Bath Elementary School Staff　76
Bauer, D.　145, 148
Beam, P.　92, 98, 150
Beard, M.　8
Beaty, J.　128
Beaumont, J.　72, 98
Beck, I.　85
Becker, H.　12, 15, 20
Behavior Research Laboratory　90
Bejar, I.　11
Bell, S.　44
Bell, T.　94
Benfort, A.　63
Berenbon, H.　39
Berger, C.　11
Bergheim, K.　141
Bertera, J.　92
Best, P.　71, 73, 98
Better, J.　169
Bevan, N.　73, 98
Beyers, C.　28
Bialo, E.　56, 61
Biddle, W.　75
Bilyeu, L.　134
Bingham, M.　55
Bitter, G.　15, 58
Bitzer, D.　6, 7, 9
Blachowicz, C.　133
Black, S.　168
Blackwell, R.　7
Blair, D.　158
Blanchard, J.　26, 27, 28, 29, 38, 61,
　65, 88, 118
Blank, D.　70, 73, 99
Blau, S.　106
Blohm, P.　78, 92
Bloor, R.　72, 98
Blum, L.　55
Blurton, C.　169

　　　　　　　　Computer applications in reading

Computer applications in reading

DATE DUE